THE
HEBER LETTERS
1783–1832

R. H. CHOLMONDELEY

LONDON

THE BATCHWORTH PRESS

PUBLISHED IN 1950 BY
BATCHWORTH PRESS LTD
20 TUDOR STREET, EC4

PRINTED IN GREAT BRITAIN BY
KNIGHT & FORSTER LTD
LEEDS

CONTENTS

ILLUSTRATIONS

7

ACKNOWLEDGMENTS

My sincere thanks are due to Algernon Heber-Percy and to Hugh Cholmondely for permitting the reproduction of some of their pictures: also to James Wentworth Day for much-needed advice and encouragement, and to R. W. K. Hinton, of the University of Reading, for his help in editing and, in particular, in supplying the historical notes.

R. H. C.

Baschurch, Salop.
April, 1949

PREFACE

THE HEBER family came originally from Yorkshire. By 1500, or soon after, the estate of Marton, near Skipton, had been acquired. The Shropshire estate of Hodnet came to them in 1752, on the death of Miss Henrietta Vernon, the last of a family that had lived there for 250 years. Miss Vernon left the property to her second cousin Elizabeth (1703-53), wife of Thomas Heber of Marton (1697-1752).

They were succeeded at Marton and Hodnet by their eldest son Richard Heber, who was born in 1727 and died in 1766, leaving two daughters only, the one Harriet who married William Wrightson of Cusworth, and the other Mary who did not marry.

On the eldest son's death the estate of Hodnet passed to the second son, Reginald Heber (born 1728), but the Marton estate did not come to him until the death of his brother's widow which occurred only in 1803. He took a scholarship at Brasenose, Oxford, in 1746, was ordained in 1753 and was elected a Fellow of the College, becoming Tutor in 1756. On his brother's death in 1766 he resigned his academic positions and was inducted as Rector of Chelsea. This benefice he held for four years, exchanging it in 1770 for the Upper Mediety of Malpas, Cheshire, about fifteen miles from Hodnet. Malpas at that time was the proud possessor of two Rectors, who performed alternate weeks duty. The benefice of the Lower Mediety was then being enjoyed by that profound but retiring scholar Dr. Thomas Townson.

Reginald Heber lived at Malpas for the rest of his life (he died in 1804), in the Rectory that he rebuilt himself. In plurality with Malpas, he became also Rector of Hodnet in 1787, which living in his capacity as Lord of the Manor he presented to himself.

He was married twice, first on 15 April 1773 to Mary Baylie who died on 30 January 1774, having had a son Richard, born 5 January 1774, and secondly, on 30 July 1782, to Mary Allanson by whom he had three children, Reginald born 21 April 1783, Thomas Cuthbert, born 21 March 1785 and last, Mary, born 2 March 1787.

Most of Reginald Heber's letters were written to his sister Elizabeth (1724-1812). She lived in London with another sister, Mrs. Gwyllim—'dear Ammy' as she is usually referred to—who suffered from very indifferent health. Most years, for as long as dear Ammy's health permitted, the two sisters made a round of country visits, in which a stay at Malpas was always looked forward to. Their London house was an invaluable *pied à terre* for all the members of their brother's family.

NOTE — Except for slight changes in spelling of place names to preserve uniformity, and, for the occasional use of capital letters and commas, the Letters are printed as in the originals. In spite of some reference books, the correct year of Richard Heber's birth is 1774.

I Letters of the
HEBER FAMILY
1783-1788

THE LETTERS of Reginald Heber and his family during the period covered by this chapter deal very little with politics. There is for instance only one incidental reference to the peace of 1783 which ended the War of American Independence. But the failure of Charles James Fox's India Bill and the appointment of William Pitt's ministry, events covering the winter 1783-4 and the first months of 1784, obtain some notice and require a short explanation.

In the Spring of 1783, Fox and Lord North, both opposed to the minister then in power, brought about his defeat in the Commons by an unequal and, it was considered, unprincipled coalition. After some weeks of manoeuvring, the King unwillingly gave power, without confidence, to Fox and North under the figurehead of the Duke of Portland. At the end of 1783 Fox introduced two India Bills. The first would have transferred to commissioners nominated in Parliament the political government of India then vested in the East India Company. The second would have removed from English administrators in India those private emoluments and benefits which later roused such criticism at the trial of Warren Hastings. It was the first bill that raised the storm. The East India Company was determined to resist it, since it would remove their patronage. The King was determined to forestall it, since it would award that patronage to Fox. The opponents of the administration, including Pitt, opposed it.

Nevertheless, having much to recommend it and being supported by a large party, it passed the Commons ; and it was defeated in the Lords only by the personal and unconstitutional interference of the King. On 18 December 1783 the King dismissed Fox and North ; Pitt accepted office and formed a ministry. He was at this time an outstanding but inexperienced young man in his early twenties.

Pitt and the King had their plans well laid. Unfavourable votes in the Commons, from members unsure of the stability of the ministry, were ignored ; time was allowed for Pitt's qualities, the King's confidence in him, and the ministry's steadiness to make their mark in the country and Parliament ; in March the Parliament was dissolved ; and when the new House assembled it was found, as the government had anticipated, that the ministry had an overwhelming majority.

The political opinions of the Hebers are evident from their letters. One sees clearly their firm Toryism, regard for authority and hatred of faction. They set themselves, in short, against the movement of the constitution towards modern practice. They were vehement anti-Foxites. For Pitt, from his first appointment, they had nothing but delighted praise, for the King nothing but sympathy, for the Prince of Wales only disapproval, for the Constitution unalterable veneration.

The Hebers were not in touch with political circles and it cannot be said that their correspondence throws light on the political world. They naturally wrote most about personal matters. Young Richard is sent to school and begins his classical education. The three children of Heber's second marriage, Reginald, Thomas and Mary, are born and thrive. Heber's sister Elizabeth, living in London, does commissions for her brother.

Although it does not appear in this selection of letters, Richard became seriously ill in the winter of 1783-4. His father came to London and consequently wrote not to his sister but to his wife. This was not the only visit to London. In 1785 and again in 1786 Heber took his family for holidays to the Assembly at Chester, and also in 1786 to visit his in-laws the Allansons at Ripon, and his cousins the Rawstornes at Preston. Their lives were by no means dull, and although travelling was not easy, they seem all to have made light of it. They appear as vigorous and good-humoured people well able to take advantage of this golden and peaceful period which followed the American war and preceded the French Revolution. We should not accuse them of complacency, for all the signs seemed to promise that public affairs would continue to run smoothly under the guidance of Pitt and that society would see no great changes in their lifetime.

*   *   *

Elizabeth Heber to Rev. Reginald Heber
21 February 1783

I have the satisfaction of acquainting my dearest brother of our safe arrival in Town after a good journey. We have had very fine weather and I found the roads good. The road through Stafford is much pleasanter than the old one. We slept there the first night and on Wednesday got to Daventry where we found dear Ammy as well as she usually is on a journey. We proceeded to Dunstable yesterday and got to Westminster soon after three this afternoon. Dear Richard is, thank God, in perfect health.

I think you would be pleased with our dear Lord North's[1] speech on the preliminary articles[2] in the old *General*.[3]

Elizabeth Heber to Rev. Reginald Heber
18 March 1783

I have the pleasure to inform you my sister Heber and I took dear Richard, as I told we intended, on Saturday last to

---

[1] Lord North (1732–92), later second Earl of Guildford ; first minister of George III until 1782 ; after 1783, in opposition.

[2] In a debate in the Commons on 17 February 1783, on the preliminary articles of peace with France and Spain and the provisional articles with America, Lord North conceded that the terms might be the best obtainable. He denied that they were either advantageous or honourable and he ended with a compliment to the American loyalists.

[3] The *General Evening Post*, founded 1733.

Greenford. We found Dr. Glasse[1] perfectly recovered, to whose care I committed my precious charge. I left him playing with his new acquaintance in good spirits and perfect health. Dr. Glasse desires his best respects and thanks for your letter and says he hopes you never have reason to repent the confidence you have reposed in him. Mrs. Glasse introduced four or five fine boys about his own age to Richard who she told him were to be his constant play-fellows. They are always in a room together and a servant with them when in the house out of school hours. He has a snug warm bed to himself and only another young gentleman sleeps in the same room. I was much pleased with the attention Mrs. Glasse paid in the particular inquiries she made in regard to diet and every particular respecting dear Richard that he might be treated accordingly. Dr. Glasse said they had a variety of breakfasts but that he recommended cocoa as the most wholesome for those boys who did not like milk. Richard, when the carriage stop'd at the door, said, 'Lord bless me, I don't know how I shall behave myself I declare,' but on a word of encouragement the embarrassment went pretty well off. Mrs. Glasse met us with a good-natured smiling countenance and began to talk to him, introduced her little boys and in half an hours time he seemed quite at home and repeated his pastoral to Dr. Glasse. The boys all look healthy and Mrs. Glasse says have been so all winter, but she promised to keep Richard in the house, while the weather was so extremely cold. It has been much warmer yesterday and to-day.

Rev. Reginald Heber to his sister Elizabeth Heber
21 April 1783

I take the very first opportunity of acquainting my dear friends that my dear Mary was, a little after three this morning, safely delivered of a fine little lad. I thank God She and the

---

[1] Dr. Samuel Glasse (1735-1812), theologian and schoolmaster ; Fellow of the Royal Society ; rector of Hanwell ; vicar of Epsom 1782, Wanstead 1786 ; prebendary of St. Paul's 1798. His son Dr. George Henry Glasse (1761-1809), classicist and theologian, succeeded him at Hanwell in 1785. Both were educated at Christ Church.

little Bab are both as well as can be expected. He is as fat as a little mole and they say looks very well.[1]

Having occasion to write to Major Lister concerning a Bill[2] now before the House brought in by the Proprietors of the Leeds Canal, I desired him to send me a few covers which arrived opportunely last night. The Major tells me he was no sooner arrived in Town after disbanding his Corps of Light Horse but he found it necessary for him to return into the country again immediately to attend the re-election of Mr. Lee[3] for Clitheroe who is appointed Attorney General in the room of Mr. Kennion,[4] and he seems apprehensive of meeting with some opposition from Mr. Curzon.

Rev. Reginald Heber to his sister Elizabeth Heber
27 April 1783

My dearest Mary having had but very restless nights on Thursday and Friday, I postponed writing to you in hopes I should be able to give you a better account this morning. My anxiety has scarce suffered me to close my eyes these two nights and the pain in my stomach which is always a concomitant of the affliction of my mind has been as bad as usual, but the joyful news I have just received that my Dearest Love is better and has had several hours of refreshing rest has quite revived my worn out and drooping spirits.

I had quite forgot to beg the favour of Aunt Pop to be a Sponsor[5] for little Reginald along with Mr. Allanson and the Rector of Marton.

[1] Reginald, first child by his second wife, Mary Allanson.

[2] A petition of the company of proprietors of the Leeds and Liverpool Canal Navigation, to amend the act under which they then operated, was referred to a committee of the Commons on 20 December 1782, and received the royal assent as a public Act on 24 June 1783.

[3] John Lee (1733-93), a lawyer known for his integrity and plain speaking. The information in this letter is not quite correct. Lee did not succeed Kenyon immediately. In April 1783 he became Solicitor-general, and in November Attorney-general. On each occasion he was forced to offer himself for re-election at Clitheroe—a constituency which was disfranchised in 1832.

[4] Lloyd Kenyon (1732-1802), Attorney-general 1782-3. Master of the Rolls 1784, Lord Chief Justice and first Lord Kenyon 1788.

[5] Reginald's godparents were :— his aunt Miss Elizabeth Heber, his uncle Rev. George Allanson, and a first cousin of his father's, another Rev. Reginald Heber, Rector of Marton who died in 1799.

Rev. Reginald Heber to his sister Elizabeth Heber
29 April 1783

I have the inexpressible satisfaction to acquaint you that my dearest Mary (I thank God) has rested extremely well these two last nights. Would you think it, she is monstrous fond of the little brat and thinks him very pretty indeed; for my part though I don't think him an ugly boy, yet I cannot as yet descry the number of beauties his Mama sees in him. His eyes are at present a dark blue but whether they will assume a different colour as dear Richard's I know not. He is, they say, a tall child. Mary ate a chicken on Sunday and some nice Hodnet perch boil'd and sparrow-grass and toast yesterday with a very good relish. Methinks, my dear Pop, I have now satisfied all your kind enquiries.

Tell dear Richard it gives me the truest satisfaction to hear he is so happy at Greenford. I desire that he will send me a list of his school-fellows. I suppose Lord Mollineaux is Lord Sefton's son.

Richard Heber to his father, Rev. Reginald Heber
7 May 1783

I have inclosed a list of my school-fellows. Corry is the best scholar in my class. Our lesson is seven or eight lines of *Cordoerius*[1] which Corry and I have done in five minutes, but James who is a dull boy keeps us in school two hours.

List of Boys in Dr. Glasse's School[2]

First Class
Clements, (from Ireland).
Second Class
Atherton and Starkie, (of Huntroyd, Lancashire).

---

[1] Corderius, or Mathurin Cordier (c. 1480-1564), French schoolmaster, wrote several Latin school-books for children.
[2] Richard's schoolfellows may be identified :—
Nathaniel Clements, later second Earl of Leitrim, b. 1768.
Atherton Legh Atherton of Atherton, Lancs., b. 1768.
Le G. P. N. Starkie of Huntroyd, Lancs., b. 1770.
George Eyre of Warrens, Lyndhurst, b. 1772.
Henry Moore, second son of sixth Earl of Drogheda, b. c. 1771. (*continued on P.* 19).

Third Class
  Eyre and Moore, (Earl of Drogheda's son).
Fourth Class
  Boyle and Molineux, (Earl Shannon and Sefton's sons).
Fifth Class
  Lloyd, (an Irish orphan).
Sixth Class
  Heber, Corry (Lord Bellmour's son), James (Sir W. James's son), Danby (Marquis of Caermarthen), Fane (Oxfordshire), and Lord Francis Osborne.

Richard Heber to his father, Rev. Reginald Heber
Westminster, 10 June 1783

We have no holidays at Whitsuntide but most of the boys go home for a few days. I return to Greenford on Friday. I am glad to inform you that I am advanced into Lloyd's class which is a great honour.

The books we now learn in are the Grammar, *Phoedri Fabulae Cordoerius* and our Exercises are in *Exempla Minora* and on Saturdays in *Selectae Veteri*. Our business on Sundays is to write out the Collect and to get it off by-heart and on Saints-days we do the Latin Testament.

We break up the 14th August.

Rev. Reginald Heber to his sister Elizabeth Heber
20 June 1783

We have fixed on Tuesday next for the Christening, Miss Allanson will be your proxy and Mr. Bridge[1] Mr. Allanson's.

Henry, Viscount Boyle, later third Earl of Shannon, b. 1771.
William, Viscount Molyneux, later second Earl of Sefton, b. 1772.
Lloyd, unidentifiable.
Richard Heber, b. 1774.
Somerset Lowry-Corry, later second Earl Belmore, b. 1774.
Edward William James, only son of Sir William James, Bt., M.P., of Park Farm Place, Eltham, b. 1774.
Earl of Danby, later sixth Duke of Leeds, son of Marquis of Carmarthen, b. 1775.
John Fane of Wormsley, Oxfordshire, b. 1775.
Lord Francis Osborne, later first Lord Godolphin, second son of Marquis of Carmarthen, b. 1777.
[1] Mr. Bridge was the Curate at Malpas.

Rev. Reginald Heber to his sister Elizabeth Heber
1 August 1783

On Saturday last we set out as was proposed on our Welch expedition. Mrs. Everard and Miss Do. Allanson in Mr. Everard's chaise and he, Mr. Allanson and myself on horseback. The weather being very fine we had a most delightful ride along the banks of the Dee to Llangollen about 20 miles from Malpas where we dined. This town is pleasantly situated in a valley surrounded by high mountains skirted with hanging woods down to the side of the Dee which dashes and roars along over a bed of huge craggy rocks which form a long string of cascades.

Upon a rising hill above Llangollen two Irish damsels[1] of Family and Fortune, a Miss Butler and a Miss Ponsonby, leaving their native land and family connections have fixed their place of residence ; friendship their bond, and reading, working and adorning the beautiful little spot they have chosen to retire to, their amusement. We had the curiosity to take a view of the premises but had not the luck to get a sight of the fair hermits. As they are both young and rich, it is not improbable but some male creature may endeavour to interrupt the tranquility and break the league of amity these romantic fair ones have entered into.

From Llangollen we proceeded in the evening all the way on the banks of the Dee with high mountains on the right hand and on the left about ten miles further to a single house called the " Druid Inn " where we slept as well as ordinary beds well stocked with fleas, and small close rooms in very hot weather would permit.

We were now about three miles distant from Llangwm, the sinecure Rectory Everard was to read in at next morning, and to which place we all intended to have accompanied him, but having prudently sent a courier before to explore the way he returned with a report the the road was impassible for a carriage. The Rector therefore and George went to the Church and I

---

[1] Miss Eleanor Butler (1739-1829)—she became Lady Eleanor in 1791 when her brother was acknowledged as Earl of Ormonde—and Miss Sarah Ponsonby (1753-1831). The Ladies of Llangollen.

proceeded a Sabbath day's journey with the ladys to a town called Bala about nine miles further over high mountains but good roads. Our inducement to go to Bala was to see a very fine pool superior to anything of the kind I ever saw before, being between three and four miles long and about two broad. It abounds with trout and perch of which we caught a fine dish on Monday morning early and George and the ladies had a pleasant row in a pretty good boat while Everard and I attended to the sport of seeing the net drawn for the fish.

From Bala where we met with pretty good accommodation we returned on Monday to Llangollen again where we slept, — breakfasted on Tuesday at Wrexham and got home to dinner where we had the satisfaction of finding dear Mary and Bab pure well: as, thank God, we all remain except poor George who has got a cold and sore throat which however is getting better.

Yesterday we dined at Iscoyd Park and are to do the like at Bolesworth Castle to-morrow, so that you see we keep it up.

I thought I had a frank[1] but cannot find it so fear you must pay double postage for this.

Rev. Reginald Heber to his Wife
Westminster, 16 December 1783

Great revolutions in the political world are expected. Everard who converses with the Great and Knowing Ones laid me a wager of half-a-crown that the East India Regulations Bill will be kick'd out of the House of Peers, and that a new Arrangement of Ministers must be the consequence.[2] Indeed the Division which took place last night in the House of Lords for an Adjournment seems to favour Everard's opinion and information on the

---

[1] Every member of Parliament was entitled to send through the post, free of charge, letters and packets not exceeding two ounces in weight, and printed matter including newspapers in open wrappers. The privilege obtained during sessions of Parliament and for forty days before and after. The member franked his mail by merely signing the envelope, and could supply his friends with envelopes so signed.

[2] Everard was right. The bill was defeated at its second reading in the Lords, on 17 December 1783, by ninety-five votes to seventy-six.

matter. He says the *Fox stinks*, for my part I think he was never sweet.

Rev. Reginald Heber to his Wife
18 December 1783

You will see in this days' paper that the Lords have rejected the East India Bill which it is said the Secretary of State brought into Parliament in direct opposition to the opinion and inclination of the King. Therefore all real friends of the Constitution rejoice that a demagogue who was vain enough to imagine that he could bind the King in chains and his Nobles with links of iron is disappointed of his insolent expectations. What changes this event, so ominous to the present Administration, may bring I know not ; some say the Ministers are determined to keep their places *maugre* this rebuff. Others are of the opinion which seems more probable that a new arrangement must take place, as the King can neither meet his present Ministers, nor they his Majesty in Council with any degree of good humour much less with confidence or cordiality.

Mary Heber to her Husband, Rev. Reginald Heber
Malpas, 19 December 1783

We are quite diverted with your account of politics. Poor Charley is baited in his turn, and has need of all his wiles and cunning to carry him safe through the difficulties he has engaged in, but as I do not comprehend the merits of the cause I don't know which side to wish for, so I will e'en be neutral till the event determines, and I wish the Prince of Wales[1] had been as prudent ; for the heir-apparent to be found in a minority is very, very sad.

---

[1] The Prince of Wales, round whom according to the practice of the century was grouped the party who had not the confidence of the King, had voted for the Bill at its first reading and merely abstained at the second.

Rev. Reginald Heber to his Wife
23 *December* 1783

Various are the opinions of the present state of political affairs and of the events likely to take place. I have seen and conversed with your old friend Major Lister, who inquired kindly after you. He is a Foxite and is positive that in case his Majesty should dissolve the present Parliament, there would not be thirty new Members returned in the next and that in consequence there would still be a great majority in the House of Commons who would adhere to and support the measures of North and Fox and that no new Ministry could go on, and of course the King would be forced to reinstate them in their places.

Rev. Reginald Heber to his Wife
15 *January* 1784

Whether Parliament will be dissolved or not there are different opinions. But it is evident to everyone that the present House of Commons will not support the present Ministry,[1] and that therefore his Majesty must either give up the Ministry of his choice or dissolve the Parliament. Alas ! his Majesty is much to be pitied.

Rev. Reginald Heber to his sister, Elizabeth Heber
11 *March* 1784

It grieves me to the heart that your last kind letter did not bring me a better account of my dear sister Gwillym's state of health. You may remember the late Mr. Preb. Mainwaring[2] often said that he had found more relief and benefit from taking a table-spoonful of the White Mustard seed every night at bed-time and washing it down with a glass of white wine than any other prescription whatsoever. If dear Ammy has not tried this remedy for any considerable time together, I wish she would try it for one month without the interposition of any other

---

[1] The ministry of William Pitt. He took office 19 December 1783.
[2] Rev. Edward Mainwaring (1709-80), Prebendary of Chester.

medicine. I took it last Spring every morning drinking half a pint of whey after it and have great reason to believe it was of great service to me in keeping off the rheumatism, and I have begun it again.

I had a letter by the last post from Mr. Rawstorne[1] in which he desires me to make what inquiry I can concerning a school at Rugby in Warwickshire, to which from the repute it bears, he seems inclined to send dear Lawrence. I have interrogated Doctor Townson[2] concerning it, who I imagined in his frequent visits to Blithfield might have heard the opinion of the neighbourhood of it. He says he has heard it much commended but is not acquainted with Doctor James,[3] the Master, or knows any particulars about it.

The d—l take the Fox, and God give a better mind and more sense to the geese who are led by him by the nose. Mr. Pitt is a prodigy, I admire him more and more. The King's reply to the last address of his faithful Commons deserves to be written in letters of gold.[4]

Rev. Reginald Heber to his sister Elizabeth Heber
19 March 1784

The weather has been extremely cold here for many days and agues are very epidemical.

Major and Mrs. Henchman[5] came to dinner on Friday and left us on Wednesday morning. The Major says they shall carry the election at Chester hollow for the Governor of Bolesworth[6] if

[1] Lawrence Rawstorne of Newhall, Lancs., a cousin of Reginald Heber's.

[2] Dr. Thomas Townson (1715-92), co-rector of Malpas. He was also Rector of Blithfield in Staffordshire.

[3] Dr. James, Headmaster of Rugby from 1778-94.

[4] The opposition had succeeded in passing through the Commons an address for an efficient administration, demanding a new ministry. The King replied on 27 February : ' Very recent endeavours have already been employed on my part, to unite in the public service ... those whose joint efforts appear to me most capable of producing that happy effect : those endeavours have not had the success I wished. . . . I observe . . . that there is no charge, or complaint, suggested against my present ministers . . . and numbers of my subjects have expressed to me . . . their satisfaction in the changes I have made in my councils. Under these circumstances, I trust, my faithful Commons will not wish that the essential offices of executive government should be vacated.'

[5] Major Charles Henchman of the 10th and later the 16th Dragoons. He retired in 1781.

[6] Mr. John Crewe of Bolesworth Castle, Cheshire. He sold the place next year to the Mosleys.

a dissolution of Parliament takes place ; but reports from other quarters are far otherwise, and Mrs. Henchman seems to think the gallant Major rather too sanguine. As the Foxites have agreed to pass the Supplys and not to put a stop to the necessary national business, I suppose the Parliament will not be dissolved till after the Summer prorogation,[1] but I rather think the present faction will not be suffered to meet again in full force, and it is generally supposed that many of the present members, strenuous supporters of the junto would not again be returned. Pitt is a genuine hero, what a glorious magnanimous stand the Stripling has made in support of the Constitution, against the Goliah of Faction and his adherents. But while the spirit of Chatham survives in his son I hope Old England will still triumph over all enemies domestic and foreign.

Richard Heber to his father, Rev. Reginald Heber
Greenford, 30 April 1784

Pray get me a ticket to go to Westminster Abbey to hear the sacred music in Commemoration of Handel.[2] Mr. Glasse's *Caractacus*[3] is a very scarce book, but I believe it is at Mr. Betham's[4] sale where I would be much obliged to you to go, there being the very best editions of the classics of all sizes. I would be much obliged to you if you would let me learn to draw.

Elizabeth Heber to Rev. Reginald Heber
17 July 1784

Mrs. Crewe was here the other day, she was very low indeed having first parted with her daughter[5] who was set out for the

---

[1] On the contrary, Parliament was prorogued on 24 March and dissolved next day. The new Parliament met on 18 May 1784, with a majority of members (as usual after general elections in the eighteenth century) for the administration, and including Mr. John Crewe, member for Cheshire.

[2] George Frederick Handel (1685-1759), composer.

[3] William Mason, *Caractacus, a dramatic poem*; in the edition of 1781, *cum versione Latina a G. H. Glasse.*

[4] ? Edward Betham (1707-83), scholar ; founded and endowed a charity school at Greenford, 1780.

[5] Miss Elizabeth Crewe married Lord Falmouth in June 1784.

Duke of Beaufort's that morning and goes from thence to Corn-wall. Mrs. Crewe told me that Sir Forster Cunliffe[1] was likely to purchase Bolesworth but that if he does not, Mr. Peploe Birch[2] is to have the next refusal. I wish he was to be your neighbour but am surprised he should think of leaving Hereford-shire.

Dear Ammy is, I think, rather better within these few days.

Rev. Reginald Heber to his sister Elizabeth Heber
6 November 1784

Everard and I took a ride on Tuesday to pay our respects to the Rector of Whitchurch whom we found at home with an Italian nobleman and his brother — Milanese, who are upon a visit. We are invited to dine with him, but alas ! without the ladies, to their no small mortification, on Monday night at five o'clock. How we are to get home, as there will be no moon that night, is a matter of some concern to our wives. If the Rector offers us beds, and I think he can do no less, I believe we shall leave our *cara sposas* to sleep alone or together, if they choose it that night.

The ladys were yesterday to take a peep at Cawarden, not without a secret hope of seeing the owner[3] thereof ,but alas, he was invisible to the females, to the no small disappointment of the beautiful Fanny and her sister Bessy who both meditated con-quest or captivation of the Mighty Nimrod. Everard and I call'd at Bolesworth and found Madam Crewe in high spirits from the agreeable expectation of seeing Lord and Lady Fal-mouth[4] there on the 20th. On enquiries being made after her ladyship, she intimated with great glee on her countenance that her daughter was *very well* though a *little sick or so* but *nothing to* complain of.

---

[1] Sir Foster Cunliffe, third Baronet (1755-1834).
[2] John Peploe-Birch of Garneston Castle, Hereford (1743-1805).
[3] William Leche of Carden, Cheshire (1729-1812). He remained a bachelor till he was seventy-six.
[4] George Evelyn Boscawen (1758-1808), Viscount Falmouth ; married Elizabeth, daughter of John Crewe of Bolesworth Castle.

Rev. Reginald Heber to his sister Elizabeth Heber
9 December 1784

Mr. Allanson[1] and I tramped it yesterday on foot to Whit-church to dine with the Rector and returned again upon our ten toes this morning. We found it very pleasant walking and per-formed it going and coming in an hour and a half without the least fatigue. We met Mr. Nedham and Archdeacon Clive[2] and Mr. Gregory and spent a very cheerful evening.

It always rejoices my heart to be assured that my dear boy continues well and minding his business. I am sorry to hear that Lord Boyle has left Greenford, he was a clever boy and I under-stood there was an honourable emulation between him and dear Richard. As you say dear Richard is very desirous of having a scarlet coat this winter, he has my consent tho' I think there are many preferable colours.

I am so glad you and dear Ammy had so near and good a view of the ascent of Messrs. Blanchard and Jeffreys,[3] the sight must excite sensations of the sublime and wonderful.

Richard Heber to his father, Rev. Reginald Heber
Undated, 1784

A few days ago I went with my aunt and my cousin Kitt to see the balloon at the Lycaeum sent from Monsieur Montgolfier[4]

---

[1] The Allanson family was as follows :—
Rev. George Allanson (1759-1826), at various times co-Rector of Malpas, Curate of Moreton Saye, Prebendary of Ripon, Rector of Hodnet. He married in 1794 Anne Elizabeth, sister of Rev. Whitehall Davies of Broughton, Flints.
Rebecca Allanson died unmarried, *c.* 1830.
Mary Allanson married Reginald Heber in 1782 (1751-1834).
Dorothy Allanson died unmarried in 1799.
Elizabeth Allanson died unmarried in 1817.
Francis Allanson married Rev. John Kirkby, Rector of Gotham, Nottingham, in 1792.
[2] Ven. Robert Clive (1725-92), Archdeacon of Salop. First cousin and brother-in-law of first Lord Clive.
[3] Jean Pierre Blanchard and Dr. J. Jeffreys were the first persons to cross the Channel in the air — this in 1785. The first person to rise into the air from British soil had done so in August 1784. In September Lunardi ascended from the Artillery Ground in London and was carried to Hertfordshire, the performance attracting enthusiastic attention. This year was the heydey of ballooning in England.
[4] One of the brothers Montgolfier, Joseph (1740-1810), or Jacques (1745-99).

which we heard was finely gilt. But it did not at all answer our expectations being nothing but a catchpenny business with the gallery on the floor. The man being asked by a young Agzonian why it was not compleat, he answered very impertinently and told him he would kick him. The young gentleman told him he would have horse-whipped him well if the ladies had not been in the room, but said he would horse-whip him well when he came to Oxford and have his balloon cut to pieces.

Rev. Reginald Heber to his sister, Elizabeth Heber
27 December 1784

Pray give my blessing to dear Richard and a guinea on his birthday on which God grant him many happy returns. I am glad to hear Dr. Glasse is better, when you receive his account you will be so good as to send me the sum total. I desire Dicky will copy the account on one side of his letter when he writes, which will save double postage these hard times.[1]

Honest George and his sisters went with Miss Davies[2] to Wrexham Assembly on Tuesday last, Fanny had the felicity of dancing with Major Williams my quondam pupil, who she says was a most delightful partner, Bessy danced with Mr. Wayne a brother of Mrs. Fletcher's, and George figured away with Miss Davies, Miss Dod,[3] and the great and mighty heiress Miss Pulstone,[4] by turns. Upon the whole they were well pleased with their evening's entertainment, tho' the meeting was neither so numerous nor so brilliant as it would have been, had it not happened to be Sir Watkin's[5] wedding day by which Festivity many beaus and belles were engaged at Wynnstay.

---

[1] The famous mail-coach system began with the dispatch of a coach bearing the royal mails from Bristol, 2 August 1784. In the next fifty years the postal service was remodelled. But the average charge for a letter was 7d. till the Penny Post began, 10 January 1840.

[2] Miss Davies whom George Allanson eventually married.

[3] Miss Dod, one of the sisters of Thomas Crewe Dod of Edge, Cheshire.

[4] Miss Francis Pulstone, heiress of Gwysanny, Flints. She married Bryan Cooke of Owsten, Yorks., in 1786.

[5] Sir Watkin Wynn, fourth Baronet (1742-89).

Richard Heber to his father, Rev. Reginald Heber
31 *December* 1784

I begun to learn Greek, almost as soon as I left Malpas and have done the first book of Ovid, the story of Phaeton, Echo Narcissus and Pyramus and Thisbe (which is 110 lines) to construe and say by heart for my Task which I got the first morning before breakfast.

You was so good to promise me that you would give me something towards Bell's Poets[1] at Christmas. I have got eight guineas.

Rev. Reginald Heber to his son, Richard
8 *January* 1785

You would all I make no doubt be quite happy on the fifth which you may be sure your friends at Malpas made a day of rejoicing and festivity as usual, with singing, music and dancing. The menials footed it in the laundry and the gentry in the gallery: little Tiddy was at first somewhat astonished to see the dancers whisking about like so many crazelings but soon became ex-hilerated, entered into the spirit of the fun and trolled about like a little fairy by moonlight. The fidler seem'd at first rather to alarm him, to whom he frequently pointed and called out ' Man, Man,' which he repeated both before he went to sleep and when he awaked the next morning.

Richard Heber to his father, Rev. Reginald Heber
13 *January* 1785

I am much obliged to you for your kind remembrance of my Birthday. It was kept here with mirth and festivity : after tea we had a quadrille and commerce-table and anticipated Twelfth Night in eating plumb cake and choosing King and Queen. The servants and their company played at cards and danced.

---

[1] John Bell (1745-1831), publisher, brought out *Bell's British Poets*, 109 vols. (1777-82).

Rev. Reginald Heber to his sister, Elizabeth Heber
23 January 1785

We propose making our long intended visit to Major and Mrs. Henchman to-morrow. My dear Richard would I hope receive a line from me on Friday last in which I mentioned our *bold design* of going to the Play at Wynnstay on Wednesday which we accomplished without being much fatigued and were very much entertained by the performance. The Play was *As you like it*, the part of Rosalind was well acted by Miss Jones a pretty girl from Wrexham ; Orlando and Jacques were pretty well done by Mr. Bunbury[1] and Capt. Horneck, and Adam and Touchstone by Mr. Wardle and Mr. Aldersey,[2] the two last were in my opinion the best of the male performers. The Farce was the agreeable surprise, a droll laughable thing in which there were some comical songs, the principal character Sir Frederick Friendly was admirably performed by Mr. Kinnersley.[3] The scenes being landscapes of various views in Wales are extremely beautiful, one of the bridge at Langothling is remarkably fine. The Theatre was very full of good Company who after the Play assembled in the Grand Room which was built on Sir Watkin's coming of age and is one of the finest I ever saw. The Company was regaled with tea, negus[4] and cakes in great abundance. I had a sight of Mrs. York[5] who inquired kindly after you, she had a number of little Yorks in her train at the Play. Sir Watkin did me the honour to recognize me. The Baronet and his Lady seemed to be both much pleased with the performance.

Would you believe it ! tho' we did not leave Wynnstay till after twelve o'clock I and my pregnant Lady came home to Malpas that night or rather morning where we arrived safe and sound at about half past three, eat each an egg upon a toast,

[1] Henry William Bunbury (1750-1811). Artist and caricaturist. He married Catherine daughter of Capt. K. W. Horneck R.E.

[2] Samuel Aldersey of Aldersey, Cheshire (1742-1803).

[3] Clement Kynersley of Loxley, Staffordshire. d. 1815. The farce seems almost certainly to have been ' The Bashful Man ' by Moncrieff, in which the daughter of Sir *Thomas* Friendly marries the bashful Edward Blushington.

[4] Hot sweetened wine and water.

[5] Philip Yorke of Erddig, Denbighshire. He had seven children.

drank a glass of negus and got to bed about four, went to our bye and kept at our bye till eleven the next day and (God be thank'd) have neither of us found any bad effects from the enterprize.

Mr. Allanson and his sisters stayed at Broughton and went to another play viz. the *Confederacy*,[1] yesterday and returned home this day to dinner. They say the *Confederacy* was better acted than *As you like it*. Kinnersley, Aldersley, Miss Jones and Mr. Cotes of Woodcote[2] and Mr. Bunbury were the principal characters and best performers.

Richard Heber to his father, Rev. Reginald Heber
London, 27 January 1785

I hope your Party were well entertained at Wynnstay and caught no cold. I was much pleased with Mrs. Abington's[3] performance both of ' Belinda '[4] and ' Lady Bab Lardoon '[5] but I prefer a Tragedy to a Comedy.

Mr. Samuel Joliffe was so good as to take me last night to the ' Eidophusikon '[6] which I admired very much ; particularly the Pandemonium with Satan arraying his troops on the banks of the Fiery Lake.

Rev. Reginald Heber to his sister, Elizabeth Heber
1 February 1785

We returned from Chester on Friday to dinner and left our friends all well. We had a very genteel and full assembly on Monday sennight, the noble Major had provided agreeable beaus to dance with Fanny and Bessey with whom they kept it

---

[1] *The Confederacy* by Vanburgh.
[2] John Cotes, M.P., of Woodcote, Shropshire. d. 1821.
[3] Frances Abington (1737-1815), actress.
[4] ' Belinda ', probably from John Murphy's *All in the Wrong*.
[5] ' Lady Bab. Lardoon ' from Burgoyne's *The Maid of the Oaks*.
[6] The Eidophusikon, a performance of moving pictures and coloured lights given by Philip de Loutherbourg, R.A. by means of intricate mechanism on a stage eight feet by six feet. The *Pandemonium* was a well known scene, as were *The Falls of Niagara* and *Winter in Switzerland*.

up till past 12 o'clock. The beautiful Miss Bouver[1] of Warrington happened to be there and danced with Sir Foster Cunliffe who says she is the finest *Woman on Earth*. She is indeed a fine well-made girl and dances country dances with great vivacity and activity. It is said she is engaged to be partner for life with Sir — Anderson, a Scottish baronet.

Rev. Reginald Heber to his sister, Elizabeth Heber
12 March 1785

Poor Mary has been tormented for this week past with a troublesome itching all over her for which she has begun to take an Electry.[2]

Rev. Reginald Heber to his sister, Elizabeth Heber
21 March 1785

Between the hours or two and three o'clock last night or rather this morning, dear Mary was safely delivered of another little boy. Tell my dear Richard I have baptized his little brother this morning by the name Thomas Cuthbert, after his paternal and maternal grandfathers.

Rev. Reginald Heber to his sister, Elizabeth Heber
9 April 1785

Richard's and Mr. Allanson's letters had been sent to Halifax, how the letter sorters make such mistakes is astonishing.

Little Thomas thrives daily. Dear Richard says he has twelve guineas in Bank towards purchasing Bell's *Edition of English Poets*, but the thirteen-guinea set being much handsomer he would like to have them. I will therefore contribute another yellow-boy now or at Whitsuntide.

The learned Cheshire Pig you mention, old Nurse says, is a native of Ireland, that the owner a poor Hibernian who had

---

[1] ? Maria Bover, daughter of a Frenchman, Capt. John Bover (de Beauvoir). She was known as the Lancashire Witch.

[2] Electuary ; a medicinal powder &c. mixed with honey or syrup.

instructed the docile animal in the service for which it is so celebrated, brought it over from Dublin to Chester and then died of a fever at the Inn, where poor piggy was left in pawn, and by your account has paid off all scores to the landlord into whose possession it came.

Rev. Reginald Heber to his sister, Elizabeth Heber
10 July 1785

The drought I complained of in my last still continues in this neighbourhood and there will be so very little new hay that they who have a stock of old hay before-hand ask a most extravagant price for it, viz., five or six shillings per hundred, and alas, I must be a buyer, dear as it is, as I shall not have more than a third part of the quantity I had last year.

Rev. Reginald Heber to his sister, Elizabeth Heber
27 February 1786

This unexpected return of hard weather makes us farmers who are short of hay for our cattle pull very long faces. I hope my dear Richard on his return to Greenford will take care not to get wet of his feet nor to go out of doors without his hat. Tommy is as brisk as a bee and has got into short pettycoats and paddles about in his little red cloth shoes.

Jolliffe the Bookseller's bill amounts to much more than I expected. I must not allow dear Richard to be so extravagant in the binding of his books as he has been. Jolliffe sent in his bill the day before we left town, you will find it on the bureau in the study, which be so good to pay what is due to him, but tell Dicky I will have no more debts contracted with booksellers or bookbinders.

Rev. Reginald Heber to his sister, Elizabeth Heber
10 March 1786

As my dear Mary and I have fixed on Saturday the 18th for our visit to Nicholas Street, and as she thinks her cloak and I think my surtout too shabby for an exhibition at Trinity Church we must beg your kind assistance in this great emergency. With regard to myself I desire you will order a surtout for me of fine cloth of the sort and colour enclosed, with respect to my other clothes, I am not in immediate want of them nor will there be time to make them now. Mary will be obliged to you to order an handsome white sattin cardinal or cloak, whichever is most fashionable, trimmed with white skin, and that you will consider her stature. If muffs are the ton, would have one suitable to the cloak. She also desires at the same time eight yards of beautiful scarlett sattin ribond an inch broad. You will be so good to see these valuables packed up very nicely in a deal box so that they may not be damaged by the friction of the coach, and send it by one of the Chester flys directed to me at Major Henchman's.

Rev. Reginald Heber to his sister, Elizabeth Heber
15 March 1786

I suppose the extraordinary Matrimonial Event[1] you mention is a fact. Mr. Smelt[2] mentioned it as indubitable in a letter to Mary by the same post. If the Great Lady should prove a breeder I fear the national consequences may be very serious. The supplications of every loyal subject for the long, long life of the present King and Queen will now be offered up with more frequency than ever.

I hope poor Ammy will soon get rid of that troublesome complaint the lumbago.

Rev. Reginald Heber to his sister, Elizabeth Heber
Chester, 20 March 1786

Accept the united hearty thanks for executing the commission we troubled you with in so expeditious and complete a manner. Mary is quite delighted with her cardinal and muff and I am not

---

[1] The Prince of Wales's marriage to Mrs. Fitzherbert had taken place on 21 December 1785. There were no children.
[2] Once Sub-Governor of the Prince of Wales, and friend of Fanny Burnsy.

less pleased with my surtout. They are both the Very Thing and meet the approbation of all beholders.

Elizabeth Heber to Rev. Reginald Heber
20 May 1786

I have bought four hundred pounds Stock in the 3 per cent Consols for £285.

We went with Mrs. Congreve and Master to Greenford on Tuesday morning and found dear Richard well. He says his cough is not gone but Dr. and Mrs. Glasse as well as Mrs. Bristowe say they never hear him cough so I hope it is of no consequence.

Rev. Reginald Heber to his sister, Elizabeth Heber
20 June 1786

We had a very grand Christening at Malpas Church on Thursday last. No less than two coaches and four ; the postillions and livery servants in scarlet and gold arrived at the higher Rectory about eleven o'clock, containing in one coach Sir John and Lady Mosley[1] and Mr. and Mrs. Baylie of Manchester, Mr. and Mrs. Mosley, their infant and nurse in the other. It being Dr. Townson's week to officiate, he received the little Christian named John into the Church. Mary and I and the Doctor went afterwards to dinner at Bolesworth where we were sumptuously entertained.

Rev. Reginald Heber to his sister, Elizabeth Heber
Ripon, 10 July 1786

George and I have taken two or three very pleasant rides in this country. One day we went to see Sir Bell Graham's[2] at Norton about four miles from Ripon, a place adorned with noble woods and beautiful and clear river and a very extensive

---

[1] Sir John Mosley, first Baronet (1732-98). His wife had been a Miss Bayley of Withington, Lancs., Mr. Oswald Mosley his eldest son (1761-89), and John Mosley his second grandson (1786-1804).

[2] Sir Bellingham Graham, fifth Baronet of Norton Conyers, Ripon. d. 1790.

meadow of one hundred acres which forms the lawn in front of an ancient mansion. Yesterday we rode to Grantley and took a circuit through the extensive woods of Studley by the shade of which we were sheltered from the heat of the sun for a mile or two. A great deal of money has been laid out on this spot — Grantley — which is pretty but not situated in so good a country as Norton.

On Saturday we were hospitably entertained at dinner at Holling Close by Mr. Wood who is *sola* there at present. This a most delightful spot indeed and commands a most extensive prospect over a fertile well-cultured country, part of which is the grand vale of Mowbray. I remember my Aunt Edward Heber[1] used to boast about the beauties of Holling Close and well she might. We are going to dine to-night with Mrs. Blacket,[2] a fine old lass of ninety.

I shall like to see Hurtley's *Craven*[3] a publication I had not heard of before you mentioned it. It is the first time I ever heard that any of our progenitors was inimical to the Royal Cause at the great Rebellion but the contrary.

Rev. Reginald Heber to his sister, Elizabeth Heber
York, 18 July 1786

We arrived at this City yesterday by one o'clock having fixed to dine with Aunt Dunne[4] at two, whom we had the satisfaction of finding pretty well. She was delighted with Reginald who was in high spirits and pleased with running about in Aunt Dunne's little garden and sending Uncle George into the cherry tree.

[1] ' Aunt Edward Heber ' was the wife of Rev. Reginald Heber's youngest uncle who was a proctor at York and had married Miss Margaret Cuthbert in 1747.

[2] Mrs. John Blackett, mother of Sir Edward Blackett, fourth Baronet of Matsen. She died in 1788 aged 93.

[3] Thomas Hurtley, *A concise account of some natural curiosities in the environs of Malham, in Craven, Yorkshire*, London, 1786. The book names Thomas Heber of Marton (connected by marriage to General Lambert) as one who declared for the side of Parliament at the outset of the Civil War.

[4] ' Aunt Dunne ', née Dorothy Heber, was Rev. Reginald Heber's youngest aunt. She married William Dunne who had been sheriff of York in 1755. She died on 7 December 1786 aged seventy-four and was buried on 22 December ' being kept above a fortnight by her own desire '.

Rev. Reginald Heber to his sister, Elizabeth Heber
Ripon, 29 July 1786

Running colds in the head prevail much in this family. I am glad to hear that Sir James Long has presented Dr. Glasse with the living of Wanstead but hope he will not reside there as the situation cannot, I think, be so wholesome or agreeable as that of Greenford.

Rev. Reginald Heber to his sister, Elizabeth Heber
Preston, 10 August 1786

This has been a very gay bustling week at Preston being a second Race Meeting under the auspices of Lord Derby. The Meeting was extremely genteel and numerous, the Balls splendid, and the sport on the Turf the best I ever saw.

Mary and I were at the ball on Monday night and had the pleasure of seeing Miss Rawstorne dance the first minuet with Lord Derby in which Bessy acquitted herself extremely well. She is indeed a very genteel fine figure and does great credit to Queen's Square. Mrs. Rawstorne attended the Ball again last night with her daughter and Miss Loxam but Mary and I stayed at home with Mr. Rawstorne. Miss Rawstorne had the honour of dancing a minuet with little Lord Stanley[1] a very fine lively boy.

Rev. Reginald Heber to his sister, Elizabeth Heber
Malpas, 30 October 1786

Many thanks for your kind enquiries after my stomach, it has been better since I have abstained from Porter and toasted cheese.

Rev. Reginald Heber to his sister, Elizabeth Heber
Malpas, 6 November 1786

Mary and her sister are bound to Chester to-morrow to purchase fripperies and sables for the Court mourning wherewith

[1] The twelfth Earl of Derby (1752-1834) and his eldest son Lord Stanley, later thirteenth Earl of Derby (1775-1851) and father of the Prime Minister.

all his Majesty's liege subjects are to be dight on Sunday next in obedience to the Lord Chamberlain's orders. I know not whether I shall accompany the ladies to Chester as they will be busy in the shops where I have no business at all. I think with you that it is monstrous base and truly horrid — as Dicky says — that the old Princess should send her Riches for which she was indebted to Old England, to Germany.[1] Methinks she ought to have bequeathed handsome legacies to her nephew the Duke of Gloucester's[2] offspring who I suppose have as much need of it as her relatives of the House of Hesse-Cassel.

Rev. Reginald Heber to his sister, Elizabeth Heber
4 December 1786

It gives us pleasure to hear that Lady Kenyon and her family were well. I think Sir Lloyd would make a very good Chief Justice but the papers give that high Office to Judge Buller.[3]

Rev. Reginald Heber to his sister, Elizabeth Heber
18 December 1786

Pray with my truest love to dear Dicky tell him I lay my absolute commands upon him not to skate at all during the holidays, as bad accidents happen, limbs are broken, skulls fractured and lives lost every winter in the frozen ponds in St. James' Park, Hyde Park and other places. I trust the boys at Greenford are not suffered to venture on the ice except in the presence of Mr. Bristowe and where the water is shallow.

[1] Princess Amelia Sophia, a maiden aunt of George III, died on 31 October 1786 aged seventy-five. She left more than £20,000 each to her two nephews of the house of Hesse-Cassel, but also about the same amount to her Ladies-in-Waiting.

[2] The Duke of Gloucester (1743-1805), younger brother of George III. He had three children.

[3] Lord Mansfield, who had been an unpopular Lord Chief Justice since 1756, resigned at last in 1788. Ministers ' hesitated long between the corruption of Buller and the intemperance of Kenyon ', but decided in the end in favour of Kenyon.

Rev. Reginald Heber to his sister, Elizabeth Heber
22 January 1787

Bessy returned safe and sound from Chester on Saturday. She was at a Ball and a concert and at routs and suppers without end. The news of the Country is that our old relative, Viscount Kilmorry[1] is going to espouse the Widow Forester of Chester. You will not be surprised at his Wedding haste when I tell you he never put on mourning for his last lady. It is also rumoured that Sir Thomas Broughton[2] is soon to be married to Lord Clive's sister, and Lord Carresford[3] to Miss Grenville, sister to Lady Wat. Williams. Thus our widowers shew their good liking for the honourable state of matrimony.

Rev. Reginald Heber to his sister, Elizabeth Heber
3 March 1787

I have the pleasure to acquaint my dear sisters that my dearest Mary was safely delivered between three and four o'clock yesterday afternoon of a daughter.[4] The infant is well and I hope likely to continue so. I will write to you again on Monday.

Rev. Reginald Heber to his sister, Elizabeth Heber
24 June 1787

I had a letter from my dear niece Harriet[5] by the last post informing me that Mr. Wrightson has made proposals of marriage to her which I make no doubt she has communicated to you, otherwise take no notice of it as she enjoins me to keep it secret from everyone but my wife. His age, family and fortune are very suitable and I trust his religious and moral principles are such as she desires in a partner for life.

[1] John, tenth Lord Kilmorey was seventy-seven at the time ; he had lost his wife only in August 1786. There is no record of his remarrying. He died in 1791.
[2] Sir Thomas Broughton, sixth Baronet, married a daughter of Lord Plymouth's in June 1787. Lord Clive's sister married Colonel Walpole in 1788.
[3] John, second Lord Carysfort, married in April 1787 Elizabeth, sister to the first Marquis of Buckingham and to Lady Williams-Wynn.
[4] Mary, third and last child of his second wife, Mary Allanson.
[5] Harriet Heber, daughter of Rev. Reginald Heber's elder brother Richard, married William Wrightson of Cusworth, Northumberland, on 20 July 1787.

Rev. Reginald Heber to his sister, Elizabeth Heber
27 December 1787

We are all as well as can be expected considering the severity
of the weather which is not calculated to cure the rheumatics
under which my wife groans as well as myself. Notwithstanding
the frost and snow the fair Frances went yesterday with the
young ladies from Broughton to a Ball at Wrexham, but they
are but young and can keep themselves warm by flirting
and dancing.

Rev. Reginald Heber to his sister, Elizabeth Heber
6 January 1788

Accept my dearest sister my best thanks for your kind letter
as well as for the Colchesters which arrived at the same time and
which afforded a delicious treat last night to Mary and myself,
Mrs. Fowler and John Bissell, the celebration of dear Richard's
birthday being postponed till Tuesday. We drank dear Dicky's
health in a copious bowl of stiff Rum Punch after our oysters,
both of which agreed very well with us all, tho' I think (*except
myself*) they were tipsy she and tipsy he.

Rev. Reginald Heber to his son, Richard Heber
Hodnet, 13 January 1788

I hope to be able to establish a Sunday School here of which a
beginning was made this day when twenty poor boys and girls
attended Divine Service and twenty poor widows in Lindsey
gowns.

Rev. Reginald Heber to his sister, Elizabeth Heber
3 February 1788

Our friends at Ripon are well but sorrowful for the loss of
their good and friendly neighbour, Mrs. Blackett who is just
dropt into the earth like a sheaf of corn full ripe.

The Heber and the Cholmondeley Families

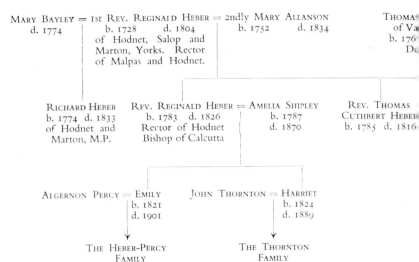

MARY BAYLEY = 1st REV. REGINALD HEBER = 2ndly MARY ALLANSON   THOMAS
   d. 1774   b. 1728   d. 1804   b. 1752   d. 1834   of Va
                  of Hodnet, Salop and   b. 176
                  Marton, Yorks. Rector   De
                  of Malpas and Hodnet.

   RICHARD HEBER   REV. REGINALD HEBER = AMELIA SHIPLEY   REV. THOMAS
   b. 1774 d. 1833   b. 1783   d. 1826   b. 1787   CUTHBERT HEBER
   of Hodnet and   Rector of Hodnet   d. 1870   b. 1785 d. 1816
   Marton, M.P.   Bishop of Calcutta

ALGERNON PERCY = EMILY   JOHN THORNTON = HARRIET
                 b. 1821   b. 1824
                 d. 1901   d. 1889

        THE HEBER-PERCY   THE THORNTON
           FAMILY   FAMILY

ondeley Families

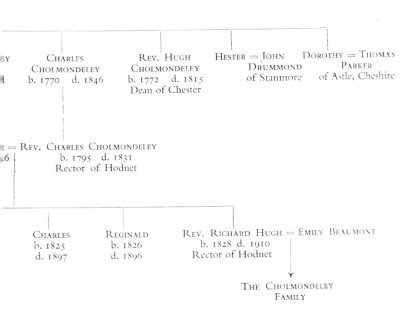

EY   CHARLES   REV. HUGH   HESTER = JOHN   DOROTHY = THOMAS
    CHOLMONDELEY   CHOLMONDELEY   DRUMMOND   PARKER
    b. 1770   d. 1846   b. 1772   d. 1815   of Stanmore   of Astle, Cheshire
                     Dean of Chester

= REV. CHARLES CHOLMONDELEY
6   b. 1795   d. 1831
      Rector of Hodnet

CHARLES   REGINALD   REV. RICHARD HUGH = EMILY BEAUMONT
b. 1825   b. 1826   b. 1828 d. 1910
d. 1897   d. 1896   Rector of Hodnet

THE CHOLMONDELEY
FAMILY

Richard Heber to his father, Rev. Reginald Heber
14 *March* 1788

By all accounts Fox is beyond everything. The night before he made those fine speeches[1] which astonished everybody both with their elegance, their sound sense and the fluency which they were delivered, this English Cicero had spent in revelling and drunkenness ; he had never been in bed and only just dressed himself in the morning before he came to the Hall.

Rev. Reginald Heber to his sister, Elizabeth Heber
27 *June,* 1788

Dear Mary had the satisfaction of hearing from Fanny yesterday that she got well to Manchester before eight o'clock that evening where she met with a kind welcome from Mrs. Fowler under whose roof she should have enjoyed a sweet repose after the fatigue of her journey had not the Watchman disturbed their slumbers with a sudden alarm at the door and cry of Thieves. Fanny says she supposes some evil-minded person allured by her baggage unloaded out of the post-chaise at Mrs. Fowler's door had taken the opportunity while the trunks were carrying in of slipping into the house and concealing himself till the family were gone to bed, she further supposes that the rogue had attempted to carry off her great trunk but finding it too heavy unlocked the front door (which the watchman found open) and went for assistance to convey away the spoil. It is not clear from Fanny's narrative that the watchman saw the thief come out of the house, but it was very well that he saw the door was open and gave the alarm before the *raparee* returned with a reinforcement as no one knows what the consequences might have been both to their persons and property.

Sir Watkin has got a plan for a Palace from Wyatt[2] which Mr. Sidebotham his House Steward told me was to be begun immediately.

---

[1] Fox spoke twice in the House of Commons on 13 March 1788 ; on and against a point in the Mutiny Bill, and in introducing his motion for the repeal of the Shop Tax, lost by 141 votes to 98.
[2] James Wyatt, R.A. (1743-1813), the well-known Architect.

Rev. Reginald Heber to his sister, Elizabeth Heber
24 July 1788

On our return from Hodnet to-day where I went with Mama, Tiddy and Tommy on Saturday last, I had the pleasure of finding my dearest Pop's affectionate letter. You will conclude I was pretty well when I tell you I held forth twice at Hodnet Church on Sunday. On Tuesday we had the honour of dining at Hawkstone where we met a great number of the race of Hills,[1] viz. Mr. and Mrs. John Hill with their daughter Jane and four of their sons and Mr. and Mrs. Robert Hill with three of theirs, and these not half the number each couple counts ; Mr. J. Hill having 13 in all and Mrs. Robert 12 and another coming, of which I think ten or eleven are lads so there is no lack of heirs male to the house of Hawkstone though the Baronet seems to be a determined bachelor.

We spent the day very agreeably a large party of the male creatures were entertained in sailing in a fine large pleasure boat on the noble canal from whence we saluted the ladies, who had chose to take a walk up to the Grotto, with repeated discharges from half a dozen carronades on board. The views of the woods and rocks from this fine piece of water are very grand and beautiful and are I think seen to the greatest advantage. Upon the whole since the completion of this Grand Canal, I think there is now — take it all together, no place in England superior to Hawkstone. Mrs. Jane Hill, as she now stiles herself, inquired very kindly after you. Miss Jane is very near as tall as her mother but will never, I think, be as handsome as she has been, indeed, she is still very handsome tho' she has had thirteen children.

[1] Sir Richard Hill, second Baronet of Hawkstone, d. unmarried 1809.
Mr. (later Sir) John Hill (1740-1828), and Mrs. John Hill, d. 1806.
Rev. Robert Hill (1746-1831), and Mrs. Robert Hill, d. 1824.

II   Letters of the

HEBER FAMILY

1788-1793

WE ENTER now on unquiet times. In October 1788 the King was taken ill and showed signs of mental derangement. For a few days he appeared to recover, but on 5 November, at Windsor, became delirious. Physicians correctly forecast that he would recover, and he resumed his duties on 10 March 1789. But in the meantime who was to exercise the function of Regent ? The Prince of Wales had an indisputable right, and Fox was allied to the Prince. Pitt proposed to shackle the Regent with parliamentary restrictions ; before handing over power, he intended to limit the new ruler's capacity to do harm. Fox on his side declared that the Prince's right by birth overrode the right of Parliament to appoint the Regent and make terms with him. So alien was this idea to the spirit of the Constiturion that he was forced to surrender the point. He also wanted the Prince to assume the Regency immediately, lest the King recover. In this he was prevented. It is indeed doubtful that he could ever have come into power with the free hand which he desired, for Pitt's Regency Bill was successfully going through Parliament when the King made it unnecessary by returning to health and sanity.

The Hebers were quite able to reconcile their high opinion of the powers of the Crown (still more evident in the next chapter) with the necessity of limiting them by the action of the legislature.

No sooner was Reginald Heber reassured by the recovery of the King than his strong feelings were again roused by a movement on the part of the Dissenters for repeal of the Test Act, which for more than a century had excluded scrupulous non-conformists from the service of the Crown. In his mind the Established Church was sacred equally with the Constitution. He regarded Dissenters as ' restless people, grasping at power, which we know by experience they would exercise, if possessed of, in the destruction of the constitution both in Church and State.' Dissenters, regicides, revolutionists, republicans : to Heber they were not only equally abhorrent but all one. ' God preserve us,' he wrote, ' from the wicked devices of republicans and dissenters of all denominations.' Although loud in denouncing those turbulent spirits, he never evinced personal concern for, or seemed to apprehend an attack on, his own property or position ; and he wrote with humour of a revolutionary escapade at his son's school, without seeming to fear that familiarity with Tom Paine would corrupt the boy's mind.

This chapter finishes at the outbreak of war between England and France. The last few letters reflect the rising excitement of these months.

The government took strong measures against dangerous democratic propaganda, to the point of behaving with doubtful legality, and although it is easy to see now that Pitt misjudged the situation and that Fox was more nearly right a great part of the nation agreed that the measures were necessary. Provocation was given by many radical societies, of which the Corresponding Society and the Friends of the People were foremost in enthusiasm and perhaps most deficient in tact. In November 1792 the former addressed a message of sympathy to the French National Convention, and the National Convention declared its support for all peoples against their rulers. If Pitt misjudged the English reformers, so did the English reformers misjudge the French revolutionaries and the French revolutionaries the English reformers. A 'society for preserving liberty and property against republicans and levellers' had been formed in the previous month ; now the mutual indiscretions of the Corresponding Society and the Convention raised more such associations, to which Heber referred in a letter with natural approval.

Rev. Reginald Heber to his sister, Elizabeth Heber
22 October 1788

We despatched John Billington on Tuesday with a letter to Mr. and Miss Cholmondeley[1] informing them that we intended having the honour of waiting on our friends at Vale Royal on Thursday and received an answer from Miss Cholmondeley that she and her brother were engaged to go to Erthwick (Mr. York's)[2] on Wednesday and after that visit were to go for ten days to Hagley after which they would be glad to see us.

Rev. Reginald Heber to his sister, Elizabeth Heber
1 November 1788

Dr. Townson has lent Mary a novell called *Emeline* or *The Orphan of the Castle*[3] which she began upon last night after our Company left us, with great avidity. It is interesting and will amuse you if you have not read it already but I don't think it the equal either of *Caroline of Lichfield* or *Cecilia*.[4]

Rev. Reginald Heber to his sister, Elizabeth Heber
19 November 1788

Mary went with Mrs. Parker and her three fair daughters[5] to the Ball at Knutsford on Wednesday 12th, which was not so

---

[1] Thomas Cholmondeley of Vale Royal (1767-1855). He was M.P. for Cheshire for many years, fought in the Wars in Flanders, created Lord Delamere 1821.

[2] Erddig, in Denbighshire, a fine brick mansion built in James II's reign, had been bought, in 1718, by John Meller, Citizen and Draper of London, whose sister, Anne, married Simon Yorke (uncle of the Lord Chancellor) ; their son, Simon, became Meller's heir.

[3] *Emmeline* or *The Orphans of the Castle* by Mrs. Charlotte Smith, published in 1788.

[4] *Cecilia* by Miss Burney, published in 1782.

[5] Rev. John and Mrs. Parker of Astle, Cheshire, had one son and five daughters who reappear constantly in these pages. They were :—

Thomas Parker (1766-1840), married in 1795 Dorothy, youngest sister of Thomas Cholmondeley of Vale Royal.

Jane Parker married in 1791 John Baskerville Glegg of Old Withington, Lancs.

Alice Parker married in 1781 Sir Peter Warburton, Bt., of Arley.

Lydia Parker married in 1784 John Dixon later of Astle.

Anne Parker married in 1793 Roger Barnston of Churton.

Mary Parker married in 1790 Peter Patten of Bank Hall, Warrington.

splendid as usual on account of a prevailing rumour of the poor
King's death, whom God preserve and restore to his pristine
health of body and soul. Mr. and Miss Cholmondeley were
there and Mary thinks our fair cousin extremely pretty but alas !
too delicate in her appearance to be healthy. She told Mary that
they were to set out on Monday for Hagley ; it is rumoured
that the young Esquire is a great admirer of Miss Betty Curzon
who I make no doubt will have a good Fortune and methinks
the match would be very suitable. They left Arley the day before
we got there and as the young Squire forgot his appointment
to dine at Astle on the Saturday before, I saw but little of him.
Mr. Tom Parker had engaged him to meet Harry Leicester[1] and
young Shakerley[2] to dinner at Astle at four o'clock and dinner
was in vain put back till past five. Mrs. Parker told him at the
Ball of the pretty trick he had play'd them and his reply was that
he was ashamed to show his face but that he never recollected
the engagement he made till Sunday morning. Mary says, his
poor pretty sister blush'd with him and for him. I hope he will
not inherit his poor father's failing in this want of punctuality.
It has been rumoured that Tom Parker admires our fair cousin
very much indeed but nothing of that was mentioned at Astle,
so *Mum*. He is a very pleasing sensible young man as he was a
boy ; his Father told me with that satisfaction better to be conceived than expressed that he had never done anything either
at Eton or Oxford to displease him or give him a moment's
uneasiness.

I grieve and grieve for the deplorable condition of our poor
good King. How unspeakably grievous must it then be to the
poor Queen and the rest of the Royal Family. Grievous it is to
every loyal subject, and calamitous it is to the State and the
Nation. Doctor Townson read me a letter this morning from his
brother which gives a more hopeful account of the probability
of his recovery and restoration to himself than I had heard
before. God grant it may prove less fallacious than others have
been !

[1] Henry Leicester (1765-1816), second son of Sir Peter Leicester, fourth Baronet.
[2] Charles Shakerley of Somerford Park, Cheshire (1767-1834).

Elizabeth Heber to Rev. Reginald Heber
24 November 1788

Yesterday we drank tea with Lady Lucy Meyrick who with her daughter and Miss Essex Cholmondeley arrived in Town about ten days since. Lady Lucy went from Vale Royal to Overleigh (Mrs. Cowper's) on her way to Mr. Yorke or would have given you a call. Mr. Charles Cholmondeley drank tea there with us. He is like his Mother and I fear inherits her delicate constitution.[1]

Our spirits have been greatly depressed on the present melancholy occasion, in which distress every good Subject must deeply sympathise. I wish I could give you any good intelligence. The accounts have been less favourable this day or two. May it please the Almighty to hear our prayers and restore our Beloved Sovereign to his afflicted Queen, his family and people. The Prince of Wales and the Duke of York have never left Windsor Castle since the King's illness, and have behaved with great sensibility and dutiful attention. God grant may have a good effect on their future conduct.

Elizabeth Heber to Rev. Reginald Heber
1 *December* 1788

Charles Fox you will see by the papers is arrived from the Continent *post haste*,[2] and has been sent on an Embassy to the Chancellor, if this report is true it augers no good. The Prince is returned to town as the paper says to-day, I fear, I fear the influence of evil Counsellors will again prevail. But enough of this unpleasant subject .

Poor Mrs. Ellison dined with us about ten days since in very low spirits indeed, well she might, her son's extravagance had at last determined his Father to discharge no more of his debts,

[1] Charles Cholmondeley (1770-1846), younger brother of Thomas Cholmondeley of Vale Royal. His mother was a Cowper of Overleigh, Chester. Essex Cholmondeley died unmarried. Lady Lucy Pitt, daughter of Thomas, Earl of Londonderry, had married Piers Meyrick of Bodorgan, Anglesey.

[2] Fox, who at this time was touring in Europe with Mrs. Armistead, returned with great speed and arrived in London on 24 November. It was sufficiently obvious that he and the Prince would make common cause against Pitt and the Queen.

he was arrested, the law took its course and he was sent to Newgate where he now is confined. I most heartily pity his parents.
He has deserved prison long ago and if he was at liberty he would
go on to the ruin of the family.[1]

Elizabeth Heber to Rev. Reginald Heber
15 December 1788

To-morrow is the great important day when I hope Mr. Pitt
will be found in a decided majority of loyal and independent
Members.[2] God grant the King a speedy recovery that he may
re-assume the government of the Country in his own person.
His Majesty, when Dr. Willis was first introduced to him, said he
remembered having heard of him above twenty years since, that
his brother the Duke of York[3] having related some anecdotes
of him. I suppose the Dr. was Fellow of Brasenose before your
time as I don't recollect ever hearing you mention him.

Rev. Reginald Heber to his sister, Elizabeth Heber
20 December 1788

Doctor Willis[4] who has now the case of His Majesty, was a
Fellow of Brasenose when I entered but resided only a short
time before he accepted Wapping.

I perceive by the papers that Fox's friends are very anxious to
get him out of the scrape he is certainly got into, by asserting that
the Prince had the right to assume the reins of Government without the sanction of Parliament and without any restrictions or
limitations. They know their Champion is wrong in Revolution

---

[1] Imprisonment for debt was not abolished until 1869.

[2] On 16 December 1788 Pitt introduced the three vital resolutions as a preliminary to
his Regency Bill. These, passed by a narrow majority, stated the right of Parliament to
provide for the Regency during the King's incapacity. Fox's contention that the Prince
ought to assume the Regency automatically, with the full power of a King, as by right
of birth, was thus defeated.

[3] Edward, Duke of York, younger brother of George III (1739-67).

[4] Dr. Francis Willis (1718-1807), fellow and vice-principal of Brasenose College ; took
holy orders ; physician, specialist in mental derangement ; of considerable reputation in
1788, although regarded by many orthodox medical practitioners as a mountebank. He
treated patients with unusual gentleness. His success with the King brought him great
fame and a large practice.

Principle, and therefore labour to avoid discussion of the question of absolute Right. But I suppose the matter of Right would be debated in the House of Commons on Wednesday or Thursday last and decided against Fox's opinion. I presume the Regent will appoint a new Administration, but mum for that. It is an ill-wind that blows good to nobody, I hope our friend the Dean of Lincoln[1] will either be confirmed in St. Marylebone or get a Bishopric. St. Asaph now vacant and worth £3,000 per annum would suit him nicely.

Richard to his father, Rev. Reginald Heber
London, 29 December 1788

You will find by the Papers that the Resolutions have been carried by a great majority in the House of Peers.[2] Their Lordships have distinguished themselves in no small degree by their good oratory in general — more particularly — The Chancellor,[3] Lord Loughbour,[4] The Marquis of Lansdowne[5] and Lord Abingdon.[6] There is, I believe I may safely say, no doubt but the Prince will discard the present Administration in favour of Charles Fox and Gang, tho' Mr. Pitt will, I dare say, have a majority in the opposition. Never (I suppose) did a Minister go out with more general and justly conceived esteem than the present. It is reported that the Corporation and City of London purpose to present him with a purse of 50,000 guineas for his eminent services to the nation : the Borough of Cambridge also intend voting him an address of thanks. I allow our friend Charles all possible merit as to the powers of oratory — alias — the powers of making a bad cause appear good — only hope that when in power he will not put his good sense to a bad end.

[1] Rev. Sir Richard Kaye, Bt., Dean of Lincoln, 1782. He was confirmed as Rector of Marylebone at this time and continued to hold that, the Deanery and the Archdeaconate of Nottingham till his death in 1809.

[2] Vote of 23 December : contents 99, not-contents 66.

[3] Edward Thurlow (1731-1806), first Baron Thurlow ; Lord Chancellor until 1792.

[4] Alexander Wedderburn (1733-1805), first Baron Loughborough and first Earl of Rosslyn ; tory ; Lord Chancellor, 1793-1801.

[5] William Petty (1737-1805), first Marquis of Lansdowne (1784) and second Earl of Shelburne ; best known by the latter title ; chief minister 1782-3 ; a whig.

[6] Willoughby Bertie (1740-99), fourth Earl of Abingdon ; politician and democrat.

Rev. Reginald Heber to his son, Richard
2 *January* 1789

I sincerely wish the City of London may present Mr. Pitt with a sterling compliment. You say it is a purse of 50,000 but imagine you have put down a cypher too many and that it should be but 5,000 which would be very handsome.[1] Such acknowledgements confer great honour and afford substantial encouragement to Political Integrity.

Rev. Reginald Heber to his sister, Elizabeth Heber
5 *February* 1789

We had a pacquet this day from Ripon from which we learn that Lord Grantley[2] has left his relict in noble plight, her income being three thousand a year, the house in Surrey and that in Lincoln's Inn Fields. He has also done handsomely by his daughter having bequeathed to her a fortune of twelve thousand pounds. To the present Lord he has left Grantley with the Yorkshire Estate reckoned £5,000 per annum, to the General only two thousand pounds and to the Baron nothing. This seems hard, methinks he might have given his two younger sons five thousand apiece as they have neither of them any money. It is current report of the gossips at Ripon, Fanny says, that brother George is to comfort and console Gracy : but she says she recommends the Dowager. But methinks an amiable good-tempered and virtuous young woman with good connections and twelve thousand pounds in her pocket is no despicable object, and I hope my friend George will be of the same opinion, as I am inclined to believe that if he puts in his plea in due time, it will be accepted.

We rejoice to read in the papers that His Majesty has had two calm days and nights, and that the Queen and the Princesses

---

[1] Pitt refused a gift from the City of London, intended to comfort his retirement, of £100,000.
[2] Fletcher Norton, first Lord Grantley (1716-89). His widow died 1803.
William, eldest son, second Lord Grantley (1741-1822).
Fletcher Norton, second son (1744-1820). A baron of the exchequer in Scotland.
General Chapple Norton, third son, d. 1818.
Grace Norton, married in 1799 John, third Earl of Portsmouth, and d. 1813.

have dined with him. O ! how glad shall I be if the greedy, Gaping Cormorants are balked of their prey at last !

Rev. Reginald Heber to his sister, Elizabeth Heber
No. 18, Milsom Street, Bath, February 1789

Here is a son of Mrs. Palmer, dear Mary's and your acquaintance who is very intimate with and I think a great admirer of the Misses Parkers, particularly of Miss Mary. They say he is an agreeable lively young man but cannot say he inherits much of his Mother's beauty or is near so handsome as his Father, having an odd cast with one eye, however he inherits a good Fortune and can clearly discern Miss Mary's charms tho' he looks ascue at them. Mary Parker is a lovely sweet girl indeed and her beauty is set off by modest diffidence and lamblike innocence so rarely to be seen among the Modern Race of *Belles*, which makes her admired the more. I must tell you a smart thing he said to Miss Mary at the Ball on Monday. Observing a little spot upon her cheek, he asked her what had occasioned it, " A gnat bit it last night," said she — " I wish I were a gnat," replied he.

Rev. Reginald Heber to his son, Richard
Bath, 26 February 1789

Bath is much fuller than it was a week ago tho' Charles Fox and Mrs. Armistead[1] are decamped. I fancy Reynard on the event of his Majesty's happy recovery, for which God be praised, will be forced to cry "The Grapes are souer." What a Bull the Irish Lords and Commons have made over the Regency business ; you see the Lord Lieutenant would not forward their address to the Prince and the King's recovery will annihilate it.[2]

---

[1] Mrs. Armistead was Fox's mistress and later his wife.

[2] The Irish Parliament, taking Fox's line, had voted full powers to the Prince as Regent. Their address was held up by the Lord Lieutenant, the Marquis of Buckingham, with Pitt's approval, until it was made irrelevant by the King's recovery.

Rev. Reginald Heber to his sister, Elizabeth Heber
Bath, March 1789

We rejoice with joy unspeakable and gratitude inexpressible for the marvellous critical restoration of our King's health.

What a ridiculous contemptible figure do the Irish Delegates cut, but their situation and conduct is characteristic of their blundering Country.

Rev. Reginald Heber to his sister, Elizabeth Heber
Bath, 12 *March* 1789

I suppose you would have the greatest rejoicings and the most splendid illuminations in the Metropolis on Tuesday last that were ever exhibited, on the joyful occasion of his Majesty's recovery being announced. This City was well lighted up last night, the Circus, the Crescent and the principal Streets made a very luminous grand appearance. Some of the Papers have hinted that there is to be a day of public Thanksgiving,[1] and that the King and Royal Family will attend Divine Service at St. Paul's. The procession from St. James' to St. Paul's and the congregation at the Cathedral will afford the grandest, most aweful and grateful a spectacle that ever was seen since the dedication of it in Queen Anne's time or that of the Temple of Solomon.

Rev. Reginald Heber to his son, Richard
15 *April* 1789

I cannot say I rejoice in the importation of the cargo of books you mention from abroad, we had before enow and too manny, ten times more than were ever read or even looked into. Of multiplying books, my dear Richard, there is neither end nor use. The *Cacoethes* of collecting books draws men into ruinous extravagancies. It is an itch which grows by indulgence and should be nipt in the bud.

[1] The King attended a service of public thanksgiving at St. Paul's on 23 April. His illness, and the terrible prospect of his son governing, greatly enhanced George III's popularity.

Rev. Reginald Heber to his sister, Elizabeth Heber
Malpas, 13 May 1789

My breakfast is a good nice smooth milk pottage and my supper a small basin of new milk mix'd with a little hot water and a spoonful of rum, both of which meals agree very well.

We had heard the report of our cousin Miss Cholmondeley's[1] approaching nuptials and rejoice to hear it so well confirmed. She is a very sensible amiable young woman and will make any good and worthy young man happy, to which description I trust Mr. Drummond is entitled, in point of fortune it will certainly be a great match for our kinswoman.

You see the Dissenters have again fail'd in their application to Parliament for a repeal of the Test Act,[2] and Lord North distinguished himself by his steady opposition to a measure so dangerous to the Established Church, of the friends of which however, I am sorry to see so small a majority. These restless people are grasping at power, which we know by experience they would exercise, if possess'd of, in the destruction of the Constitution both in Church and State.

Rev. Reginald Heber to his sister, Elizabeth Heber
Chester, 20 January 1790

Yesterday evening we drank tea and played a game of Whisk at Mrs. Kennyon's and passed the time very agreeably, Sir Thos. Hanmer, Mr. Falconer and a few others being of the party.

I must beg the favour of you to send my annual present of a Cheshire Cheese of about 40 lb. weight to Freshingfield.

Rev. Reginald Heber to his sister, Elizabeth Heber
Malpas, 27 January 1790

I am glad dear Richard by favour of Lord Kenyon was at the House of Lords to hear his Majesty's speech and the Addresses

[1] Miss Hester Cholmondeley, elder sister of Thomas Cholmondeley of Vale Royal, married John Drummond of the famous banking house on 11 June 1789.

[2] Mr. Beaufoy's motion for the repeal of the Test and Corporation Acts was debated in the Commons on 8 May 1789 and was defeated by 122 to 102 votes.

worded thereon.[1] 'Twas a pity the lady's high head dresses
intercepted his view of the King and the speakers on the occasion.
It is very extraordinary that the maniacs male and female should
loose their rage and fury against His Majesty,[2] it is a mercy the
consequences have been no worse. God defend His sacred person
from all his enemies, mad or malicious.

Rev. Reginald Heber to his sister, Elizabeth Heber
February, 1790

Mr. Whitehall and his friend Tennant are still in the Country.
I accompanied the old hero a hunting on Thursday and had
good sport. Would you think it, the two young men were too
indolent to be of our party, what will the effeminancy of the
age come to ?

The Clergy of Malpas were invited to attend their Reverend
Brethren of the Archdeaconry of Chester at the Chapter House
on Monday to consider the stir made by the Dissenters in all
parts of the Kingdom for a repeal of the Test Act which meeting,
my brother Rector being then in Staffordshire, I attended alone,
or rather *solus cum sola*, for *chara sposa* went with me. The chief
intention of the Assembly was to give the lie direct to an assertion
advanced by the Dissenters at almost all their Meetings and
published in the Newspapers " That the Clergy of the Established Church approved of, and were in general friendly to their
Petition to the Legislature for the repeal of the Test Act ",
which unwarranted and impudently assumed sanction of their

---

[1] In his speech on opening the session, the King referred to war on the continent but
did not anticipate that Britain would be involved. He recommended a measure for
preventing the export and encouraging the import of corn. In proposing the Address of
the Commons, a speaker spoke in these terms : ' While discord, with all her direful train,
stalked abroad, we were in the full enjoyment of profound tranquillity. . . . Our revenue
was considerably increased ; our manufactures prospered ; and our commerce flourished
in every quarter of the globe.'

[2] There were several attacks on George III.

1. 1786, Margaret Nicholson, a lunatic, tried to stab him in St. James's Park.
2. January 1790, a stone thrown through his coach window by James Frith, also a lunatic,
   when he was on his way to open Parliament.
3. October 1795, again at the opening of Parliament, a mob met him in the Park,
   stones were thrown and a shot fired from an air-gun.
4. February 1796, a stone thrown at him on his way to the Opera.
5. May 1800, shot at in Drury Lane Opera House by John Hadfield.

proceedings it was judged proper to do away. The meeting was numerous and respectable, the unanimous resolutions and declarations in flat contradiction to the assertion of the Dissenters were agreed to, which you will shortly see in the *General Evening Post* and other Papers. There are I fear a set of men in this country at this time, ripe for mischief, ready formed to pursue the baneful example of the unprincipled insurgents and abettors of licentiousness, anarchy and infidelity so unhappily prevalent on the Continent, and all this is carried on under the fictitious mask of a love of liberty. May God's good providence protect us from their wicked machinations.

Rev. Reginald Heber to his sister, Elizabeth Heber
24 *February* 1790

You may possibly have seen the Resolutions of the Rev'd Clergy of the Archdeaconry of Chester in the *General Evening Post*. Mr. Fox you see has given notice of his intentions to make his Motion for the repeal of the Test Act on Tuesday next, and I am glad to see that Mr. Pitt has fix'd the preceding day for a call of the House, which I heard was very ill-attended the last time this matter was agitated, the Friends of the Constitution being too secure and free from apprehension of the success of the dissenters, which supineness and remissness occasioned the Petition then to be rejected by so small a majority as twenty. But as the Friends of the Church and King are now roused out of their lethargy, I hope the present petition will be thrown out by a great superiority of persons.

Tiddy and Tommy both attended Church this morning to say their catechism with the other boys, and Mary went to hear them, being the first time of her appearance in the Congregation.

Rev. Reginald Heber to his sister, Elizabeth Heber
1 *March* 1790

I am very glad my dearest Richard will have so good an opportunity of hearing the Debates in the House of Commons to-morrow of which I shall expect a particular account from his pen. Heaven grant that the Friends and Advocates of the Constitution of Church and State may triumph over the insidious attempts of their malevolent foes to undermine and subvert them. I hope the House will be full and the majority against the Dissenters so great and respectable as to give these restless turbulent men a set down, as you say for years to come. But they are become so impudent and arrogant that scarcely any checks will restrain them from pursuing their mischievous intents.

Mary had a letter from Miss Parker by this post. Miss Anne is better and 'tis to be hoped by a change of scene will ere long recover her health and spirits. The wretch whose behaviour hurt her so much is returned to England with a French Madam. Anne certainly had a happy escape.

Elizabeth Heber to Rev. Reginald Heber
10 March 1790

Mr. and Mrs. Booth called on us yesterday and we rejoiced together at the defeat of the Non. Cons.[1]

Dear Harriet was but indifferent after her journey and very nervous ; Dr. Denman says that is her chief disease, and tells her she must live well to recruit her strength, eat oysters and drink porter at noon and night or any other shell-fish. This regimen is both palatable and agrees with her.

Rev. Reginald Heber to his sister, Elizabeth Heber
20 March 1790

Little Tommy has had the resolution on his own accord and at his own request to abstain entirely from animal food and subsist wholly upon vegetables ever since his brother began to be ill, and I really think he has by this regimen which he proposed and prescribed to himself, evaded the fever.

---

[1] Fox's motion for the repeal of the Test and Corporation Acts was debated in the Commons on 2 March 1790. Pitt opposed it. The motion was lost by 294 votes to 105.

I wish you would get for me the Debates in the House of Commons on the proposed repeal of the Test Act to which the names of the Members who voted pro and con are annexed.

Rev. Reginald Heber to his sister, Elizabeth Heber
2 April 1790

The Paper to-day says Doctor Horne[1] has refused the Bishopric of Norwich and that he pleads his indifferent state of health as his apology. If he must resign his headship of Magdalene College, Oxford, worth £600 and Deanery of Canterbury worth £1,400 his income would not be mended by his accepting the See of Norwich but his expenses would be increased ; so that perhaps the Dean judges well in an economical light. He married a lady with very considerable fortune and has only two daughters who will be amply provided for. He is a worthy, pious, orthodox Divine and deserves a mitre. I was in hopes Dr. Glasse would have got something good in this scramble for Loaves and Fishes but fear he has no one steady potent friend.

Rev. Reginald Heber to his sister, Elizabeth Heber
9 April 1790

Mama ventured out to Doctor Townson's on Easter Monday to meet Mr. and Mrs. Dod and one of her sisters where they spent a very pleasant day, and, being Malpas Fair, the Ladys had the felicity of perambulating the streets and buying bargains, viz. toys, gingerbreads and Welch blankets.

I heard that (on the matter of the Test Act) Sir Richard Hill was neither bird nor beast but a *blind bat*. Good Sir Rowland[2] would not have turned his back on the Church of England on such an occasion. The Friends of the Church are much displeased but I hear of no opposition for the County.

---

[1] Dr. Horne was consecrated Bishop of Norwich in 1790, but died in 1792.
[2] Sir Rowland Hill, first Baronet and father of Sir Richard. d. 1783.

Rev. Reginald Heber to his sister, Elizabeth Heber
23 April 1790

Methinks our excellent Prime Minister has opened the Budget
with great *eclat* and I doubt not will make good all his comfortable promises at the expiration of the present year and that the
public income will then be equal to the expenditure exclusive
of the Annual million appropriated to the liquidation of the
National Debt ; which tho' in bulk a mountain will soon be
melted down to a molehill, if it please God to continue us in
the blessings of Peace.

Rev. Reginald Heber to his sister, Elizabeth Heber
12 June 1790

I was glad to hear Pop had a peep into Westminster Hall
among others to see the ceremony of Hasting's trial,[1] am sorry
it was not the day on which Fox summ'd up the evidence, tho'
I should think an harangue of five hours must be rather tiresome
to the audience as well as to the orator.

Rev. Reginald Heber to his sister, Elizabeth Heber
16 June 1790

As every newspaper since the Dissolution of Parliament costs
a shilling postage, I desire you will be so kind to stop Lasham
from sending any more till he can get them franked.[2]
There are to be Oratorios at Whitchurch this race week.

Rev. Reginald Heber to his sister, Elizabeth Heber
18 June 1790

I hear of no contested Elections in this county or in Cheshire :
indeed, the majority of the late Representatives behaved so well

[1] The impeachment of Warren Hastings (1732-1818) lasted from 1788 to 1795.
[2] *See* footnote on page 21.

on some trying occasions that I think they are deserving of the confidence of their Constituents.[1]

Rev. Reginald Heber to his son, Richard
18 July 1790

As to Music it is so apt to take of the attention of its votarys from more useful pursuits, I must own that it is an art in which I do not wish you to become a proficient. I think you are employing your time far better at Greenford than in thrumming cat-gut. I had rather you would persist in improving your acquaintance with the ancient poets, orators and historians than with modern musicians. If when you go to the University, you should wish to amuse yourself with the German flute or forte piano, which are the fittest instruments for a *Gentleman*, you will have more leisure than you can well spare now.

Rev. Reginald Heber to his sister, Elizabeth Heber
Parkgate, 30 July 1790

We arrived on this coast last night which is just twenty-seven miles distant from Malpas, we had a fine day and the children bore the journey without being coach-sick. The lodging houses are small but we occupy the whole of this except three apartments. If the weather holds fair I think the sea air and bathing will be of service in strengthening and bracing both Mama and her babes.

Rev. Reginald Heber to his sister, Elizabeth Heber
5 August 1790

Though we have had a good deal of wind and some rain since we came to this place, yet no day has been so bad as to prevent Mama and her babes taking a dip in the salt water or me from

---

[1] The members returned at this general election by the counties and boroughs of Shropshire and Cheshire differed in one name only from those returned at the previous general election.

taking an airing on horseback. The air, the exercise and the bathing agrees very well with us all — the last indeed I have not ventured to try but almost every day have taken a glass of sea water which sits easy on my stomach and has I think done me good.

The roads about this place (except the sands which are heavy) are extremely fine. We made an excursion one day to the New Ferry about eight miles from hence where we had a fine prospect of Liverpool which is on the opposite side of the Mersey. If the weather should be fine it would be a temptation to take a trip over to take a peep at this imposing noble sea-port, which Mary never was at and which I am told is almost as big again as when I last saw it almost twenty years ago.

Rev. Reginald Heber to his sister, Elizabeth Heber
Hodnet, 12 November 1790

I sincerely congratulate you and all lovers of Peace on the fair prospect of a re-establishment of that blessing, a blessing cheaply purchased by the expenditure of three or four millions without bloodshed which by means of war and slaughter would not have been obtained for forty millions, so prudent an economist I am persuaded our wise Minister has been by his vigorous tho' expensive preparation for War.[1]

I have sent for Mr. Burke's book on the French Revolution[2] which everybody reads and I hear everybody but your Prices[3] and Priestleys[4] and rank Republicans and King-Killers approves.

[1] The affair of Nootka Sound, in the spring of 1789. Political boundaries on the Pacific coast of North America were not at this stage defined. The Spaniards certainly had a good claim to Nootka Sound, but the British were in possession. The Spaniards ejected the British. The British government immediately prepared for war. Overawed, the Spaniards gave way : a convention was signed in October 1790. The event was a notable diplomatic success.

[2] Edmund Burke (1729-97), published his *Reflections on the French Revolution* in November 1790.

[3] Rev. Richard Price (1723-91), mainly known as a writer on politics and finance ; took the part of the American colonists and warmly welcomed the French Revolution.

[4] Dr. Joseph Priestley (1733-1804), theologian and scientist. It is said that some injudicious remarks of his in a pamphlet issued just before Fox's motion of 2 March contributed to its defeat. In July 1791 a mob attacked his house ; so general was the confusion in the public mind between liberal and republican thought.

The Ladys walked up the Parks this morning through the Wood and round by Kenstone making a circuit of four miles at least, while Papa and Reginald amused themselves by coursing five hares in the Parks which shewed fine sport tho' the dogs were beaten four times out of five.

Rev. Reginald Heber to his sister, Elizabeth Heber
26 December 1790

Tell my dear Richard if he has not **read** Burke's book he has a great pleasure to come. I have perused it with uncommon pleasure and admiration and think it a capital performance. Having truth for its basis, sound sense and argument in its composition and fine classic language for its embellishment.

Rev. Reginald Heber to his sister, Elizabeth Heber
21 December 1790

Miss Allanson, I and Tiddy paid our annual Christmas visit yesterday to Mrs. Bridge to partake of her goose, pye and other good X's cheer while poor Mama was indulging upon water gruel in her bed.

Rev. Reginald Heber to his sister, Elizabeth Heber
No date

Pray inform my dear Richard that his Tutor, Mr. Churton[1] has secured the same apartments in College for him that my dear brother had, which are very pleasant having a window to Radclyffe's Area and another to Exeter Gardens with a convenient study, the only inconvenience is the smallness of the bed-place but everything to be wished is not to be expected in any situation or at any time of life.

[1] Ralph Churton (1754-1831), fellow of Brasenose College, Oxford.

Rev. Reginald Heber to his sister, Elizabeth Heber
5 June 1791

We had fine weather in our excursion into the pleasant Vale once the residence of Owen Glendower, now better known by the name of Llangollen. We took up Mr. Whitehall Davies[1] at Broughton and made our first halt at Ruabon, where we had the pleasure of joining Misses Davies and Eaton, close to Wynn-stay Park which they traversed with us and where we discovered many beautiful scenes.

Having finished our perambulation and regaled ourselves with a cold beef sandwich at the Vicarage, we proceeded through one of the most beautiful Vales in the Principality of Wales to Llangollen where we took up our abode that evening. In the cool of the evening we strolled to view the ruins of the ancient Abbey of St. Cruce, *alias* of the Holy Cross, which is about a mile from Llangollen, which is the most sequestered spot you can imagine surrounded by an immense wall or boundary of cloud cap't mountains with only one narrow entrance into a green vale fringed with wood, through which a crystal stream meanders, and where the mouldering walls of the Abbey appear, which altogether put us in mind of Paracletes ' White Walls and Silver Springs '. A more recluse spot, more secluded from the world, or better calculated for the religious retirement of devotees, ' The world forgetting, by the world forgott ' could not be chosen.

The next morning we took a peep at the elegant cottage of the two celebrated Irish friends, Lady Eleanor Butler and Miss Ponsonby, the prospects from this little habitation are romantic, their garden a little paradise and the habitation a cabinet of curiosities. But the great curiosities, the ladies themselves, were not to be seen which we regretted.

From Llangollen we returned by Chirk Castle which stands on a bold eminence and makes a grand appearance in the midst of a beautiful, well-wooded park and gives one the idea of the residence of an ancient British Baron. The apartments in the

---

[1] Rev. Whitehall Davies (1764-1824), of Broughton, Flints.

Castle are spacious and grand specially the saloon, gallery and the drawing-room and very suitably furnished. In short Chirk is the finest old fortress I ever saw except Windsor.

Rev. Reginald Heber to his sister, Elizabeth Heber
14 June 1791

I went with Reginald and Thomas to Hodnet on Saturday but did not take the Ladies with me not having at this time convenient accommodation for them ; having no bed in the old Tapestry Room which is taken down in order to have it plastered and papered. I had promised my boys that they should be present at the pulling down of the old tapestry, which operation they saw yesterday morning by six o'clock in eager expectation of finding hidden treasure behind the arras, an expectation which they had fostered in their imagination ever since the alteration was proposed. But alas, how vain and fallacious are our hopes ! Not one doit save a solitary sixpence was found. However, as most sublunary pleasures consist rather in idea than reality, they have for some months enjoyed the pleasing anticipation of discovering huge bags full of Queen Elizabeth's broad pieces of gold and silver.

However, though their expectations were disappointed in their object they were much entertained with another amusement which they did not expect :— namely, a procession of two hundred men with White Staves and a Band of Music to Hodnet Church on Whit Monday, attended by a great crowd of spectators. You must know there is an Amicable Club or Society in Hodnet Parish who have an annual meeting on Whit Monday, when they attend Divine Service, hear a sermon and afterwards spend the day in festivity. The object of this Institution is to provide a fund by mutual contributions in order to relieve each others distresses and bear one another's burdens under misfortunes, old age and sickness. On which occasion at their request I gave them a sermon and I think to a larger congregation than I ever saw in Hodnet Church before.

Rev. Reginald Heber to his sister, Elizabeth Heber
4 *July* 1791

Do you not grieve for and lament the hard fortune of the poor captur'd King and Queen of France,[1] I do most sincerely.

Elizabeth Heber to Rev. Reginald Heber
7 *July* 1791

We very heartily join in your lamentations for the miserable Royal Captives whose situation is now dreadfull indeed : they are in the hands of merciless enemies ; and I fear, notwithstanding the threatenings in the Marquis de Bouilie's[2] letter to the National Assembly, the powers of Europe will find other employment than that of arming in their defence. A general peace is not I fear at hand. God preserve us from intestine commotions which are by many strongly apprehended, but I trust Government will keep a watchfull eye on our Revolutionists and not suffer themselves to be surprized as was the case in the year eighty.[3]

Rev. Reginald Heber to his sister, Elizabeth Heber
12 *July* 1791

I heartily join with you in your good prayer devoutly to be prefer'd by all real friends to their Country that it will please God's good Providence to preserve this happy land from intestine commotion and from all the wicked machinations, plots and devices of restless mischevious Revolutionists over whose Cabals and Conventions I trust the vigilant Pilots at the Helm will keep a watchful eye : or we shall soon have only two Parties in the Empire, the Plunderers and the Plundered, those who have something to lose and those who have nothing. As is now the case in France.

[1] On 20 June 1791 the French King and Queen, virtually prisoners, fled secretly to the frontier. They were intercepted at Varennes and brought back, and from that moment were prisoners in name as in fact.
[2] The Marquis de Bouillé was the Royalist general at Metz.
[3] 1780 was the year of the Gordon Riots, when an inflamed Protestant mob attacked Roman Catholic chapels, demonstrated at Westminster, burnt Newgate prison, destroyed private houses, and was not dispersed until some 300 rioters had been killed.

Elizabeth Heber to Rev. Reginald Heber
1 December 1791

I am sorry we can't rejoice with you on the capture of Seringa-patam but have the loss of many of our brave officers and soldiers to lament.[1] However things are better than was at first supposed and Lord Cornwallis[2] was on the whole victorious but it is grievous to think of the fresh hazards and difficulties he and his army must again sustain if they make a second attack on the place.

Rev. Reginald Heber to his sister, Elizabeth Heber
6 December 1791

It is to be lamented that the monsoons stop'd Lord Cornwallis in his career and rob'd him and his brave army of the fruits of their victory. But as the periodical rains generally abate or cease in Sept'r, 'tis to be hoped they might rally and return to the charge and Seringapatam may now be in the hands of his Majesty's troops.

Rev. Reginald Heber to his sister, Elizabeth Heber
26 December 1791

What a shocking fire there has been at the Duke of Richmond's the conduct of the Duke of York[3] appears to have been highly laudable and benevolent and will I hope entirely extinguish any remaining heart-burnings occasioned by the Duel with Colonel Lenox.[4]

[1] A reference to the third Mysore war. Tippoo Sahib, ruler of Mysore, having attacked an Indian ally of the British, Lord Cornwallis undertook the campaign of 1791 to take Seringapatam. That year he failed, but next year succeeded in utterly defeating Tippoo, and partitioned his territory.

[2] Charles Cornwallis (1738-1805), first Marquis and second Earl Cornwallis. Governor-general of India 1786.

[3] *The Times* of 22 December 1791, reporting this fire which gutted the Duke of Richmond's house on the evening of the 21st, commented : ' The Dukes of York and Clarence were also present, the former very active, and gave orders to a party of his regiment to work the floating engines.'

[4] Charles Lennox (1764-1819), while a captain in the Coldstream Guards in 1789, challenged and fought the Duke of York, whose conduct in the affair was exemplary. Lennox's ball carried away a curl of his wig. Lennox was nephew and heir of the third Duke of Richmond (1735-1806), whose house was burned.

Rev. Reginald Heber to his sister, Elizabeth Heber
2 January 1792

I had the satisfaction of receiving your kind letter at Whit-church on our way to Hodnet on Saturday which proved a tolerable pleasant day. This morning I have been in the Parks with my two young sportsmen a coursing and killed one puss and found another which the dogs never got sight of, and the air being extremely cold we didn't stay out long. Had the weather been more favourable and our success better it was my intention that you should have shared the fruits of our labour with us, but we must reserve what we have for dear Richard's birthday . . . I have just been told that since we left the field another fine hare was killed, which is your humble servant.

I hope my dear Richard's young noble contemporary is likely to become an agreeable friend and associate. The Grenvilles are a worthy, good family of Constitutional Principles in Church and State and with such I should wish my son to be connected. As I am sure from experience there is neither religion, honour nor honesty existing in the opposite Party. I shall never have any objection to dear Richard's acceptance of Lord Temple's[1] invitation to Stowe having a good opinion of the principles of the family, Civil and Religious.

Elizabeth Heber to Rev. Reginald Heber
5 January 1792

Richard was last night at the Play to see the New Theatre graced with the presence of their Majestys and five Princesses in one box, opposite to them sat the Prince of Wales, Duke and Duchess of York and Duke of Clarence.

[1] Richard Temple-Nugent Brydges Chandos Grenville (1776-1839), son of the first Marquis of Buckingham, matriculated from Brasenose College, Oxford, in 1791. His grandfather was George Grenville (1712-70), contemporary and associate of the elder Pitt. His uncle was William Wyndham Grenville (1759-1834), a prominent member of the younger Pitt's ministry. He later threw himself on the side of Catholic emancipation, of which Heber would hardly have approved.

Elizabeth Heber to Rev. Reginald Heber
12 January 1792

Two weddings are speedily to take place at Oulton, viz. Miss Egerton to Charles Leicester, Sir John's youngest brother, and Miss Mary gives her hand to Capt. Broughton, second son of the Baronet.[1] Woful matches both, and far from meeting the approbation of their Mother and Aunts. Poor Mrs. Egerton is much to be pitied, who no doubt has far superior views for her daughters, who are accomplished fine young women and were much admired.

Elizabeth Heber to Rev. Reginald Heber
19 January 1792

I am glad that *Celestina*[2] has afforded you some entertainment. It is as you truly describe it, perplexing and vexatious and often put me out of all patience, especially with Willoughby whose credulity and hasty conclusions on every unfavourable appearance make him scarce worthy of a Celestina.

The Papers would inform you of the Pantheon being burnt down. Opera houses seem to have a fatality attending them.[3] It is a thousand pities that beautiful building should have been destroyed.

Rev. Reginald Heber to his sister, Elizabeth Heber
22 January 1792

Malpas bells have been ringing these two days for the birth of a young lordling who has his title from this place.[4] Lady Cholmondeley it is said presented her Lord with a son and heir at Paris, no very eligible place I should think for her ladyship's confinement.

---

[1] Miss Heber has got the news the wrong way round. Mary Egerton married Charles Leicester, third son of Sir Peter Leicester. Elizabeth Egerton married John Delves Broughton, second son of Sir Thomas Broughton.

[2] *Celestina* by Mrs. Charlotte Smith, published 1792.

[3] The King's Theatre was burnt down in 1788, the Queen's Theatre in 1789 and the Pantheon in 1792.

[4] George Viscount Malpas (1792-1870), succeeded as second Marquis of Cholmondeley.

Elizabeth Heber to Rev. Reginald Heber
26 January 1792

The Duchess of York on the Birthday[1] made literally a brilliant appearance from tip to toe. She was so much fatigued with the weight of her finery that her attendants came to undress her at the Queen's house as soon as they were come from Court where she stayed till the Royal Family went to the Ball and then retired to York House, Piccadilly. She caught a violent cold on her passage to England which she has never got the better of and seems at present unequal to the fatigues attendant on Royalty.

This is a dismal rainy day and makes me wondrous stupid.

Elizabeth Heber to her nephew, Richard
18 February 1792

Ammy complains of rheumatic pains this severe weather. She is sitting by me perusing the Minister's speech of yesterday on opening the Budget.[2] You see how Charley and Sherry envy him and plainly shew their teeth when they cannot bite.[3] The Paper Cabinet is dead and buried. No great loss.

Rev. Reginald Heber to his sister, Elizabeth Heber
26 February 1792

Methinks Mr. Mason the Music Master's bill is very high, his last which you know I paid to you up to X's, 1790, came to £11.12.0 and now this you say is £16.13.0 making together

---

[1] Princess Frederica of Prussia married the Duke of York in September 1791. The birthday was Queen Charlotte's, officially celebrated on 18 January. The 'Queen's House' is Buckingham Palace.

[2] 'There never was a time in the history of this country,' said Pitt in his budget speech on 17 February 1792, 'when, from the situation of Europe, we might more reasonably expect fifteen years of peace than we may at this present moment.' He regarded the troubles in France as matters of domestic concern. So far was he from anticipating war with a country which he had every reason to regard as exhausted and impotent, that he repealed taxes and reduced the armed forces.

[3] Sheridan (1751–1816), ally of Fox, who spoke after Pitt, severely criticized the trifling nature of the tax repeal. Fox's line was to attack the increasing arrogation of power by the government. Pitt had presented the House with a measure and challenged them to take it or leave it ; but the function of the House was to debate and advise on — not merely to accept or reject — the measures by which the nation was governed.

£28.5.0 for Tweedledum and Tweedledee[1] which I never thought he (Richard) would make anything of, nor ever approved of his attempting. However, before you discharge the scraper's demand which strikes me as very exorbitant, I desire you will send the bill or a copy to dear Richard for his examination, and if the demand be just I desire you will pay it. But I must say Richard is very inconsiderate and very unreasonable in contracting debt after debt for me to pay. Since his return to College he has had the conscience to make a demand for £39.0.0 to pay his Wine Merchant's bill over and above his allowance under pretence that I made him a promise to furnish him with a stock of wine at his first setting out. I might say I would make him a present of a few dozens but never dreamt of his being so unconscionable as to expect me to pay for a pipe.

Elizabeth Heber to Rev. Reginald Heber
1 March 1792

Mr. and Mrs. Charles Leicester are in town which their friends think are imprudent step, six guineas a week for lodgings will go deep into his pocket besides all other expenses.

Rev. Reginald Heber to his sister, Elizabeth Heber
30 March 1792

I had a letter by the last post from Mr. J. Cayley of the Lower Hall communicating the melancholy tidings of the sudden death of poor Sir Thomas Cayley, who after a few days indisposition which seemed to be but slight, was carried off in an apoplexy or paralytic complaint on the 15th instant. How soon has he followed his father ' to that bourn from which no Traveller returns '.[2]

---

[1] The names ' Tweedledum and Tweedledee ' hark back about fifty years to a musical controversy between the German and the Italian schools that among other things embittered the relations between George II and his son Prince Frederick of Wales.
[2] Sir George Cayley (1707-91), fourth Baronet of Brompton, Yorks.
Sir Thomas Cayley (1732-92) fifth Baronet, his son.

It is to be lamented that he did not live to see his son of age, by whose aid and in conjunction with whom he might have made a better provision for his relict and children, who it is to be feared will be very poorly provided for. Sir George, I hear, tied up everything so strictly by his will that it was not in his son's power to do anything for his wife and children without the concurrence of his eldest son, Sir George never having been reconciled to his son's match, tho' Lady Cayley has been a most frugal and excellent wife and it is generally thought had the worst of the bargain in her match with Sir Thomas from first to last.

Rev. Reginald Heber to his sister, Elizabeth Heber
6 April 1792

We rejoice to hear that the Slave Trade is to be gradually abolished, the determination does credit to the humanity of the People of the Country and the wisdom and justice of their Representatives in Parliament.[1] Their hearts must have been harder than the nether millstone who could vote for the continuance of a traffic so abominably cruel, inhuman, and unchristian as the Slave Trade has been indisputably proved to have been. My Paper gave us Mr. Wilberforce's affecting speech, those of Mr. Pitt and Fox we are to expect to-morrow.

Elizabeth Heber to Rev. Reginald Heber
10 April 1792

I was just now surprised with a sight of Mr. John Bissell. He is come to town on a very unpleasant occasion. His brother

---

[1] The best men of all parties agreed that the slave trade was abhorrent and ought to be abolished. But for the opposition of the West India interest it would perhaps have been abolished in 1789. Since then, the revolt of slaves of St. Domingo and the rise of those dangerous Jacobinical principles associated with the French Revolution had rather reduced the support for the abolition movement. The King, for instance, would no longer countenance it, and Pitt was therefore restrained from lending it the support of government. William Wilberforce (1759-1833), proposed a motion for the total abolition of the trade on 2 April 1792. Pitt and Fox spoke warmly in favour. But the vote was left free. Finally, after an all-night sitting, a motion for ' gradual ' abolition was carried by 230 votes to eighty-five. The crucial amendment introducing the word ' gradual ' had been carried by only 193 to 125. Reginald Heber seems to ignore that the abolitionists had in fact suffered a reverse.

William who has been tried by a Court-Martial at Plymouth for sending a challenge to his superior officer, is sentenced to two years imprisonment in the Marshalsea Prison. He looks well, but is much hurt at William's bad behaviour, who he says is very miserable and sensible of his fault.

Rev. Reginald Heber to his sister, Elizabeth Heber
14 April 1792

What execrable scoundrels these Regicides are. I hope in God the poor King of Sweden will recover and live to avenge himself of his adversaries. The sudden death of the Emperor[1] and the desperate attempt on the King of Sweden[2] had I doubt not their origin in the same accursed Jacobin Club.

Rev. Reginald Heber to his sister, Elizabeth Heber
29 April 1792

Pray have you received the letter I wrote you on the 14th, that which I sent by the same post to Messrs. Hodsoll & Co. enclosing a Bill for £15, reached their hands on the 27th having been thirteen days in travelling from Whitchurch to London, and I am inclined to suspect that if I had not written to my Bankers to stop payment and to Miss Spencer who conducts the office at Chester, as well as to the post-master at Salop, acquainting them that I was determined to trace the matter to the fountain head, lost sheep would not have been found. I very much fear that there is something rotten in the state of the office at Whitchurch. The postmaster at Shrewsbury returned my letter to him, which he suspected and which I am certain had been opened at Whitchurch.

[1] The Emperor Leopold of Austria died suddenly on 1 March 1792, and was succeeded by Francis II, a man of inferior capacity and far less fitted than Leopold for the troubled times of the Revolution.
[2] Gustavus III of Sweden was shot by a Swedish officer on 16 March and died on the 29th. His successor being a child, a Regent was appointed ; the Regent reversed Gustavus' pro-Bourbon policy and placed Sweden in a position of absolute neutrality. These two deaths thus greatly favoured the rise of revolutionary France, although there is no evidence that Jacobins had any hand in them.

I shall be obliged to you to write to Mr. Heawood ordering a coat, waste-coat and breeches of best black cloth for me and at the same time to order Mills to make me a dark grizle peruke.

Elizabeth Heber to Rev. Reginald Heber
3 May 1792

Lady Bromley's son is by his own desire going to China with Lord Macartney.[1] He is a very fine, well-disposed boy, thirteen years old.

Elizabeth Heber to Rev. Reginald Heber
24 May 1792

You see there is a proclamation issued,[2] not before it was wanted. God preserve us from the wicked devices of republicans and dissenters of all denominations.

Rev. Reginald Heber to his sister, Elizabeth Heber
22 June 1792

On our return home yesterday from our weeks' tour through a considerable part of North Wales I had the satisfaction of finding your welcome letter dated the 16th instant.

The weather being very favourable and cool and fair made travelling from place to place over the mountains and far away, very pleasant both for us and our cattle. On the first day, viz. Friday the 15th, we visited Wynnstay, Chirk Castle and Llangollen where we slept, and the next morning after viewing the cottages we proceeded through the beautiful romantic Vale of Glendower to Llanroost where we roosted that night, and large as our party was met with good accommodation.

---

[1] Later Admiral Sir Robert Bromley, third Baronet (1778-1857). Lord Macartney's Embassy to China set out in 1795.

[2] Given on 21 May and debated in the Commons, not without acrimony, on the 25th, a proclamation ordered sheriffs and magistrates to 'make diligent enquiry in order to discover the authors and printers of such wicked and seditious writings', and also to 'take the most immediate and effectual care to suppress and prevent all riots, tumults and other disorders . . . which on whatever pretext they may be grounded, are not only contrary to the law, but dangerous to the most important interests of this kingdom.'

The next day we proceeded through another delightful valley with woods and high rocky mountains on one hand and the fine full winding River Conway on the other, to Conway town surrounded with ancient walls, castle, towers and battlements, commanding a fine view of the sea : the town is half encompass'd on one side by the bay and on the other by castle's redoubts and indented battlements with high rocky mountains covered with woods towering above them and hanging over them, making a most grand and picturesque appearance.

Having much to see and admire in this delightful place, we tarried all night, having attended Divine Service at the Parish Church in the morning, which was partly in Welch and partly in English. Having a recommendation from Mr. Davies of Broughton to Mr. Holland of this place we were accommodated in his pew, Mr. Holland being confined with a fit of the gout, his first attack tho' upwards of seventy years of age. His sister a very agreeable sensible maiden lady who lives with her brother who is a bachelor, came to us to the Inn and attended us to the Church of which he is a Patron, and after to the Castle of which he and his ancestors have been governors for many generations. This Mr. Holland is uncle to Mrs. York, Lady Lucy Meyrick's[1] daughter-in-law, who was expected to be with them the day after we left Conway on our return. He is a very gentlemanlike, agreeable, grey-headed man, the principal person in the place, has a good fortune and a very respectable character. On our return to Conway on Tuesday 19th, we drank tea with him and his sister in the afternoon, and had the pleasure of taking a very pleasant walk on a hill planted with trees and flowering shrubs which he has named Arcadia, and which commands a view of the bay on one side and overlooks the town and fortifications of Conway on the other.

But to return : on Monday morning the 18th, we cross'd the bay in boats in order to proceed to Bangor Ferry ; on our way we passed over a stupendous road along the sea called Penman-Mowar, which is supported by arches for more than a mile,

[1] Diana Wynne married first R. Owen Meyrick (d. 1773) and secondly in 1782 Philip Yorke of Erddig, Denbighshire.

bounded on the left by mountains and rocks and on the right by the sea and Isle of Anglesea, of which you have a fine view of many miles extent : on our way nearer Bangor, we went to see Lord Penrhyn's new house, not quite finished ; thence we proceeded through Bangor to the Ferry, which is an Inn delightfully situated on an arm of the sea between Wales and the Isle of Anglesea, where we rested that night and met with good accommodation at bed and board.

The next morning we went to Carnarvon to breakfast, where the castles and fortifications erected by Edward the First have a very grand appearance and are more extensive than those of Conway and on a larger scale ; they command an extensive prospect of the sea and the Strait of Menai. We climbed one hundred and forty-seven steps to the top of a tower, and saw the Chamber were the unfortunate Edward of Carnarvon was born.

After examining the works and eating a hearty breakfast, we returned to Bangor Ferry to dinner, after which all the party except myself and Mary, ventur'd to take boat for Anglesea, tho' the evening was cold and the Straits rather rocky and rough, but the voyage was voted by a majority and go they would to see Lord Buckley's beautiful seat near Beaumaris ; during the absence of our fellow travellors Mary and I took a walk to Bangor to see the Cathedral and the Bishop's Palace which are very neat and pleasantly situated. On our return we were rather in panic for the voyagers, the evening being very cold and the wind rising. However we had the happiness of seeing their boat approaching and hearing them hail us on the shore about half past nine in the evening, and saving a few rheumatic complaints in his shoulders of which Mr. Rawstorne complained the next morning, I don't think the navigators suffered by their trip over the Straits of Menai.

Our excursion was pleasant upon the whole, but would have been more so but for the cruelty and cold indifference of Harriet[1] who much to the disappointment of her parents, has rejected the tenders of a worthy unexceptionable admirer who would have

[1] Harriet Rawstorne apparently never married. The worthy admirer was George Allanson.

made her a good and tender husband ; but *it is over*. Her good Mother has suffered much on the occasion, but the likings and dis-likings of young folks are unaccountable. I think she has some prior attachment which she is afraid to disclose.

Rev. Reginald Heber to his sister, Elizabeth Heber
20 *July* 1792

Poor Archdeacon Clive died on Sunday last when we were at Hodnet, he had been in a bad state of health for many months. I am invited to attend his obsequies at Moreton Saye tomorrow morning. The benefice which is said to be worth eighty or one hundred per annum is at my disposal as Rector of Hodnet, to which Moreton is a Chapel of Ease, and I have offered it to my brother Allanson and believe he will accept it, being tenable with any other preferment at any distance.

Elizabeth Heber to Rev. Reginald Heber
9 *August* 1792

If Mr. Allanson is still with you, we beg our best regards and wish him joy of his preferment, which I am glad is so agreeable to him as to induce him to pass some of the Summer months in Shropshire. I once went by Moreton to Drayton and admired the place very much.

This day's paper announces the death of Lord Guildford [Lord North], much lamented by his family as he would have been by the nation some years since.

Rev. Reginald Heber to his sister, Elizabeth Heber
Ripon, 12 *November* 1792

We spent a very pleasant day, evening and morning at Gis-burne Park. Mr. Lister[1] gave me and Richard the meeting at Monk Bridge, in order to conduct us through his extensive plantations and other improvements which are great and

[1] Thomas Lister of Gisburn, Yorks., created first Lord Ribblesdale, 1797.

ornamental. He assured me that he had never planted fewer than thirty thousand trees each and every year since he came of age all of which have thriven amazingly.

We had the satisfaction of finding our dear Tommy very well and grown above an inch since he left us, and his mental improvements have kept pace with the increase of his stature ; we have been agreeably surprized to hear him repeat the *Hermit of Warkworth*[1] and Goldsmith's *Retalliation*[2] by heart perfectly both of which poems of considerable length, he got off of his own accord, understands and enters into the spirit of them.

Rev. Reginald Heber to his sister, Elizabeth Heber
5 December 1792

I am sorry to see that the apprehensions entertained of approaching troubles and commotions have sunk the Stocks so considerably in a few weeks, but I trust in the accustomed goodness of Providence to us that the threatening storm will soon blow over and be succeeded by serene and tranquil skies. It is wise and provident in Government to be forewarned and forearmed against the evil designs of turbulent and seditious spirits, as it is easier to prevent than to quell insurrections. The precautions taking in the Tower are to secure the armory and prevent any sudden attempt of the Mob against that arsenal and the stores therein contained.

Rev. Reginald Heber to his sister, Elizabeth Heber
14 December 1792

I rejoice to see the numerous Associations both in the Metropolis and populous Country Towns to protect and defend the lives and properties of the peaceable and most willing members of the Community against the wicked machinations and bold menaces of Levellers and Republicans. I trust the Good Providence of the King of Kings who stilleth the raging of the wave

---

[1] Thomas Percy (1729-1811), Bishop of Dromore, *The Hermit of Warkworth* 1771.
[2] Oliver Goldsmith (1728-74), *Retaliation, a poem*, 1774.

and the madness of the people will protect us from the barbarity and cruel depredations of Lawless Democrats and the bandittis led by them to plunder and massacry. It is astonishing to find that such diabolical wretches should find any advocates or abettors endued with common-sense or possessed of, or ever likely to be possessed of any property.

Rev. Reginald Heber to his sister, Elizabeth Heber
22 December 1792

The Man of the People and his adherents methinks make a despicable miserable figure in the debates and divisions in St. Stephen's Chapel.[1] The Wily Demagogue has certainly shot beyond his mark on the present occasion and has lost many of his friends, the fewer he retains the better for the Country. For it appears now to be evident that he would stick at nothing to gain his own ambitious ends. However it is fortunate that he has at length opened the eyes of the men who are not wilfully blind or wilfully bent upon the same schemes of anarchy, confusion and mischief that he is.

Rev. Reginald Heber to his son, Richard
29 December 1792

Mama went to Whitchurch to fetch Reginald home on Sunday evening on account of the sickness that he complained of.

---

[1] In a speech of 13 December 1792 on the address of thanks, Fox used these words : ' We are come to the moment, when the question is, whether we shall give to the King, that is, to the executive government, complete power over our thoughts ; whether we are to resign the exercise of our natural faculties to the ministers for the time being, or whether we shall maintain that in England no man is criminal, but by the commission of overt acts forbidden by the law. This I call a crisis more imminent and tremendous than any that the history of this country ever exhibited. . . . What is the course prescribed by law ? If any doctrines are published tending to subvert the constitution in church and state, you may take cognizance of the fact in a court of law. What have you done ? Taken upon you by your own authority to suppress them. . . . You have gone upon the principles of slavery in all your proceedings ; you neglect in your conduct the foundation of all legitimate government, the rights of the people ; and, setting up this bugbear, you spread a panic for the very purpose of sanctifying this infringement, while again the very infringement engenders the evil which you dread. One extreme naturally leads to another. Those who dread republicanism, fly for shelter to the crown. Those who desire reform and are calumniated, are driven by despair to republicanism. And this is the very evil that I dread ! '

It was lucky for him he came home as he thereby avoided getting into a scrape with others of his schoolfellows, who according to the prevailing Rage of the Times of standing up for the Rights of Boys, adopted Tom Paine's principles and doctrines and rebelled against King Kent, who however soon taught the young insurgents who barred him out of the school on Monday morning that he had a prerogative to maintain, and by cutting off all supplies of provisions soon reduced the Rebel Garrison by famine to surrender at discretion to their rightful Sovereign. So may all Rightful Monarchs ever prevail against Levellers and Republicans, the pests of Society.

Rev. Reginald Heber to his son, Richard
5 January 1793

Loyalty triumphs in every corner of the Kingdom. Tom Paine[1] was first shot through and through and then burnt in effigy at Malpas Cross on Wednesday, and a Band of Music pervades every street, playing and singing ' God save Great George Our King' and Mr. Heaton says there was not a housekeeper in the town, however indigent, who did not contribute his mite to testify their Loyalty and Love of their King and the Constitution of their Country, and their utter abhorrence and detestation of Republicans and Levellers and disturbers of the Public Peace !

Tiddy, Tom and Missy amused themselves yesterday in dressing up two figures to represent Tom Paine and Demourrier[2] which they carried about stuck upon their hunting poles all day long, and in the evening suspended them from the balustrade at the top of the stairs, where they are still hanging.

[1] Thomas Paine (1737-1809), democrat, author of the *Rights of Man*. Sympathized with the French Revolution and was in France during its early stages.

[2] Charles Francois Dumouriez (1739-1823), French general of the old school. Minister of foreign affairs 1792. Planned and executed invasion of the Austrian Netherlands. Defeated Austrian army at Jemappes, 20 September 1792. He had thrown in his lot with the Revolution, but he neither liked nor was trusted by the Jacobins. Success at first upheld him. Failure at the battle of Neerwinden (March 1793) ruined him. He went over to the Austrians and eventually, in 1804, came to England, where he was employed by the War Office, and where he died.

I am glad you got into the House to hear Burke's speech and see the effect of his action when the produced, displayed and hurled the Birmingham dagger into the midst of the House.[1]

Rev. Reginald Heber to his sister, Elizabeth Heber
11 *January* 1793

The French National Assembly will fill up the measure of their insanity by rousing the British Lion. A war with France is never disagreeable to this Country and would now be popular.

Elizabeth Heber to Rev. Reginald Heber
26 *January* 1793

Alas poor Lewis,[2] the papers are full of dismal accounts. I have wept over his Will.

Rev. Reginald Heber to his sister, Elizabeth Heber
27 *January* 1793

It is rumoured that the poor King of France was murdered by his inhuman subjects on Monday last ; surely this heinous crime will draw down the Vengeance of Heaven on this devoted Race of barbarians.

Rev. Reginald Heber to his sister, Elizabeth Heber
4 *February* 1793

Between friends, methinks Miss Motte's projected expedition to France[3] a very mysterious business. Committing herself to

[1] The speech of Edmund Burke on the Alien Bill (which endowed the executive government with wide discretionary powers) on 28 December 1792, is reported in the Parliamentary History as follows :—
'. . . He mentioned the circumstances of three thousand daggers having been bespoke at Birmingham by an Englishman, of which seventy had been delivered. It was not ascertained how many of these were to be exported, and how many were intended for home consumption.' (Here Mr. Burke drew out a dagger which he had kept concealed, and with much vehemence of action threw it on the floor.) ' This,' said he, pointing to the dagger, ' is what you are to gain by an alliance with France: wherever their principles are introduced, their practice must follow . . .'
[2] Louis XVI (1754-93) was guillotined on 21 January.
[3] France declared war on England on 1 February 1793.

the sole care of a French courier hired here, till she arrives at Pandemonium, for so I call Paris, and intending to hire a she-devil there for her *fille de chambre*, makes me conclude that she must be already a demoniac herself. An Intrigue ! an intrigue ! depend upon it ! But this *inter nos*.

Dear Reginald returned to school in good health on Thursday last. His stomach continued in a weakly state for two or three weeks after he came home but Bark draughts with Acid Elixir of Vitriol was of vast service to him.

My dear Mamma

I am extremely obliged to you for your kind Letter and am in perfect health and so are Tommy and Mary I hope you and papa are the same Tommy improves in his Lesson I am very well at present I hope to see you at Rippon soon I hope Aunts at york are well Mary still loves Miss Davies Tommy sends 20 Kisses Our duty to papa: your Affectionate Son

Reginald Heber

I EARLIEST LETTER WRITTEN BY REGINALD HEBER

(afterwards Bishop of Calcutta)

John Hoppner, R. A. (c. 1800)

II 'PAPA'

Rev. Reginald Heber, Rector of Malpas, 1728-1804.

III   Letters of the

HEBER FAMILY

1793-1799

AR WAS declared between England and France on
1 February 1793. The various radical movements that had
worried Heber for the past four years now became sub-
merged in a wave of patriotism. Although Fox and others
continued to speak in favour of peace and to resist the tendency to
make the war ideological, they were in the minority. The great
weight of public opinion swung over to support the war and to
oppose anything French, in fact to join Heber. The letters in
these years, when they depart from the private matters which are
still their main concern, refer chiefly to the fighting itself and
secondly to the warlike measures of the government. When they
talk of war they are essentially the letters of civilians and when of
affairs of state, of ordinary people who read their newspapers.

These were years of great stress in England. Yet it does not
so appear from the letters as clearly as one might expect. The
Hebers devoured their newspapers and paid their taxes, but
seem to have felt no personal responsibility for what went on,
to have had no sense of personal urgency, to have been spectators
rather than actors of the great struggle. Naturally correspondence
within a family which knew itself well would not need to
emphasize the deeper feelings that could be taken for granted ;
also a certain formality of style tends to conceal from the
twentieth-century reader what the eighteenth-century writers
really thought. Nevertheless, because it is observable that they

6

wrote more formally of public affairs than of private, it may be inferred that their minds were fundamentally more occupied with private than with public business. War did not press so hard upon them as upon English people of the twentieth century.

The war began for England with a British expeditionary force landing in Holland under the command of the Duke of York, himself under the command of the Austrian general, the Prince of Coburg. The allies were immediately successful in driving the French army out of the Austrian Netherlands. France was considered so disorganized as to be incapable of supporting a long war, and her army so distracted as to be powerless. Time was thought to be on the side of the allies. It soon appeared, however, that this estimate was wrong. After some indecisive manoeuvring on the French frontier, Coburg attempted a major action with the object of not merely defeating but annihilating the French army. At Tourcoing in May 1794 the event went the other way. That defeat was followed by others. The Austrian and Dutch Netherlands were lost. In April 1795 the British contingent returned home.

Heber's reaction to this failure was to pin his hope (one might say rather, his faith) on the navy and a protracted naval war. There was much justification for this view, for the navy had not been unsuccessful ; and especially when the troubled state of Ireland began to invite a French invasion, and the French seemed disposed to make one, it was evident that the main defence must be at sea. These were indeed critical years : but they did not, so far as we can judge, disturb the normal tenour of the Heber family's life.

*   *   *

Rev. Reginald Heber to his sister, Elizabeth Heber
3 March 1793

I hope the British and Hanoverian troops in conjunction with the Hollanders will repulse the *Sans Culetts* and drive them back into their own country.

Rev. Reginald Heber to his sister, Elizabeth Heber
18 *March* 1793[1]

We rejoice to see in the last paper that the Troops are safe landed at Helwet Slyzs. The *Sans Culetts* seem to carry all before them, but I hope will soon meet with their desserts.

Rev. Reginald Heber to his sister, Elizabeth Heber
24 *March* 1793

I congratulate you and all good people on the successful commencement of the campaign in Brabant against the French scoundrels, whose day of retribution is advancing with gigantic strides, and whose atrocious deeds and damnable doctrines and principles will I trust soon meet with their just recompense.

Rev. Reginald Heber to his sister, Elizabeth Heber
7 *April* 1793

Have you heard of the terrible Crash among the Bankers at Chester and Liverpool ?[2] One Caldwell at Liverpool has failed for a very large sum and has involved poor Hesketh and Thomas in his ruin. Everybody is sorry for the Chester Bankers who it is said are taken in for at least sixty thousand pounds between Caldwell of Liverpool and Forbes a Banker in London, who it is said is decamp'd for France, the land of rascals, with seven hundred thousand pounds to be laid out in the purchase of Church lands which no power on earth has any right to alienate or convey to a purchaser. I pity not these villainous speculators but I am sorry for the many, many innocent sufferers drawn in by them. Many of the Bankers in the Country Towns have stop't payment, and no one now will accept their notes. The anti-Ministerialists attribute these failures to the War, but the fact is

---

[1] On this day the great battle of Neerwinden was fought, between the Austrians under the Prince of Coburg and the French under Dumouriez. The latter were decisively defeated.

[2] ' The Corporation of Liverpool intend to mortgage the revenues of the docks there, to sustain the credit and engagements of their bankers and commercial people.'
The Times, 3 April, 1793.

the mischief has been done by these avaricious speculators who expected to make enormous gains by the purchase of French estates. But with the Dog in the Fable, they have lost the substance by snatching at the shadow.

Rev. Reginald Heber to his sister, Elizabeth Heber
Bath, 14 April 1793

We arrived at the Bear Inn yesterday at half past two. Bath seems very full of Company. We are to succeed Lady Stowell and Lady Bromley in very pleasant Lodgings in Milsom Street, No. 41, which they evacuate to-morrow morning.

The remnant of the Republican Army after the losses they have sustained by slaughter and desertion, and after having been abandoned by Dumourier and their best Officers, will not be able to make headway against the Victorious Allies with the Prince de Coburg at their head.

Rev. Reginald Heber to his sister, Elizabeth Heber
Malpas, 25 November 1793

There was an Assembly at Chester on Friday for the purpose of raising a sum for the purchase of flannel shirts and Welch stockings for our brave soldiers in Flanders, the collection amounted to one hundred and seventy guineas. And a benefit Play for the same laudable purpose in which Mrs. Siddons[1] acted, produced seventy more : the play was produced the week before we went but we contributed to the Assembly. These collections have been very generous all over the Kingdom and it is said were first put on foot on the recommendation of the Princes Royal.

Rev. Reginald Heber to his sister, Elizabeth Heber
2 December 1793

You ask how Reginald and Thomas were entertained with Mrs. Siddon's performance of *Jenny Shore*[2] — They were both

[1] Sarah Siddons (1755-1831), actress.
[2] *Jane Shore* by H. Rowe, 1713.

very attentive and affected by her distresses, Tommy turned to me and said, ' I am *very sorry* for her ', while the tears ran down his face.

Elizabeth Heber to Rev. Reginald Heber
21 December 1793

We were happy to hear that Mrs. Parker is in better health and that her good man looks so well. I hope they will both live to enjoy much comfort from their daughter Ann's marriage with so worthy a man as Major Barnston. I am glad the noble Capt. (Tom Parker) obtained leave to attend the occasion. Now his sisters are so well disposed of, he has nothing to do but look out for a wife. Miss Hunt is still at liberty.

Rev. Reginald Heber to his son, Richard
7 January 1794

I question if the poor Royalists in Normandy and Brettaigny will be able to secure a safe landing place for Lord Moira and his Forces, yet if it should be practicable to succour them it would be a pity to leave them to be cut to pieces by the *Sans Culots*.[1]

Rev. Reginald Heber to his sister, Elizabeth Heber
28 April 1794

You will be so kind as to escort Reginald to Neasdon in the course of the next week; his Mama desires thus :— Will you be so good as to tell Mr. Bristow that he has been used to a blanket under and one or two over as suits the weather. We suppose he is to have a bed to himself and a bureau for his exclusive property.

---

[1] Revolt broke out in Vendée in March 1793. By October government forces had won the ascendancy. Lord Moira (Francis Rawdon-Hastings, 1754-1826), soldier and administrator, was placed in command of a British supporting expedition in October, arrived off the French coast in December, found no forces with whom to co-operate, and had no alternative but to return. Had he arrived a month earlier the story might have been different.

As he is just begun the Greek Grammar, I would not wish him to learn French till after X's next.

Rev. Reginald Heber to his sister, Elizabeth Heber
28 May, 1794

We are sore hurt and griev'd at the severe check our brave countrymen have met with in Flanders[1] but everything considered, think with you that it is as well it was no worse. The poor Duke of York appears to have been in great jeopardy and imminent danger. His escape was hair-breadth indeed. His division seems to have been ordered upon the most hazardous service and to have been ill-supported by the Austrians. Who was to blame, God knows, but such disasters are common events in war and ought not to dispirit us.

Elizabeth Heber to Rev. Reginald Heber
5 July 1794

Lady Warburton called on us yesterday, Sir Peter[2] and she had been to Portsmouth, went on board the *Royal Charlotte*[3] and saw the superb and elegant diamond sword presented by His Majesty to Lord Howe.[4]

Elizabeth Heber to her nephew, Richard
19 August 1794

So the reign of Robespierre[5] is at an end. His successors in office will probably have a shorter period. It is to be hoped their dissensions will (under providence) prove favourable to us.

[1] The battle of Tourcoing. An allied offensive designed to annihilate the French army resulted in defeat. The British contingent under the Duke of York took a prominent part.

[2] Sir Peter Warburton (1754-1813), fifth Baronet of Arley ; married Alice Parker in 1781.

[3] The *Queen Charlotte* launched in 1790. The *Royal George* was a sister ship.

[4] The presentation sword was in recognition of the battle of 1st June. It was valued at 3,000 guineas. Richard Howe (1726-99), Earl Howe, admiral of the fleet and victor of the First of June.

[5] Robespierre was guillotined on 28 July.

Rev. Reginald Heber to his sister, Elizabeth Heber
24 *January* 1795

I hope dear Richard would be well entertained at the House
of Lords on hearing the debates on the Duke of Bedford's[1]
motion for a Peace.[2] A consummation devoutly to be wished,
but I think quite impracticable in the present situation of affairs.
The French Republicans are too much elated with their successes
in the Austrian Netherlands and the United Provinces to treat
with us but upon the most unreasonable and degrading terms.
I suppose they are now in possession of Amsterdam, and it is
to be feared of the Dutch Navy and Naval Stores, and for that
reason the best policy that can be pursued by the government
of this Country will be to increase our Navy, and I trust under
the Blessing of Providence, our Wooden Walls will prove an
impregnable defence if the Sons of Britannia prove but true to
themselves. In the American War the British Fleet beat the
combined Naval Powers of Holland, France and Spain, and, I
fear not, will fight them and conquer again and again. A protracted Naval War which I trust will be glorious, will be much
better for Old England than an ill-timed, hasty and ignominious
Peace.   So much for my Political Opinion at the present crisis.

I desire Hatchard the Bookseller will procure for me the follow-
ing Publications in addition to those I before ordered viz. Payleys
Evidences of Christianity,[3] Observations on Dr. Priestley's
Emigration, Stockdale pr. 1s. 6d.,[4] Russel's History of Aleppo,[5]

---

[1] Francis Russell (1765-1802), fifth Duke of Bedford ; friend of Fox and the Prince
of Wales.

[2] The Duke of Bedford moved in the House of Lords, on 27 January 1795, 'that any
particular form of government which may prevail in France, should not preclude
negotiation or prevent peace, consistent with the interest, the honour, and the security
of this country.' He here expressed a view which had been voiced by Fox before the
outbreak of war : that British relations with France should not be affected by the form of
government chosen by the people of France. This was not the view of the King, of the
government, or of Reginald Heber, who regarded the French government as a horrible
faction temporarily dominant, a treaty with whom would be immoral and without
stability. It was also said that France was weakening and that time was on the side of
Britain. Bedford's motion was decisively negatived.

[3] William Paley (1743-1805), *Evidences of Christianity*, 1794.

[4] William Cobbett (1763-1835), *Observations on the emigration of Dr. J. Priestley and
on the several addresses delivered to him on his arrival at New York*, London, 1794.

[5] Alexander Russell (1715?-68), *Natural history of Aleppo*, 1765.

Peacock on the House of Commons, Debrett, 2s.,[1] Taylor's[2] Architecture Octavo 8s., The Age of Infidelity in answer to Thos. Pain's Age of Reason[3] by a Layman,[4] 6 dozen Country Carpenter's Confession of Faith 2d. or 25 for 3s,[5] Revington Anecdotes of the Life of the late Earl of Chatham 4th Editn., 3 vols. Octavo,[6] A Visitation Sermon before the Bishop of London by George Henry Glasse May 14th 1794,[7] Bishop of London's Last Charge, do, the Revd J. Whitehouse's Odes Moral and descriptive.[8]

Elizabeth Heber to Rev. Reginald Heber
27 January 1795

Richard attended a long and warm debate in the Commons on the suspension of the Habeas-Corpus Act[9] last Friday. He admired Mr. Pitt's speech wonderfully which he thinks the finest he ever heard on any occasion and that it is not possible that any reporter can give it justly. Your papers will shew he had a respectable majority. We have got all the Royal Family from Holland. Old England is the general asylum of those who flee from their own country. Continental Alliances I have little hopes from. The French has had no doubt a great acquisition to their Navy, as it was impossible that the Dutch shipping could be got off in the hard frost.[10] Lord Howe has gone out once more and I trust will be able to give a good account of the enemy squadrons where ever he may fall in with them.

[1] Daniel Mitford Peacock, Considerations on the structure of the House of Commons .. 1794.
[2] ? Sir Robert Taylor (1714-88), architect.
[3] Thomas Paine, Age of Reason, 1793.
[4] Thomas Williams, The Age of Infidelity . . . 1795.
[5] Hannah More (1745-1833), A country carpenter's confession of faith, 1794.
[6] Perhaps an error for John Almon's Anecdotes of William Pitt, Earl of Chatham, 1792 and frequently reprinted.
[7] George Henry Glasse, A sermon . . . at the visitation of . . . Bishop of London, 14 May 1794.
[8] John Whitehouse, Odes moral and descriptive, 1794.
[9] A Bill for the continuance of the Habeas Corpus Suspension Act, passed in the last session, was introduced by ministers on 16 January and debated at its second reading on the 23rd. A minority offered very pungent opposition. Pitt's speech, as Richard foretells, does not appear in the Parliamentary History as a great one, though certainly clear and to the point.
[10] After Tourcoing followed other successes for the French which culminated in the winter in the capture of the icebound Dutch fleet by cavalry. The Dutch surrendered and the Prince of Orange sailed for England 17 January 1795. The British contingent was evacuated.

Rev. Reginald Heber to his sister, Elizabeth Heber
31 January 1795

It is pleasing to see in the papers, the many noble donations and contributions which have been made for the relief of the indigent in many parts of the Kingdom, this severe season when so many labourers are out of work and the necessaries of life are so very dear. This general bounty of the affluent will I hope satisfie the People at large that they could not be in better hands or live under a better government than that of Old England.

Rev. Reginald Heber to his sister, Elizabeth Heber
14 February 1795

Sir Richard Hill having prepared a Bill to be brought into Parliament immediately for the purpose of dividing or enclosing certain common or waste lands within the parish of Hodnet,[1] a copy of which I have seen and find some clauses which I do not approve and which I think very unjust and injurious to my interests. I have determined to come to Town immediately in order to make my appearance in the Committee room to oppose and offer my objection to such clauses.

Rev. Reginald Heber to his sister, Elizabeth Heber
17 February 1795

Having reason to suspect from the close and reserved conduct of Sir R. Hill's agents in their proceedings, that they want to smuggle the Inclosure Bill through the House as rapidly as possible, that they may not steal a march on us, I desire my dear Richard will inform himself on what day the Bill will be first presented, and to take such steps as are usual and necessary to prevent it being passed without our having an opportunity of opposing it.

[1] To enclose land within the parishes of Prees, Stanton upon Hineheath and Moreton-Saye ; the Bill to be prepared by Sir Richard and Mr. Hill. Having met with no opposition in committee (Commons Journals, vol. 50, p. 276) but somewhat amended, in what direction is not known, the Bill became law on 5 March 1795.

Elizabeth Heber to Rev. Reginald Heber
7 April 1795

The Princess, the papers will inform you, arrived on Sunday.[1] The rain after Church prevented our going out at the usual hour, or we should probably have seen her Highness make her grand entree into the City of Westminster, she came from Greenwich over Westminster Bridge and through the streets to St. James', where she showed herself at the window to the populace who received her with loud applauses. The marriage is to take place to-morrow evening. The guns at the Tower and in the Park have been firing this day and the bells ringing merrily. I hope for good news from Admiral Hotham[2] who has had an engagement with the French. Our Princess was I hope the forerunner of a Victory and arrives under happy auspices. We are just informed she is exhibiting at the windows, so are going to take a peep at her.

Elizabeth Heber to Rev. Reginald Heber
21 April 1795

I think Lady Warburton will be in no haste to have her picture finished which was the ostensible errand to town. She says Sir Peter tells her she had bribed Romney[3] to go on slowly with it.

The brilliant appearance at the Royal Nuptials and the succeeding Drawing Room furnishes sufficient topics for the gay world. Our servants went to gaze amongst the multitude at the Princess, who was very affable and attentive to the people in shewing herself from the windows of St. James' Palace, Cleveland Row; they think her beautiful and she is allowed in general to be a pretty little woman, very lively and pleasing in her manner. May she long continue pleasing in the eyes of her Lord and Master.

[1] Arrival of Caroline of Brunswick to marry the Prince of Wales. They were married on 8 April.

[2] Admiral Hotham (1736-1813) was at this time watching the Toulon fleet. In March he fought an indecisive action, taking two prizes.

[3] George Romney (1734-1802), painter.

Elizabeth Heber to Rev. Reginald Heber
12 *May* 1795

Dear Richard attended the Debate in the House of Lords on the recall of Lord Fitz-William's.[1] He says there were some good speeches but most of them irrelevant to the Question, which was lost by a considerable majority against the Enquiry.

Rev. Reginald Heber to his sister, Elizabeth Heber
3 *June* 1795

We are diverted with the report of dear Richard's sufferings in his struggles to get admittance into St. Stephen's Chapel on Mr. Wilberforce's Motion,[2] however I find the entertainment of the subsequent debate compensated for the loss of the flap of his coat and the temporary inconvenience of sitting without shoes.

Elizabeth Heber to Rev. Reginald Heber
30 *June* 1795

Now the Parliament is prorogued the Town will soon be deserted excepting the Jacobins who begin to be busy. Some thousands of people were assembled yesterday in St. Geroge's

[1] 8 May. Debate in the Lords on the Duke of Norfolk's motion for the House to be informed of the reason for the recall of the Earl Fitzwilliam from the lord-lieutenancy of Ireland ; lost by 100 votes to twenty-five. A similar motion by the opposition in the Commons was also lost. Fitzwilliam had held the appointment for three weeks only ; he was the victim of what may charitably be described as a complicated misunderstanding about the future treatment of Roman Catholics in Ireland. His disgrace caused great discontent in Ireland, where hopes had been entertained that the status of the Catholics was to be improved ; and this discontent led to repression, and repression caused the Irish to look to France.

[2] 27 May. Debate in the Commons on Mr. Wilberforce's motion ' that the present circumstances of France ought not to preclude the government of this country, from entertaining proposals for a general pacification ; and that it is for the interest of Great Britain to make peace with France provided it can be effected on fair terms, and in an honourable manner '. Pitt declared that ' by a vigorous prosecution of the war for a short time longer, we have every reasonable prospect that we shall be able to procure for ourselves a solid, permanent and honourable peace.'

Fields,[1] they were not however riotous but bills put up in several places signified their intention of procuring annual Parliaments and universal suffrage. His Majesty, it is said, was treated disrespectfully by the mob as he went to and returned from the House of Lords. I am glad Lord Bridport's victory[2] afforded them a sugar-plumb at parting. The news came very seasonably and I trust will be followed by repeated successes. Poor Mr. Edward Maynwaring's son Charles was on board the *Sans Parrelle* and I was happy to find his name not amongst the kill'd or wounded. His Father called upon us after he had been with him at Portsmouth. As he found it impossible to dissuade him from entering the Service he made interest with his friends to get him on board a Man-of-War as soon as he could. I wish he may succeed in the profession he has chosen but it is one which will give many a pang to the heart of his parent.

Elizabeth Heber to Rev. Reginald Heber
14 *July* 1795

May God send us a good harvest, the present scarcity of Wheat is a very serious calamity, and will increase the discontent of the People already too much inflamed and inclined to mischief. The rioters on Sunday night went from Charing Cross to Downing Street, where they broke Mr. Pitt's windows and were proceeding to greater acts of violence when they were stopp't by the Military. *What has Billy done ?* He can't send rain or sunshine and is contented to partake with the poor of their brown bread. The Wedgwood pies will be in great request

---

[1] Extract from *The Times* of 30 June 1795, referring to a meeting in St. George's Fields promoted by the London Corresponding Society : ' We can evidently trace in it the progress of French anarchy, and the exercise of those measures which have been of late pointed out in some of our Jacobin newspapers, to instigate the lower orders of the people to acts of rebellion against Government, as being the source of the present scarcity of bread ; whereas no government ever took greater precautions to prevent it.' Tickets of admission to the meeting were sold at 6d. each, and biscuits were distributed bearing the slogan ' Freedom and plenty, or slavery and want '.

[2] Lord Bridport (Alexander Hood, 1727-1814) engaged a French fleet off Belle-Isle on 23 June 1795. The action has been much criticised, but was publicly regarded as a victory. The *Sans Pareil* (captured at the Battle of 1 June) lost ten killed and two wounded.

being the only appearance of pastry allowed to fill up the table, if we follow the advice of the Privy Council to forego all luxurious crusts and puddings till a more plentiful season.[1]

Elizabeth Heber to Rev. Reginald Heber
2 November 1795

You would be shocked to hear of the insults offered to his Majesty in going to and returning from the Parliament House.[2] His life was certainly in imminent danger from the ruffians who surrounded him in his private coach on his way through the Park from St. James' to the Queen's House, had not the Guards come up at that instant, he must have fallen a sacrifice to their brutal rage.

Rev. Reginala Heber to his sister, Elizabeth Heber
7 December 1795

Mr. Allanson and Mr. Davies had been at the County Meeting at York which was called by Fox's friends who thought to carry all before them, but the spirit of the friends of good order being rous'd, the Democrats were completely foiled.

Mary Heber to her sister-in-law, Elizabeth Heber
14 December 1795

Please let me know the boys know the day they are to set out that they may be ready. They must travel in their great-coats

---

[1] ' The Privy Council have come to a determination to recommend a general use of household or brown bread, and have already adopted the measure themselves.' *The Times* of 14 July 1795, which about that day gave the following recipe : 2 lbs. potatoes boiled and mashed, 1 pt. milk, 3 eggs, 2 ozs. moist sugar ; mix and bake in an oven for three quarters of an hour, and call the result Cottage Pudding.

The price of wheat (which had been 36s. a qtr. at the beginning of the century) stood at 56s. in 1790, whence it rose steadily during the French Wars, being 83s. in 1800-10 and 106s. in 1810-3. By mid-century it had dropped to 50s. or 60s.

[2] A ball apparently from an airgun broke the window of the King's carriage. Stones were thrown. A gang of men kept pace with the carriage, shouting insults. There were cries of ' No war. Down with George.'

and never take them off at the Inns. Please to mention this, that the great-coats may not be put in the trunks.

Rev. Reginald Heber to his sister, Elizabeth Heber
21 *December* 1795

We shall be obliged to you to take the trouble of ordering 2 pounds Hyson Tea at 8*s.* per lb., 2 pounds Soushong at 6*s.*, 3 pounds Congo at 4*s.*

Elizabeth Heber to Rev. Reginald Heber
28 *January* 1796

We were alarmed on Sunday morning with (as we apprehended) the shock of an Earthquake but it proved an explosion of the Powder Mills at Hounslow.

Rev. Reginald Heber to his son, Richard
7 *May* 1796

The Candidates for the Borough of Shrewsbury are spending or rather spilling a shower of gold, and various and mutable are the opinions of the by-standers of the result. Mrs. J. Hill and her fair daughters have resided there some time in a house which it is said the Baronet purchased, furnish'd and presented to her. Will Hill, *the Lad*, alias *Tu Brute* as Sir Richard denominates him, is I hear quite an Adonis and the favourite of the Salopian females, young and old.

So our friend and relative is still a croaker and persevering adherent to Charles Fox and *Misery's side*. For my part I can see no cause for depressing and foreboding apprehensions of a *Crash*. If I had forty thousand good pounds in ready Rino, I would invest them in the Funds without delay, so firm is my opinion of the stability of Government security.

Elizabeth Heber to Rev. Reginald Heber
24 May 1796

Dear Richard is very anxious for his cousin Cholmondeley's success at the Election.[1] Mr. Glegg tells us that Lord Gray[2] has declined standing but it is thought Mr. Egerton of Tatton[3] meant to offer himself. I hope our kinsman will not stand a contest which he can by no means afford. His address is in true Cholmondeley style, I wish he may be brought into Parliament by the unanimous voice of the County as his forefathers have always been.

Rev. Reginald Heber to his sister, Elizabeth Heber
June 1796

I went with my neighbour Dod on Monday to Northwich as proposed to attend the nominations of the Candidates Crewe and Cholmondeley to represent the County Palatinate of Chester. The day was very rainy but not so stormy as by your account it was in London. The Assembly of Electors was very respectable and numerous. Sir Peter Warburton proposed Mr. Crewe, and Mr. Dod, our kinsman, which office he undertook and performed in a very clever sensible manner at Mr. Cholmondeley's particular request and with great *eclat*. Mr. Egerton of Oulton[4] seconded Mr. Dod, and Sir Thomas Broughton backed them both in a long harangue which was chiefly directed against the election of the sons of Peers in the Commons House of Parliament which he averred was totally inconsistent with the spirit of the Constitution and subversive of it and ought not to be tolerated by the Electors. Both the Candidates came forward in their turn and addressed the Electors, and it afforded the friends of our kinsman great pleasure to hear him acquit himself with great fluency, propriety and, ability. The wetness of the day prevented

[1] At the general election of 1796, John Crewe and Thomas Cholmondeley were returned for Cheshire.
[2] 'Lord Gray' is Sir Thomas Egerton, seventh Baronet, cr. Lord Grey de Wilton 1784 and Earl of Wilton 1801.
[3] William Egerton of Tatton, Cheshire (1749-1806).
[4] John Egerton of Oulton, Cheshire (1766-1825).

the Nomination being, as is usual in fine weather, out of doors, and the room being small where the Sheriff opened the business would but admit of few of the vast number of Free-holders assembled to support their favourite Candidate. However, no sooner was the Nomination of Mr. Cholmondeley announced without doors than the multitude made the air resound with 'Cholmondeley for ever', and as soon as he went out of the house they carried him in their arms and hoisted him into a Chair surrounded with Oak Boughs which formed an arbour and carried him on their shoulders as far as he would suffer them, at least two miles towards Vale Royal.

Elizabeth Heber to Rev. Reginald Heber
7 June 1796

We will make all the enquiries we can after a governess for little Mary, but such as are in every respect eligible are difficult to be met with and their terms very high. There are plenty of emigrant ladies, some of the rank of Viscountess, to be had, but I think you would not prefer a French-woman, and I am sure would not take a Roman Catholic into your house. We have just hired a governess for Mary Ann, her wages or salary is to be forty guineas a year, her washing done at home or paid for, and she is to eat at their own table. She undertakes to instruct her pupil in English, French, Geography, Music, Writing and Arithemetic. The wages are now, it seems, thought low, fifty or sixty pounds or guineas being frequently given.

Rev. Reginald Heber to his sister, Elizabeth Heber
11 June 1796

The Shrewsbury struggle which has been very warm and monstrously expensive is concluded, as far as the power of the Mayor, the Returning Officer extends, in favour of Sir William Pulteney and the Hon'ble William Hill, but it is said that Mr.

By courtesy of Brig. Heber-Percy of Hodnet.

III   REV. REGINALD HEBER

1783-1826

The young Rector of Hodnet, afterwards Bishop of Calcutta.

George Richmond, R.A. (1826)

IV   MARY CHOLMONDELEY

Daughter of Rev. Reginald Heber (' Papa ') and wife of Rev. Charles
Cholmondeley.

John Hill will appeal to the House against the return of the latter.[1] The question in dispute is whether the assessed Burgesses *only* are legal Voters or all Burgesses assessed or not assessed. Mr. William Hill had a majority of eighty-nine of assessed Voters over Mr. J. Hill but Mr. J. Hill on the other hand had a majority of forty-four of assessed and not assessed Burgesses. The Mayor's opinion was in favour of the former who usually reside in the town and pay Lot and Scot, the latter are non-resident collected from all quarters, tag, rag and bob-tail fresh imported on this occasion, far fetched and dear bought indeed if they turn out mere cyphers.

Rev. Reginald Heber to his sister, Elizabeth Heber
21 *August* 1796

Sir Richard Hill you may be sure was not a little proud of the honour of entertaining His Highness of Orange[2] at Hawkstone, nor a little vain of the dashing paragraphs inserted in the newspapers.

Rev. Reginald Heber to his sister, Elizabeth Heber
31 *August* 1796

I hope Richard will be with us at the commencement of the Partridge Shooting which is now postponed by Act of Parliament to the middle of September.

As I had mentioned in my last letter I went with Mr. Davies to attend the Nomination of the Candidates to represent the County of Flint[3] at Mold on Tuesday last, where there was a

---

[1] The result of the Poll was :—

Sir William Pulteney	370
William Hill (later third Lord Berwick) ..	242
John Hill (later Sir John Hill third Baronet)	153

John Hill petitioned the House against this verdict but, after some delay, withdrew.

[2] William of Orange-Nassau, fifth and last Stadtholder of the Netherlands, fled to England in 1794, on the people throwing in their lot with the French revolutionaries. His son was recalled, in 1813, as King and the modern Kingdom of the Netherlands (Holland after 1830) came into existence.

[3] A single-seat constituency.

numerous and respectable meeting in support of Sir Thomas
Hanmer,[1] who was nominated in a very handsome manner by
the old hero of Broughton with great applause. On the other
hand the Dean of St. Asaph,[2] after a long eulogium or, as one of
the speakers called his speech, a Funeral Sermon on their late representative, Sir T. Mostyn, proposed his son the present Sir Thomas
tho' under age to succeed his Father.[3] This was forcibly objected
to by a Mr. Williams of Ruthin, a young Counsellor, as illegal
and unconstitutional, Minors being incapacitated from sitting or
voting in the House of Commons by an express Act of Parliament in the time of William and Mary. The Dean, nevertheless,
persisted in his nomination of the young Baronet, insisting that
Minors to his certain knowledge had been permitted to sit in
both Houses of Parliament in the last two sessions. In short,
Sir T. Hanmer being afraid of the expenses of a contest as is
supposed, left his friends in the lurch and declined standing a
Poll to the no small chagrin and disappointment of his adherents.
Had he stood it out like a man, he must have been the sitting
Member, even supposing his disqualified opponent had had a
majority of votes, of which however there was little probability.
Sir T. Hanmer by his pusillanimity has lost an opportunity of
representing the County of Flint (in which he has a better estate
than any other man) which may never offer again to himself
or any of his family. Tuesday last the day of the Nominations
was extremely sultry and tho' the scene of action was a large open
field, the intense heat was almost insupportable.

Rev. Reginald Heber to his sister, Elizabeth Heber
3 September 1796

The Flintshire Freeholders are very indignant at the insolent
conduct of the Dean of St. Asaph in attempting to impose an
unqualified ineligible Minor upon them to represent them in
Parliament and I have reason to believe that Lloyd Kenyon.

[1] Sir Thomas Hanmer, second Baronet (1747-1828).
[2] Rev. William Shipley, Dean of St. Asaph. d. 1826.
[3] Sir Roger (not T.) Mostyn died 26 July 1796.
His son Sir Thomas Mostyn, sixth Baronet, died 1831.

Lord Kenyon's eldest son, will be set up in opposition to Sir T. Mostyn.

The pusillanimous behaviour of poor Sir T. H., or rather his parsimony, has made him the object of ridicule and contempt.

Richard to his father, Rev. Reginald Heber
20 October 1796

In one respect I was glad I was in town as I had by that means an opportunity to be present at the first night's discussions in the H. of C. Hodson and I agreed in thinking Mr. Pitt very brilliant, and Mr. Fox more embarrassed and less eloquent than usual. We likewise thought that the Minister's speech gave but little prospect of a termination of the War. Since that period, nothing like a debate has taken place till Tuesday night when I was fortunate to witness a most interesting and animated attack and defence on Mr. Pitt's proposal for a national armament against invasion. The Plan which Government seem resolved to adopt is indeed vigorous and immense,[1] not on too large or serious a scale if they have any probable reason to apprehend an invasion, though surely likely to produce much trouble and some evil in detaching many hands from industrious occupations. The arming of the game-keepers at first produced no little amusement in the House tho' perhaps it may not be without its use. Mark must renounce the poor partridges, woodcocks and rabbits for a more formidable and resisting game. At all events this confirms me in the convictions that Peace cannot be expected.

Rev. Reginald Heber to his son, Richard
24 October 1796

I think Mr. Pitt's proposal for embodying the game-keepers a fair one, and if the Frenchmen become Birds of Passage, these

[1] On 18 October 1795 Pitt proposed, in order to meet the threatened invasion and as a means of reinforcing the overtures for peace, a levy of 15,000 men to the regular forces, of 60,000 to form a supplementary militia ; of an auxiliary force of irregular cavalry ; and of a corps of gamekeepers, both gentlemen and servants. Fox denied the emergency and considered these great forces a dangerous addition to the power of the executive government.

marksmen will be ready primed to knock them down like Woodcocks.

Rev. Reginald Heber to his son, Richard
3 November 1796

Your fowling-piece burst in Mark's hand, a piece a foot long flew off the barrel but did no mischief. I suppose there must have been some flaw in the part; it was well it was not nearer the breech.

Rev. Reginald Heber to his sister, Elizabeth Heber
7 November 1796

Mr. Pulestone of Emerald after having made love to Miss Owen our neighbour Dod's niece for some time and the wedding day being fix'd, has left her in the lurch and trained off. This shameful usage of the Fair Lady, you may be sure is very highly resented by her brother Owen,[1] her uncle Dod and all her friends. The former sent Pulestone a challenge to single combat for the insult about ten days ago, when the matter was patched up by Pulestone signing a paper acknowledging himself a scoundrel. But such ulcers are not easily healed and are apt to rankle and break out afresh : as has been the case in the present instance. Dod and Pulestone met it seems at the Tarporly Hunt and in consequence of what passed there, of which I know not the particulars, another challenge ensued between Dod and Pulestone, who met with their seconds at Barnhill on Saturday, but fortunately no blood was shed. It is said that Mr. Morral the surgeon who was sent for to attend in case of need, prevailed on the combatants not to proceed to extremities.

Rev. Reginald Heber to his sister, Elizabeth Heber
15 November 1796

Mary and I waited upon our neighbours at Edge on Monday sennight and found Mrs. Dod pretty well. She gave us a detail

---

[1] William Mostyn-Owen of Woodhouse, Shropshire.

of the affair at Barnhill between her husband and Pulestone, by the latter of whom the challenge was given, as is supposed, to regain his credit for prowess with his brother officers in Sir Watkin's Corps of Fencibles, to whom it was known he had cried 'Peccavi', and had declined a combat with Captain Owen whose eldest sister he had used so scurvily. Some mischief-making busy-body had told Puleston that Mr. Dod had made an *improper use of his name* for which he demanded satisfaction. Mr. Dod conducted himself with great good sense and temper on the occasion. When they met at Barnhill with their seconds, viz. Mr. Patten and Mr. Kennyon of Kevin, Mr. Dod asked Pulestone with what views he had called him out, for tho' he was afraid of no man, yet he was not inclined rashly to expose his own life or run the hazard of taking away that of another; if Mr. Pulestone meant or supposed by challenging him or by spilling his blood to wipe out the stain upon his character which had been contracted by the unjustifiable behaviour to his niece and his acknowledge-ments to her brother, Captain Owen, he might be assured that by taking away his life, if such should be the event, so far from lessening would aggravate his delinquency in the eyes of all men.

Mr. Patten then asked Pulestone to explain why he had challenged Mr. Dod and for what offence. Mr. Pulestone re-plied, because Mr. Dod had made an improper use of his name. Mr. Dod asked him who told him so, he wished to know his authority, this Mr. Pulestone declined. Mr. Dod then said he neither had nor could make an improper use of Mr. Pulestone's name; then replied Pulestone, 'My quarrel with you is at an end as you deny it', 'I deny nothing', says Mr. Dod. 'Produce your informant and I will repeat and abide by whatever I have said of or concerning you'. Mr. Pulestone refusing to name his in-formant, the seconds interfered and the affair ended.

Elizabeth Heber to Rev. Reginald Heber
26 November 1796

Various are the opinions and surmises respecting the opening of the Budget, what Billy means to do with our Property will soon be known. Times and taxes I know are hard enough upon us already, but one would give up a great deal rather than to be subject to the domiciliary visits of the Jacobins.

Rev. Reginald Heber to his sister, Elizabeth Heber
8 December 1796

I see in the *Chester Chronicle* of to-day that twenty millions, two millions more than were required, were subscribed in the short space of three days after the Books were opened at the Bank, such an instance of promptitude in raising the supplies for the service of government is I believe unparalleled in the Annals of Funding ! This proclaims to the world in a voice of thunder how little this Queen of Isles fears any efforts of the combined Powers of France and Spain to disturb her repose !

Richard to his father, Rev. Reginald Heber
10 December 1796

What say you to the Budget ? Voluntary contributions ? New Taxes ? This morning's paper brings an acc't of the trimming Billy has received for his subsidy to the Emperor — without leave of Parliament — which I think he richly deserves.[1]

Rev. Reginald Heber to his sister, Elizabeth Heber
9 March 1797

I rejoice with you and all true friends of Old England on the glorious Victory[2] gained by Sir John Jervis[3] and his gallant tars over the Spanish Fleet, tho' two to one in number of men and guns. I hope this brilliant achievement will raise the drooping spirits of the dastardly Cockneys, and dissipate their cowardly apprehensions and fears of an invasion. The Foxites will be

[1] Pitt introduced his budget for 1797 on 7 December 1796. The expenses of the war for 1797 were estimated at nearly £28,000,000, of which £18,000,000 was to be met by a public loan at £5 12s. 6d. per cent. It was revealed that ministers had paid, and proposed to continue, at their discretion, considerable subsidies to the Austrian Emperor.
[2] Battle of Cape Saint Vincent, 14 February 1797.
[3] Admiral Sir John Jervis (1734-1823). cr. Lord St. Vincent in 1797.

grievously chagrined at the good news, who were no doubt
contrivers and plotters of the late Run on the Bank of England,[1]
by spreading alarms and persuading all they could influence to
hurry with their notes to the Bank for specie. But the wicked
machinations, thank Heaven, proved abortive; and I verily
believe the Bank of England to be the firmest security upon this
habitable globe.

Elizabeth Heber to Rev. Reginald Heber
11 *March* 1797

I had the pleasure of a letter from Bessy with a long acc't of
the invasion at Milford Haven[2] and the consternation occasioned
by a false alarm of sixty thousand of the French being landed
in Monmouthshire. The Marquis of Buckingham and Lord
Temple headed the Military and were marching to oppose the
enemy, but returned in about four hours, being informed by one
of the King's Messengers the report was without foundation.
The gentlemen of this town turned out as Volunteers and, headed
by the Mayor, undertook to guard the French Prison in which
are thirteen hundred prisoners; in short the Merchants and
principal inhabitants at Bristol shew the firmest loyalty and
warmest zeal on the occasion in supporting and assisting the
Government.

Richard to his father, Rev. Reginald Heber
26 *April* 1797

Politics wear but a gloomy complexion. Do guineas ever
make their appearance in your quarters or are they as here super-
seded by paper.[3]

---

[1] The great cost of the war, which absorbed as much as 30 per cent. of the total
income of the nation, caused in 1797 a financial crisis. The Bank of England could not
meet its note issue with coin. Cash payments were in part suspended, and bank-notes
became inconvertible currency.
[2] In February 1797, 1,500 French landed at Fishguard. They were captured without
firing a shot.
[3] Cash payments of sums over £1 were suspended in 1797.

Elizabeth Heber to Rev. Reginald Heber
9 May 1797

Great preparations for the Royal Wedding,[1] methinks it is ill-timed when the public distresses accumulate every day. The Emperor leaves us to fight our own battles with the French,[2] and what is still worse our seamen continue in a state of Mutiny.[3] How this will end, God only knows.

Rev. Reginald Heber to his sister, Elizabeth Heber
4 November 1797

I hope this will find dear Richard with you and in perfect health after his excursion to Sheerness and highly gratified by the triumphant Review of the vanquished Batavian Squadron.[4]

Rev. Reginald Heber to his sister, Elizabeth Heber
12 November 1797

We are happy to be assured of dear Richard's safe return from Rochester with his friends Nicholson and Cleaver. I am glad they did not attempt going to the Nore but contented themselves with going on board the *Venerable*, the *Monarch* and the Dutch Admiral's ships and had the gratification of cheering and being cheered by the Noble Admiral on his passage from one ship to another. 'Tis a pity the King did not go by land to Chatham and then proceed down the Medway to Sheerness.[5]

---

[1] The Princess Royal was married on 18 May 1797 to Frederick, King of Wurtemburg.

[2] Austria signed the Preliminaries of Loeben on 27 April and the Peace of Campo Formio in October.

[3] The mutinies at Spithead, 16 April-15 May, and at the Nore, 12 May-14 June 1797.

[4] Eight line-of-battle ships were taken by Admiral Duncan in the action against the Dutch fleet at Camperdown on 11 October 1797.

[5] On 30 October the King embarked at Greenwich to go and congratulate Duncan who was lying at Sheerness. The weather was, however, too much for His Majesty who went home again.

Reginald (aged 14) to his father, Rev. Reginald Heber
from his school at Neasdon, 13 November 1797

On Sunday the fifth we were agreeably surprised by a visit
from brother Richard who came when we were at dinner. He
gave us a very entertaining account of his journey to the Nore.
Mr. Bristow's former pupil Edwards was here at the same time,
and presented one of the oddest figures I ever saw. His beard was
almost as long as that of a Turk, his hair long and disshevelled
hanging about his shoulders without powder, and to crown all
he had a green neck-cloth.

Rev. Reginald Heber to his sister, Elizabeth Heber
18 November 1797

Poor Mary Mo has got a swelled toe, which makes her very
lame and I tell her is the gout, but others say nay, and that it is a
chillblay.

Richard to his father, Rev. Reginald Heber
28 November 1797

Everything at Oxford wears a most martial appearance. The
haunts of the Muses are molested by the din of arms and nothing
but words of command and volleys are to be heard from morning
to night. A corps of five hundred men and upward has been
raised and embodied for the defence of the University, composed
indiscriminately from all ages and ranks. As to parochial arma-
ments they are I fancy quite gone by. Government can afford no
more money, and the farmers and peasants have other means of
employing their time without shouldering their firelocks to the
neglect of their spade and pitch-fork. The Oxford Regiment at
present are indefatigable in attending to their drill twice a day,
having regular sergeants to instruct them. Their uniforms are
determined upon but not arrived yet.

Elizabeth Heber to Rev. Reginald Heber
13 April 1798

We are happy to hear that dear Mary's cough is better. I trust asses' milk will speedily remove it.

The French now seem determined to attack us in good earnest, but in the present state of Ireland[1] I should think their chief force would be directed there where it is to be feared they will find too many friends.

Elizabeth Heber to Rev. Reginald Heber
29 May 1798

I hope your Paper has been duly sent since you returned home. One is anxious for news these eventful times. Billy Pitt, you will see has fought with Tierney[2] and both come off with honour and unhurt.

You would grieve with us for the unfortunate capture of our brave soldiers at Flushing.[3] It was a glorious enterprise and success attended it as far as human efforts could accomplish it, and I trust the enemy will now find it no easy matter to convey their gunboats, artillery, etc. to their seaports for the purpose of an invasion. Shocking acc'ts from Ireland. I hope the horrid conspiracy has been found out in time to prevent further mischief.

Elizabeth Heber to Rev. Reginald Heber
23 June 1798

Mrs. Vaughan poor woman is under great and heavy apprehensions of an invasion of which she thinks the Suffolk coast most

[1] Rebellion which had long been in the air of Ireland broke out in May 1798. It was suppressed in June, but the state of Ireland continued to be dangerous.

[2] Tierney, a member of the opposition, spoke against the hurrying through of a certain bill concerning the manning of the navy. Pitt suggested that he was not over-zealous for the defence of the country. Tierney challenged. The duel was fought on 27 May on Putney Heath, without damage but with honour.

[3] A military side-show to destroy the lock-gates of the Bruges-Ostend canal. This result was accomplished, but hardly had the result hoped for. High seas prevented the troops being taken off, and 1,100 surrendered at discretion. Elizabeth Heber voices the official view.

likely to be attempted. The paper gives an account this morning
of a Revolution in Holland,[1] which seems favourable to us at
this juncture !

Reginald to his Mother
Neasdon, 23 June 1798

Mr. Bristow read aloud to us the other day a private letter
from Ireland which differs considerably from the accounts in the
newspapers; the letter says the Rebels in one of the late engagements were twenty-five thousand strong, mostly armed with
pikes, with a few pieces of cannon. They were drawn up regularly
by parishes, each parish headed by its priest. It was very fortunate
that they were so ignorant of artillery that they were obliged to
make their prisoners fire their cannon, but they took care to
point their guns so high as to do no mischief to the King's Troops.
The Rebels are composed of two sorts, Papists and Presbyterians.
The aim and intention of the Papists may be collected from the
following oath which was found in the pockets of some of them:
' I swear by our Lord J. C. and the B. Virgin Mary to burn,
murder and destroy all Heretics, up to my knees in Blood '.
The intention of the Presbyterians it seems, is the destruction of
the Episcopacy and the Monarchy. Several of these last have
returned to their allegiance.

Elizabeth Heber to Rev. Reginald Heber
30 June 1798

Yesterday His Majesty prorogued His Parliament to the 8th
August but I hope nothing will happen to make it necessary for
them to assemble before the usual time. Affairs in Ireland I trust
are mending and we flatter ourselves that Admiral Nelson will

---

[1] *The Times* of 23 June 1798, under the headline ' Counter-Revolution in Holland ',
gave a long account of the *coup d'état* carried out on the 12th by General Daendels against
the Legislative Assembly. It was a two-day wonder which did not affect the general
situation.

fall in with and give a good acc't of the French Fleet and Buonaparte.[1] The rumour of his having taken Constantinople had not
reached us and we conclude it premature, tho' I should not be
surpriz'd to hear it confirmed, the Turks having many French
emissaries amongst them and a rebel Pasha making great devasta-
tion in their country, and as *Charity begins at home*, I should rather
wish this formidable Fleet might steer their course toward them
than Ireland. I entirely agree with you that the completion of the
Prophecys are fast approaching, as whoever attends to the Signs
of the Times must be convinced of.

Elizabeth Heber to Rev. Reginald Heber
7 *July* 1798

The Lancashire Militia have offer'd their services in Ireland for
which place they were actually embarked, whether they have
gone or no is uncertain, our paper yesterday says all these
Regiments of Militia had received counter orders, no more
troops being wanted there, but to-day we are all *abroad again* by
accounts of the Rebels having appeared in great force in the
Counties of Wexford and Wicklow.

Buonaparte you see has taken Malta. Admiral Nelson had been
very unlucky in his intelligence or he must have fallen with his
fleet.

Elizabeth Heber to Rev. Reginald Heber
25 *August* 1798

I have not a word of news to write. Buonaparte is supposed to
have made his landing at Alexandria but I think the accounts
seem to want confirmation, at all events it is to be feared that
he has got clear of Admiral Nelson's Fleet.

---

[1] Napoleon Bonaparte and his army sailed from France in May 1798, evaded Nelson,
captured Malta, and occupied Alexandria on 2 July.

Richard to his aunt, Elizabeth Heber
27 August 1798

You will see in the paper the French have landed a few hundred men in Ireland at Killale[1] and taken the Bishop prisoner. Of course the reports vary. A nobleman who passed thro' Chester for Ireland said two thousand three hundred had disembarked. Bishop Cleaver's letter from Dublin said a few hundred only.

Elizabeth Heber to her nephew, Richard
15 September 1798

Mrs. Booth writes that Lord Rolles Regiment of Militia were ordered to embark: when they got to the water-side they refused to go: but that by the persuasion of their officers two-thirds were afterwards embarked.

Elizabeth Heber to Rev. Reginald Heber
4 October 1798

I must now congratulate all our dear friends on Admiral Nelson's glorious Victory.[2] This great news makes us at last ample amends for the long and anxious suspense we have been kept in respecting his having fallen in with the French Fleet, of which there have been such various reports. The rejoicings here have been beyond all bounds. Illuminations for two nights past are it is said to be repeated again to-night. The boys heard the news at Stratford where they say the people were all intoxicated with joy and drink. On this Occasion may we, with our brave and pious Admiral give due Praise to Almighty God who has so singularly Blessed his Majesty's Arms in the late Battle.

---

[1] The expedition of Humbert, consisting of about 1,000 men, was the first and the only effective one of several designed by the French government, at the instigation of Wolfe Tone, to take advantage of Irish discontent. Humbert landed in Killala Bay on 22 August 1798, defeated General Lake, and surrendered to Cornwallis on 8 September.

[2] Battle of the Nile, 1 August 1798. Only four of the French ships which had conveyed Napoleon to Egypt escaped.

Elizabeth Heber to Rev. Reginald Heber
20 November 1798

I shall be obliged to you as soon as convenient after Xmas to assist me with the odd hundred remaining on the Bond of which two hundred is already paid off, — to enable me to answer Mr. Pitt's demands the ensuing year. How do you approve of the new Budget ? I think it will be attended with greater difficulties than the present mode of gathering the assess'd Taxes.

Elizabeth Heber to Rev. Reginald Heber
13 December 1798

I had the pleasure of a letter from Mrs. Glegg a few days since : she hopes her husband will be this next Taxation rewarded for his honesty in paying a full tenth of his income,[1] as I trust we all shall, or it will be a hard case indeed on those who gave a fair statement of their income.

Rev. Reginald Heber to his sister, Elizabeth Heber
29 April 1799

The chilly blasting north-east winds have check'd all vegetation in the field and garden and to add to the distress of the farmers they are most of them destitute of hay or straw or any fodder for their cattle. On our return from Hodnet last week we over-took a dozen wagon loads of hay going out of Staffordshire to Chester, none being to be had nearer. Another grievance is that butcher's meat is rapidly advancing in price and wheat which a few weeks ago was under eight shillings a measure is

---

[1] Originally instituted in April 1798 the income tax was rather a codification of existing assessments than a direct charge on income. In December it was recast in the form which is now familiar. Incomes under £60 were exempt, between £60 and £200 paid a small tax, and over £200 paid the full tax of 10 per cent. The tax lapsed during the Peace of Amiens, was renewed, and was abolished in 1815, when all papers referring to its collection were ordered to be destroyed. Although universally unpopular, the income tax was from the first a highly efficient revenue collector.

now risen to half a guinea and is to be feared will be much dearer, the corn factors and millers having bought up all the farmers had at the above low price; and have it now in their power to put any price upon this necessary article of life their unconscionable avarice may dictate.

THIS CHAPTER opens with an account from Richard, now twenty-five years old and down from Oxford, of his tour in Scotland. He was in the company of Hobhouse and a servant, John France. Young Reginald, now sixteen years old, wrote from his school at Neasdon; he had had a serious misunderstanding with his schoolmaster. Their father visited the industrial marvels at Coalbrookdale. In the same year a second British expeditionary force to Holland failed to achieve its object. A great coalition had again been assembled against France; it seemed to be on the point of victory when all was lost. Richard Heber went to London, to the New Forest and then to Exeter. Hobhouse, Eyre, Richardson, Froude, Pering and Cholmondeley are named as his friends. With John France he descended to the bottom of a copper mine. There are references to high prices and to social discontent. At last the war ended.

Immediately Richard extended his travels to France with Eyre, and visited Paris. His activities at this time may be supplemented from letters to him collected in Chapter vi. There was no incongruity in this quick acceptance of the French as friends, but when the war seemed about to be renewed they came back hastily and were wise to do so, for the French interned all English visitors who outstayed the peace : an action which caused great discontent.

At last, the war broke into the private lives of the Hebers. All three brothers became involved in the great expansion of the armed forces with which the threat of invasion was met. They wanted to bear their part. But they entered not the regular army, not the reserve, not the militia, but the volunteers — a collection of civilians in uniform, the least warlike of all the military organizations. Their father thought that attendance at a university ought to exempt his two younger sons (for young Reginald and Thomas had followed Richard at Oxford) from service.

The letters in this chapter show Richard a grown man taking his place in the county, apparently beginning to represent the family in society and to take over social duties from his father. He is obviously an energetic and adventurous man, destined to go through life with a greater degree of *élan* than his father.

*   *   *

Richard to his aunt, Elizabeth Heber
Edinburgh 31 August 1799

Our time has been a good deal taken up with seeing sights in and about; such as the Castle, Register Office, Bridewell College, Advocate's Library, Holyrood House and in the neighbourhood the seats of the Duke of Buccleugh, Lord Hopetown, Lord Rosebery, the Marq. of Lothian, etc. We have received much civility from Professor Dalzell[1] who has taken us about and given up a great deal of time to us, we dined with a party he asked to meet us on Wednesday and we are to dine with Dr. Gregory the Medical Professor to whom he introduced us. To-morrow we spend the day with the *Man of feeling and family*[2] at his country house not far from Edinburgh called Achindinny, on our way to Lanark and Glasgow.

Rev. Reginald Heber to his sister, Elizabeth Heber
5 September 1799

Mr. and Mrs. Booth have been much troubled of late with rheumatism both attribute it to the same cause, too extensive a walk up hill and down on a hot day at Hawkstone and sitting down to rest on a cold stone in a state of perspiration. You will

---

[1] Andrew Dalzel (1742-1806), professor of Greek in Edinburgh University.
[2] Henry Mackenzie (1745-1831).

say, and so say I and they, a very imprudent experiment. However they are both better.

Richard to his aunt, Elizabeth Heber
Glasgow, 6 September 1799

. . . I should first tell you that the day before, we dined at Lanark, after having viewed the falls of the Clyde and gone over the very grand Cotton Mills erected there by Mr. Dan Dale[1] of Glasgow which he has lately disposed of to a Company for £60,000 down and an annuity of £1,500 a year. We reached Glasgow on Tuesday. Wednesday we passed in looking about us seeing the University, etc. and yesterday we went to Paisley, a town about seven miles off to see a great many manufactures such as cotton spinning, ribbon weaving, lawn-making, tanning, etc.

The good news has just arrived, it seems our troops have landed, been engaged and taken Helde, that Admiral Mitchell has taken all the shipping in the Texel and that Admiral Nelson has re-instated the King of Naples in his Dominions and reduced Capua and Gaeta, and that Suwarrow has defeated Joubert's army and killed the General himself.[2] Surely all this is worth firing, ringing and illuminating for. But I forgot all this will be old news when my letter reaches you.

Richard to his aunt, Elizabeth Heber
Perth, 17 September 1799

The first object that arrested our attention was Dumbarton Castle, a fortress standing upon a bold craggy rock which rises out of a spacious plain on the banks of the Firth of Clyde. We ascended it just in time to witness the ceremony of firing the cannon on receipt of the news from Holland. The Lieutenant

[1] David Dale (1739-1806), industrialist and philanthropist; in 1785 built the first cotton-spinning factory, on Arkwright's patent, at New Lanark on the Clyde; sold out to a Manchester firm in 1799.

[2] General Abercromby's expedition on to the coast of Holland had an initial success which he himself did not expect. Helder was captured, and a large Dutch fleet, with very slight casualties. In the same month (August) the Russian general Suvarov defeated Joubert at Novi in Italy. There was promise of a quick and successful conclusion to the war of the second coalition.

of the garrison, a hearty old soldier, seemed to enjoy our success
full as much as anybody I have met with and was very anxious
to have another lick with the French rascals himself. We dined
at Dumbarton and got that evening to Luss, a small Inn on the
banks of Loch Lomond. Thence we continued our voyage up
the loch which is about twenty-six miles in length to the foot of
Ben Lomond one of the highest hills in Great Britain. Ben however would not be persuaded quite to take off his night cap.
. . . We crossed the ferry in the morning and arrived at Oban,
a rising little seaport opposite Mull. The evening being fine we
hired a wherry hoping to reach Aros (in Mull) about thirty
miles off the same night, but finding that impossible were content
to take our supper and nights lodging at Achnacraig. Next
morning we were again in our boat and partly by the help of our
oars, partly our sails, got to Aros at twelve. There we break-
fasted and hired three horses to carry us across Mull to Ulva.
I only wish I had both room and talent to send you a caricature
of ourselves and our equipments. In the first place the Island only
afforded one saddle, a half, and one bridle for three of us; of
these the whole saddle and the bridle were borrowed from a
gentleman in the neighbourhood. Hobhouse having a lame horse,
thirty years old, was indulged with these; I was mounted on a
very small dun galloway with half a saddle and a halter instead
of a bridle. Our servant had the best pony, having the saddle-bags
to carry, but no saddle and a halter like myself. For each of these
we paid 6s. hire, the full value of the fee simple of the beasts,
besides the expenses of a man to look after them while they grazed
on the heath. Fancy us therefore three horsemen and footmen
marching at a foot's pace across the Isle of Mull, through a rugged
mountain sheep walk covered with broken stones and arriving
after four hours so employed at the end of a ten mile stage.

Rev. Reginald Heber to his sister, Elizabeth Heber
18 September 1799

We were well enough on Tuesday to make an excursion to
Coalbrookdale to see the Curiosities thereof, and Mr. Rose's

ingenious China Manufactory which is very curious and elegant and afforded us much amusement from the inspection of the whole process of moulding and forming the clay to the finishing, painting enamelling and burnishing of the divers articles of the useful and ornamental ware.

Rev. Reginald Heber to his sister, Elizabeth Heber
29 September 1799

Sugars ought to be cheaper, or I hope the merchants who have imposed shamefully upon the Public a long time, will meet with no purchasers.

Rev. Reginald Heber to his sister, Elizabeth Heber
21 October 1799

Poor Mr. Cholmondeley of Vale Royal, you may have heard, had the bad luck to be wounded in the shoulder and taken prisoner in the severe engagement in Holland on the sixth instant,[1] in which too many of our brave troops were slain, wounded or made captives. This enterprise, alas ! which commenced in so promising a manner by the surrender of the Dutch Fleet, turns out full of dangers and difficulties and blood-shedding to our land Forces. The obstacles, it seems, are now found so unsurmountable that the prospect must be abandoned.

Reginald to his father, Rev. Reginald Heber
Neasdon, 28 October, 1799

I now write to you an account of a dilemma of quite a novel kind. I am engaged in circumstances which I have never been engaged in before, and hope I never shall again ; I mean a difference with Mr. Bristow. On Saturday last Mr. Bristow went out

---

[1] Action of 6 October near Alkmaar; indecisive and costly. No further advance in north Holland so late in the year was possible. Retreat seemed advisable. The army re-embarked in November.

and not returning till much past the usual dinner hour, we began
to conclude he would not come back to dinner. Miss Bristow
was not well, so we did not like to disturb her, otherwise I am
convinced dinner would have been immediately ordered. I
sent to the servants to desire they would send up dinner. They
positively refused. We grew angry and said, 'If Mr. Bristow did
not come home by four, we would have the dinner,' on which
they set us at defiance. At four having given up all expectations
of Mr. Bristow's coming, I, according to my promise to my
juniors which I conceived myself bound to keep and thinking
besides that we were very ill-used, went into the kitchen and
took off in triumph a dish of pork chops and another of potatoes.
We carried these into the parlour, the servants refusing to wait
on us and sat down to it. In about half an hour or a little more
Mr. Bristow came in. He only said ' You will excuse me sitting
down with you ', and without staying to hear what we had to
say for ourselves went out. He has not spoken to any of us since,
nor will he eat at the same table. Since it is impossible to go on
in this way, pray give me some directions for my conduct in
this disagreeable business.

Reginald to his father, Rev. Reginald Heber
2 November 1799

I am sorry I troubled you with my last letter, but the affair
wore more than a serious face than it has done since. Mr. Bristow
has, I am happy to say, accepted my apology and the whole
disagreement seems in a fair way of termination.

Elizabeth Heber to Rev. Reginald Heber
1 January 1800

Our kindest love and best wishes attend our friends that the
18th Century may be a propitious era replete with Blessings for
many succeeding generations to Old England.

Rev. Reginald Heber to his sister, Elizabeth Heber
26 January 1800

Your next will I hope bring the tidings of dear Richard's safe arrival in London after an absence of so many months in a strangh land, which I marvel should have afforded any inducement to detain him so long from his far better native soil.

Rev. Reginald Heber to his sister, Elizabeth Heber
17 April 1800

What a lucky man is Mr. John Hill[1] of Prees who comes in for three shares out of five of the thirty thousand pound prize in the Lottery drawn last week. Mr. Clarke the purchaser of Peplow, and Downward, Sir R. Hill's steward, are the other favourites of fortune.

Rev. Reginald Heber to his son, Richard
21 May 1800

I hope the villain who attempted to assassinate our good and gracious King at the Play-house will swing.[2] If he is suffer'd to escape under the plea of insanity, the plea will afford encouragement to other malcontents to commit the like atrocious crimes.

Elizabeth Heber to Rev. Reginald Heber
31 May 1800

We have had very pleasant weather of late — a great deal of haymaking in the King's Road Fields.

---

[1] Probably Colonel John Hill (1769-1814), nephew of Sir Richard Hill.

[2] John Hadfield shot at the King in Drury Lane theatre, 16 May 1800. He said that ' he was prompted by some Divine power and talked in a mysterious way of Dreams . . . that he knew he was to be a martyr and was to be persecuted like his great master Jesus Christ.' A witness said that ' he knew very little of Hadfield, but knew where he worked, and had heard a good character of him, but that the least drink affected his head.' Hadfield had been badly wounded in the head in the Low Countries under the Duke of York. His trial before Lord Kenyon was a model of justice and mercy, good law and good taste. At Kenyon's suggestion a verdict was brought in of ' Not guilty; he being under the influence of insanity at the time the act was committed.'

Rev. Reginald Heber to his sister, Elizabeth Heber
2 July 1800

I am very glad to hear that there are to be no more Races at Shawbury. Mr. Corbet being about to remove his abiding place to Acton Reynold and to inclose the Race Ground and convert it to arable land, which will be putting it to far better use than that of galloping over it.

Elizabeth Heber to Rev. Reginald Heber
5 July 1800

The Duke of Somerset[1] is going to be married to Lady Charlotte Hamilton the present Duke's[2] eldest daughter. Her father when shewing the house took the young Duke into his daughter's apartments where they found the young Lady surrounded with books, on further inspection, the Duke was so much pleased with the collection in which she had shewn so much taste and judgement, that an offer of marriage immediately ensued and was accepted. The daughters of Duke Hamilton were all well educated under the eye of their excellent Mother.

God grant the corn may turn out well but there is certainly about London an artificial scarcity, as bread costs as much as eighteen pence the quartern loaf, while there are many ships loaded with corn in the river at this time, that there is not room for in the warehouses.

Rev. Reginald Heber to his sister, Elizabeth Heber
31 August 1800

Dear Richard returned with his Companion from Liverpool yesterday where they had fared sumptuously every day at the plentiful boards of the wealthy Merchants. In particular they partook of two elegant entertainments at the house of his Worship the Mayor of Liverpool who is no other than Pudsey

---

[1] Edward Adolphus Seymour (1775-1855), eleventh Duke of Somerset 1793.
[2] Archibald Hamilton (1740-1819), ninth Duke.

Dawson, Esq. the eldest son of our old and respected friend and physician, the late Doctor Dawson,[1] who you will remember sent his son Pudsey to Holland to be educated in the mercantile line in which he has been very successful. His income is estimated at six thousand per annum and his splendid style of living is correspondent thereto.

Richard to his aunt, Elizabeth Heber
Lyndhurst, 22 September 1800

The dear little ladies begin I suppose to think it high time to hear from their vagrant relation — who goes on very simply and quietly enjoying the shades of the New Forest. On my arrival at Southampton I employed the spare time on my hands after breakfast in looking after little John whom I found just getting out of bed. He told me he had seen Mrs. Booth who desired to be informed of my arrival whenever it took place. I had not leisure to call then as we found the Lymington coach waiting for us on our return to the Inn, so into it I got, and proceeded to Lyndhurst. Eyre[2] I found very well, he was alone, the Thorntons[3] being removed to Christchurch for sea-bathing, but soon after my arrival Mr. Thornton called in his curricle on his way to town on business (whence he returned yesterday). Before dinner John Richardson made his appearance having heard that Eyre was gone to Salisbury, he pursued me to propose an excursion to Portsmouth with his sisters and brothers by water. So after dinner I rode back with him, time enough to hire a boat for the next day and to enable him to follow his sisters to the public Assembly.

I slept at the Dolphin Inn and breakfasted early with the Richardsons. About nine we set sail in a very large, commodious vessel and tho' we had a pleasant sail did not reach Portsmouth owing to a contrary wind till three o'clock or past. We then

[1] Dr. Ambrose Dawson, M.D., F.R.C.P. (1707-94).
Pudsey Dawson, his son (1752-1816).
[2] George Eyre of Warrens, Lyndhurst (1772-1837).
[3] Probably Samuel Thornton (1754-1838) of Clapham and Albury Park, Surrey.

proceeded to the Dockyard which I had seen before but had great pleasure in going over again : after which we adjourned to the Crown Inn to a late dinner, which tho' by no means nicely served or comfortable was acceptable to all, especially the Ladies, who had had rather a fagging day.

The next morning was rather bustling to John Richardson and myself. We took a hot but pleasant walk four miles and back to Langstone Harbour to see a convict at present in the hulks but under sentence of transportation to Botany Bay. He was once a servant of Mrs. Puleston, and Whitehall Davies interests himself about him very much. His offence was taking half a guinea out of a letter while he was letter-carrier at Liverpool : previous to the offence he bore an unimpeachable character and since his sentence was passed he has behaved with great propriety. To a superior young man as he is, the society of so many abject and degraded wretches must have been worse than the hard labour to which all the convicts are there condemned, so that his removal to Botany Bay will be rather a relief than a punishment. He spoke of his situation with great propriety and seems not to despair of returning after six years (the term of his exit) to retrieve his character as a useful member of society. He is very handsome and well-made and only twenty-seven.

As the *Lord Cornwallis* transport in which he is to go is on the eve of sailing there was no time to correspond with W. Davies in the interim, I determined to supply him with cloth for a suit of clothes at Portsmouth and assortment of such articles of hardware such as knives, razors, scizzors, combs, thimbles, needles, as he might exchange at Botany Bay for ten times their value here; all these with a bible, prayer book and *Whole Duty of Man*[1] we saw packed up and obtained a promise from the Transport officer would be sent with him. This delay kept me till three o'clock before we sailed, but we had a charming sail back and dined on cold meat on board. Jack I daresay never before feasted his eyes with so many wonders as were afforded him by a sight of the Dockyards, Spithead.

---

[1] *Whole duty of Man*, 1658, generally attributed to Richard Allestree (1619-81), royalist divine.

On arriving at Southampton I drank tea with the Richardsons and after calling on Mrs. Booth, who was not at home, rode quietly back to Lyndhurst, where I found Eyre not gone to bed; he had expected me back to dinner, having a party at home, but they were all separated when I got in. Since then we have had some charming rides about the Forest and I have had the supreme honour of seeing Prince William of Gloster[1] who comes occasionally to a house his father has as Ranger.

Rev. Reginald Heber to his sister, Elizabeth Heber
24 September 1800

It is to be lamented that the misguided populace in many places are so mischievous and riotous. The ill-treatment of the farmers and the distruction of their property or the taking it from them by rapin and violence is far from being the way to induce them to bring the necessaries of life to Market or reduce the price which is certainly enormous. I trust his Majesty's gracious Proclamation[2] will powerfully excite the Magistrates to put the laws in execution against forestallers and monopolizers of every denomination.

Reginald to his brother, Thomas Cuthbert Heber
29 September 1800

As to the Masquerade, the messenger we sent proved tardy, for when he got to Wynnstay he found the gates shut, but next morning he got the tickets. We called at Prees on our way to Malpas to borrow a military sash for Crockett. Mrs. Hill was very full of the masquerade and among other things said, ' One gentleman, I don't know his name, went into a milleners at Shrewsbury and bought a quantity of old glass beads and an

---

[1] Prince William of Gloucester (1776-1834), nephew of George III.

[2] 'Whereas it has been represented to us that riotous proceedings have taken place in several parts of our kingdom, in consequence of the high price of provisions, and that in some instances corn and some other articles of provision have been violently taken from their owners, and in others the prices of those articles have been reduced by threats and intimidation . . .' all executive officers of the civil government are ordered strictly to prevent and suppress such tumults. *The Times*, 22 September 1800.

enormous old-fashioned hat, he must be a strange figure indeed '. As I was the very person she alluded to I could scarcely help laughing, but however I avoided all suspicion. The pilgrims' staff stuck out of the chaise window like a bowsprit or a barber's pole, and looked very ridiculous.

We got to Wynnstay without accident except that Hock who was sent to borrow a dagger at Broughton lost his way

'And roamed beneath the Moon's pale ray
By Druid Deva's murm'ring Tide '.

The number of masks was not great, and on the whole I was rather disappointed. There was a troop of Cottons[1] and a legion of Tomkinsons. Lady Kilmorey was an Otaheite Chief, her Lord[2] an old woman. Some tolerable characters there were, in particular Whitehall Davies as a Jew Rabbi, J. Cotton as a Jew Pedlar, Mr. K. Powell[3] was a monk, and made a very good one. I had been plaguing him a little and telling him that if he had made pilgrimages instead of remaining lazy in his convent, he would have been as thin as I myself. He came up to me as I was speaking to some ladies and said, ' Ah, son, if you ramble about and pay your vows to so many saints at once, you will still be thinner than you are now '. He attacked W Davies and told him he was a monk and would confess him, to which Whitehall answered with much humour, ' I am a Chew and like no Monkey tricks '. There was a dreadful number of flower girls and Indian dancers and three harlequins one of whom had a wooden leg, and the other seemed, as Mr. Cholmondeley who was there observed, to be not quite awake. I had no opportunity of speaking my verses which I had very much enlarged and rather improved. I had also the misfortune to break my rosary. The finest women in the room were Miss Price and three Miss Warringtons, and next to them Mrs. Barnston, who looked remarkably well. The Curries were not there. James Cotton distinguished himself very much. It was not like the Vale Royal ball either in splendour or in management.

[1] Dr. George Cotton (1742-1805), Dean of Chester. He had seven children. His wife was a Tomkinson. His second son, James Cotton (1781-1862).
[2] Robert, eleventh Lord Kilmorey (1746-1818).
[3] John Kynaston-Powell (later Sir John), d. 1822.

I was out a-shooting with Crockett this morning but was interrupted by the rain. I had three shots but killed only one.

Richard to his aunt, Elizabeth Heber
Totnes, 7 October 1800

I left Eyre on Thursday evening, the 26th, in a chaise with my man John and got safe to Salisbury the same night. Early next morning I was in readiness for the mail which however proving full, I stayed looking about me till evening. During my stay the Duke of Gloster came through. I was detained in the Inn for about an hour by the apprehension of a deserter from his regiment in the Guards who had been seized by a recruiting party in the town that morning and had made a voluntary confession of being the sole murtherer of poor Mellish.[1] He said he had never been easy in his mind since and could no longer retain the secret. He was accordingly committed for trial and will of course expiate his crime at the fatal time. He is a handsome respectable looking young man.

Tho' no stranger to Salisbury and its vicinity I had great pleasure in revisiting the Cathedral and walking up to Old Sarum. In the evening we set out again on our journey and reached Exeter the ensuing evening. There I found Froude[2] waiting my arrival.

You must know that Froude has acceded to my proposal of exploring not only Devonshire but Cornwall.

Mary Heber to her sister-in-law, Elizabeth Heber
8 October 1800

I beg the favour of you to get me a ticket in the Lottery for the Piggott Diamond[3] and send it in the next letter. Wish me

[1] Murdered by highwaymen near Hounslow in April 1798.
[2] Rev. R. H. Froude, archdeacon of Totnes, father of the historian.
[3] The draw for the Pigot Diamond took place in January 1801. 11,428 tickets at two guineas were sold.

good luck and let this be a great secret from all but Papa. It is but 11427 to one — and what is that if a woman has luck !

Reginald to his brother, Richard
13 October 1800

I could have told you a great deal about the Races and Masquerade and all the other remarkable things which have taken place since you left Shropshire, but I believe that my father has already given you an account of the principal of them. My letter can only be taken in the ' paralegomena ' which are few and of no great consequence. He has perhaps not told you that a little time after you went, we went *en masse* to Shrewsbury, where we saw one day's racing, and at night went to a miserable room which they call Theatre.

The races were very bad, but pretty much crowded. When we got first to the heath, Crockett, Tom and myself got out of the carriage to reconnoitre, we found among many others, Mr. Cholmondeley, Joddrel,[1] Vernon[2] and Sir Watkin.[3] We advised the Ladies to drive up to the stand, which, while Williams who was our postillion *pro tempore* was endeavouring to do, he broke the traces and turned sharp with the two fore horses into the midst of the stewards and the other grandees, Mr. Vernon very coolly and characteristically said ' Pray, Sir, don't drive over us, for this is Sir Watkin, and it is not reckoned polite to drive over Sir Watkin '. The Ladies were however far more alarmed and darted out of the carriage like ' a fleecy cloud before the summer's wind '. The Lady most generally admired was Lady C. Forester[4] and next to her two Miss Prices.

My Mother and aunts went away the next morning but we stayed over that day's race too, which was much better than the other. The crowd of pedestrian spectators was great and their contrivances to get a peep very curious. The trees were covered. In coming back the Corbets of Sundorn driving prodigiously

---

[1] Francis Jodrell of Yeardsley.
[2] Henry Vernon of Hilton, Staffs. (1748-1814).
[3] Sir Watkin Williams-Wynn, fifth Baronet (1772-1840).
[4] Lady Catherine Forester, daughter of the Duke of Rutland, wife of Cecil Forester of Willey, Salop (later ffirst Lord Forester).

fast came on me in a very awkward situation, having a bank on one side and horses before and behind, and almost took away my left leg to Sundorn along with them : and going about a hundred yards further they contrived to drive over a buggy with an old man and his wife. These two incidents together and the conversations which followed have served instead of a formal introduction, and Mrs. Corbet has always spoken since, wherever I have met her.

Crocket, you perhaps know, was furnished with a very elegant Polish dress for the Wynnstay Gala, from the theatre at Shrewsbury, but my father has perhaps not told you that the scheme was first thought of, tickets procured and dresses got all in the space of thirty hours. We dressed at Malpas and went in the chaise with Hockenhull as outrider, who contrived to miss the road, and ' Roamed beneath the Moon's pale ray '. He was in pocket by our masking as Cholmondeley who was there gave him a guinea. Hock said afterwards, ' he was a very nice man '. The Tomkinsons were very numerous at the Masquerade, the Mother bird is, to use Mr. Dod's expression, ' More than a plain woman, a damned ugly fellow ', ; they were going to introduce me to her and the heads of the family but I contrived to shirk it very neatly. The most beautiful women in the room were Miss Warrington and Mrs. Barnston, how the latter had contrived I don't know but she looked so well that I could scarcely recollect her at first.

I suppose my father told you of the duel between one of the Hills and an Irish Officer. The family at Hawkstone seem very much discomposed at it. It was a strange business altogether but John Hill was generally not at all blamed.

Rev. Reginald Heber to his sister, Elizabeth Heber
18 October 1800

I hope the reduction of Malta[1] will restore and secure the valuable Levant commerce to Old England of the best part of

---

[1] A revolt of the Maltese against the French broke out in September, 1798, was supported by Nelson and in September 1800 forced the French to capitulate.

which the French had possessed themselves before the War : it will also debar them from sending any succour to their Army in Egypt which will soon be reduced to the necessity of surrendering at discretion or of perishing.

Rev. Reginald Heber to his sister, Elizabeth Heber
22 October 1800

I am glad our Relatives the Rawstornes in the East are in good health, their style of living in that land of Lacks of Rupees and Pagodas is so luxurious and Raja-like that their native land will never satisfy their vitiated palates. They had best live and die where they are.

Richard to his aunt, Elizabeth Heber
Cornwall, 29 October 1800

Now for a long chat with the little Ladies in Westminster. Here I am at my ease on a sofa in a snug room, curtains drawn, and fire blazing at an Inn in the little Port of Fowey, on the point of completing my Cornwall jaunt. Both my companions are fled, ' the one to his farm the other to his merchandise ', for you must know I have had two fellow travellers both parsons, one Froude, the other Pering, but it is so long since I wrote that I must carry you back as far as Oct. 7th, on which day Froude and myself rode to Brixham, a little fishing town at the head of Torbay.

We were in high spirits at finding the Fleet had not sailed, as was reported further inland, and immediately determined to go aboard. Having a letter of introduction to Lord St. Vincent we took advantage of one of his ships' boats which happened to be putting off, and after a short but tempestuous sail found ourselves on board the *Ville de Paris*.[1] The Admiral was extremely civil to us, supplied us with an officer to conduct us through every part of the ship and pressed us very cordially to stay to dinner, when

[1] The *Ville de Paris* captured by Rodney in 1782.

we met not only the officers of his own ship, among whom was
no less a man that the gallant Sir Thos. Troubridge,[1] first Captain
of the Fleet, and Grey[2] first Captain of the ship (son to Sir Charles
and brother to the Senator) but Sir Richard Strachan[3] and
Captain Harvey both pleasant men and gallant officers.

The wind increased so as to make it scarcely safe or even
possible to return ashore, so we were fain to make up our mind
to sleeping on board which we did (John France included) and
I was slung up to the ceiling in a room adjoining to Grey on one
side and Troubridge on the other. Before mounting my pendant
couch however, I took advantage of the fineness of the night,
to enjoy one of the most interesting walks I ever took on one of
the proudest terraces that can be trode by an Englishman, the
Quarter deck of a 110 gunship, commanded by Lord St. Vincent,
having in my view 26 line of battle ships, upwards of 14 of which
were three deckers. I did not prevail on myself to retire
till it was rather late and then the extreme windiness of the
weather, the continual visits paid by the men on watch to
Troubridge for orders, not to mention the creakings of the tim-
bers and especially the quacking of ducks contributed somewhat
to interrupt my slumbers. However, I rested very well and by
the help of John's art menial and Capt. Grey's dressing apparatus,
where I found all the conveniences of a man of fashion, I made a
very spruce appearance at the Admiral's breakfast table. Lord
St. Vincent takes especial care to have his table well-supplied and
I confess I was quite surprized to be regaled with a great variety
of well-cooked dishes of all kinds, of the best liquors from
Cockagne cyder to Claret Frontignac, which is most remarkable
of all, not only good in quality but well kept.

After breakfast the Admiral would not let us go till we had
witnessed a private ceremony of his which he enforces strictly
every morning, this is, the drawing up of the Marines on deck
in the presence of the whole ship's company, for the purpose of

[1] Admiral Sir Thomas Troubridge, d. 1807.
[2] Capt. George Grey, R.N. (1767-1828, third son of General Sir Charles Grey,
cr. first Earl Grey (1729-1807), and younger brother of Charles, later second Earl Grey
(1764-1845), who was Prime Minister, 1830-4.
[3] Admiral Sir Richard Strachan (1760-1828), commander of the naval forces in the
Walcheren expedition.

going through their manual exercises, after which the band, which is a very good one, played ' God save the King ' every individual on board in the meantime standing uncovered. Three or four other tunes are then played and the business is concluded. Froude and I stood on either side of the Admiral during the whole; and a very impressive spectacle it was, I assure you.

We then took our leave after receiving from Lord St. Vincent a very friendly invitation to dine with him as often as we pleased during our stay in the bay. I had a great deal of conversation with him on a variety of subjects, as well as with Troubridge and Grey, the latter of whom expected a visit from his wife and Lady Northesk the day we went. You must not, however, fancy the *Ville de Paris* a stranger to the sight of a Lady, for since her arrival in the bay, the Admiral gave a very gay ball on board her, and the wind proving boisterous, most of the Ladies slept on board, one or two of the officers followed his example and Torbay has been the head-quarters of festivity, music and mirth.

A *Ville de Paris* boat put us on board Admiral Sir Charles Cotton's[1] ship with whom Froude was acquainted. He is a very gentlemanlike, pleasant man, and pressed us to dine with him but this we found it necessary to decline, so he furnished us with a boat to put us on shore and we went to see the garrison's works at Berry Head.

Our ride home to Dartington was diversified by the discovery of a crippled cobbler dead drunk on the turnpike road, with his horse standing by him, whom we had some trouble to re-instate on his beast and almost as much to convince him he had not sinned against the Holy Ghost. This at length Froude accomplished and besides doing the more essential service of sending a servant home with him to his wife.

. . . (On the descent of a copper mine near Land's End).

Accordingly we were provided with miner's dresses but previously stripped ourselves naked to the very skin, we wore no stockings but put on a dirty flannel shirt, a pair of small clothes or trousers in no better plight, a waistcoat and jacket not a little the

---

[1] Admiral Sir Charles Cotton, d. 1812.

worse for wear, and old pair of shoes, a coarse nightcap perfectly black and greasy and a large broad brimmed slouched old hat, a candle was suspended to my button and another lighted was carried between my finger and thumb. Froude, Pering and John France were accoutred in just the same manner and down we all went into the coppery abyss. The method of descent is by ladders perfectly perpendicular. At the foot of every one of which there is a kind of cross-beam by way of landing place but not sufficient by any means to prevent your falling if your foot should slip. Close at your side the rod of an immense steam engine moves up and down with unceasing violence and a very loud noise, pumping up the water at the rate of many hundred gallons a minute, which would otherwise inundate the miners below.

Our journey was not completed till we had accomplished a descent of one hundred and ten fathoms (660 feet) the extreme depth of the mine. Here we had an opportunity of examining the situation of the different lodes and strata and of seeing the process of excavating and blowing the rock with gunpowder. The men labour night and day, six hours each set, so that the work never stands still.

Before we re-ascended we groped our way to a very considerable distance along some of these subterranean channels which connect with each other to an immense extent. I think the horizontal method of travelling more irksome than the perpendicular for a tall man at least, for he is obliged to stoop very low on account of the rock overhead while he is walking in a stream of water reaching up to the calves of his legs. This did not prevent our enjoying a glass of brandy apiece underground over which we joined in ' God save the King '.

Our ascent was, you will readily believe, to the full as fatiguing as our descent; going up a ladder perfectly straight, supporting the whole weight of your body on your hands and feet cannot be very easy travelling, but we are more familiar than we were when we descended with the nature of the business and accomplished our labour most gallantly. Excepting a blister or two on my hands and a stiffness in the fingers from the strain the sinnews had undergone, I felt not the least the worse. John France went through it very well, but made I believe a pious resolution never to dive again so deeply into the entrails of the Earth.

Rev. Reginald Heber to his sister, Elizabeth Heber
15 December 1800

We learn this week from Ripon that little Beatrice Allanson has been inoculated with the cow-pox[1] and has got well through the novel experiment, which I hope will have the desired effect as an antidote against the small-pox. But I own I should have been loth to have infus'd matter from the pustules of any diseased beast into the veins of a child of mine.

Rev. Reginald Heber to his sister, Elizabeth Heber
7 March 1801

We rejoice to hear a more comfortable account of the health of our beloved Sovereign who God preserve. The perilous times predicted by the Prophets appear to be approaching if not already come.

Rev. Reginald Heber to his sister, Elizabeth Heber
21 April 1801

Most heartily do I congratulate you and all Friends of Old England on the glorious news from the Baltic. God be praised in the first place for the providential goodness and favour to our Native land eminently displayed at this Momentous Crisis. 'Well may Israel now say', etc. You I am sure will cordially join the holy Psalmist in the rest of his pious thanksgiving to the Supreme Disposer of all events.

---

[1] Dr. Edward Jenner (1749-1823) published his first book on small-pox in 1798. Country people had long known that one who had been infected by the cow-pox was immune from small-pox.

The defeat of the Danes,[1] the death of the Tyrant Paul,[2] and the Dissolution of the Confederacy of the Northern Potentates[3] at the same moment, are events of such consequence to Great Britain as are beyond computation.

Rev. Reginald Heber to his sister, Elizabeth Heber
2 August 1801

I am sorry we had no better luck in the Lottery. I am of your opinion that as we never have been fortunate in that Wheel we never shall.

Rev. Reginald Heber to his sister, Elizabeth Heber
6 August 1801

I hope our enemies will not be able to set foot on our *terra firma* and interrupt our peasantry in getting our Harvest home, it would be unfortunate to be under the necessity of converting our labourers into soldiers and their sickles into swords.

Rev. Reginald Heber to his sister, Elizabeth Heber
15 August 1801

I am surprised the price of bread in London remains so shamefully high. All the corn markets in the Country having fallen so considerably, that is from upwards of twenty to twelve shillings a measure.

Rev. Reginald Heber to his sister, Elizabeth Heber
22 August 1801

It is much to be lamented that the last attempt to destroy the enemy's boats and shipping at Boulougne fail'd and that

[1] Battle of Copenhagen, 1 April 1801: the Danish fleet was withdrawn from the northern confederation hostile to Britain.
[2] Assassination of the Tsar Paul, a man not only insane but infatuated with admiration for Napoleon, 24 March.
[3] These events caused the dissolution of the Neutral League of the North, designed by Napoleon to destroy the influence and trade of Britain in the Baltic, from which area the bulk of British naval stores were drawn.

with the loss of so many brave men. Capt. Parker, second son of the late Mr. Parker of Broxholm, you will see in the papers is wounded; I hope not as severely as was reported at first.[1] He has the character of a very spirited brave young officer and a great favourite with Lord Nelson with whom he had served at the Battle of the Nile and Copenhagen, and was the Admiral's aide-de-camp on the coast of France.

Rev. Reginald Heber to his sister, Elizabeth Heber
29 August 1801

The best wheat now sells for ten shillings a measure, which a few weeks ago fetched twenty-five shillings.

Rev. Reginald Heber to his sister, Elizabeth Heber
20 September 1801

Accept, my dearest sister, my best thanks for your affectionate remembrance of the year 1728, and the day of that year whereon I was born. I am thankful to God for all his mercies to me during the long term of seventy-three years completed on the 15th day of this month.

Dear Richard joined our party here in time to go to Shrewsbury Races with our Oxonians on Wednesday last and attend the Annual Infirmary Meeting at St. Chad's Church, hear Dean Cotton discourse and hold the plate for the Collection as Lady Rotchley's supporter to which post of honour he was nominated by Sir Corbet Corbet who was president. Mama was of Lady Corbet's Party and went with her to the Ball. Tomorrow morning we are all engaged to wait on Lord and Lady Killmorey and beat up the Shavington Domain for game.

---

[1] An attempt to destroy Bonaparte's invasion barges assembling at Boulogne. Parker who was only twenty-one, died a few days later.

Rev. Reginald Heber to his sister, Elizabeth Heber
30 September 1801

On Thursday evening last our young Oxonians, Mama and Mary Mo attended the Ball at Drayton where the genteelest families in the vicinity assembled. This was the first Ball Mo ever danced at, I hear she acquitted herself very laudably. They were all well entertained and pleased as you will suppose when I tell you they did not get home till near three in the morning.

Reginald to his brother, Richard
September 1801

The Drayton Ball was wonderfully crowded and brilliant to the great satisfaction of the managers, Lord Kilmorey and Mr. Clive. Some of the company told me that they had no doubt that the Drayton Ball (tell it not in Gath) would soon equal the Knutsford. A Chester beauty, Miss Mytton, was there, and much admired; of the Shropshire *belles* Miss Chetwood and Miss Fanny Crewe were pre-eminent. The evening appeared to pass off with the utmost harmony, but the devil who sleepeth not, and Mrs. Davies of Drayton who is equally active, have been already sowing quarrels and picking offence. She says that Miss Chetwood did not call her two dances in turn and that if Sir John[1] and Lady Harriet took up the matter properly they would be much incensed with the managers : as, however, I have only heard the fact on her (Mrs. D's) authority, I do not believe it, and were it true the Chetwoods are the most unlikely people in the world to trouble themselves about so trifling an accident.

Andrew Corbet[2] and Mr. Offley Crewe are managers next ball. I dined with both the day before yesterday at Crocket's, I never met Mr. Crewe before but like him very much. There was also a Yorkshireman, Sir Thomas Tancred,[3] a very gentlemanlike, quiet man, who has half promised to spend a day with us. They

[1] Sir John Chetwode, fourth Baronet (1764-1845).
[2] Andrew Corbet of Moreton Corbet, Shropshire (1766-1835).
[3] Sir Thomas Tancred, sixth Baronet (1780-1844).

went out with us yesterday with Hill's hounds. I took out Regulus
and got on as well as one awkward fellow usually does when he is
carried by another; at the peril of my neck I managed to save
my distance very well, but Mr. Wood is almost distraught at the
number of posts and rails which your horse's hind legs broke
down on Hyne Heath. John Hill, however, says Regulus only
wants a little practice to *lep* very well. Dined at Hawkstone,
Hills innumerable. In the beginning of the week passed two days
at Adderley where we saw some very curious drawings brought
over by Lady Clive. Tom has become a mighty hunter before
the Lord and Belle carries him very nicely. He had a famous run
the other day with Hill's hounds upwards of 23 miles from
Preston Brockhurst to Smyth-Owen's at Condover.[1]

Rev. Reginald Heber to his sister, Elizabeth Heber
14 October 1801

On Saturday last we were invited by Sir Richard Hill to a
Gala at Hawkstone to celebrate the pacification[2] and keep Major
Hill's birthday. The party consisted of the whole family of the
Hills, the remaining trio of the Hebers and one or two others.
After dinner we all ascended the hill to the Column which was
lighted up and from the top of which squibbs and rockets were
exhibited — nothing capital. We drank tea in the Octagon
Tower which you will remember was a favourite edifice of the
late Sir Rowland and his first lady. Hence we had a view of the
Citadel and Hawkstone Inn illuminated and had a good effect.
We then returned down the walk on the side of the Beechen
Grove and had a very fine view of the extensive front of the old
Mansion which was lighted up and made a brilliant appearance,
especially the portico from which was suspended a flag on which
was inscribed ' Peace and Plenty, 1801 — God save the King '.

[1] Nicholas Smyth-Owen (1769-1804) of Condover, Shropshire.
[2] Preliminaries of London, 1 October 1801; ratified at the Peace of Amiens, 25
March 1802.

Rev. Reginald Heber to his sister, Elizabeth Heber
24 October 1801

On Thursday we had a Gala at Hodnet on occasion of the Peace. One Sheep was roasted whole and two divided and baked with plenty of potatoes to fill the bellies of the poor, to which feast many of the farmers and others contributed their guineas, half-guineas and crowns apiece. The day was conducted with decency, sobriety and hilarity, the bells rang, the Octagon Tower was illuminated, and some of the houses were lighted up with candles, and the countenances of the inhabitants with joy and gladness.

Elizabeth Heber to Rev. Reginald Heber
9 March 1802

We will keep a good look out for lodgings for you. That where Lord Ribblesdale was would be too small for your family, neither would the noisy Bond Street suit you by any means. I hope to be able to meet with one in the central part of the town but supposing you could be well accommodated on the other side of Oxford Street, viz. Welbeck, Wimpole, Wigmore, Henrietta Streets, Cavendish Square, would you have any objection that situation ?

Elizabeth Heber to Rev. Reginald Heber
31 May 1802

Richard with his friend Hugh Cholmondeley[1] joined the numerous assembly at Merchant Taylors' Hall to celebrate the Birthday of William Pitt.[2] The whole was very well and quietly conducted. Richard was much pleased by the Songs which were

[1] Hugh Cholmondeley, youngest brother of Thomas Cholmondeley of Vale Royal (1772-1815).

[2] The long ministry of Pitt, so fiercely criticized both then as now for its conduct of the war but able always to command an overwhelming majority in Parliament, broke down in 1801 over the Irish question. Pitt's intention was to accompany the union of the governments with a measure of relief for Irish Roman Catholics designed to unite the people also. To the latter, the King could not consent; the excitement brought on a period of insanity; Pitt resigned on 14 March 1801.

well performed, particularly that written by Canning, *The Pilot who weathered the Storm.*

Elizabeth Heber to Rev. Reginald Heber
18 *June* 1802

His hair powder Tax[1] (being entered as my inmate) Richard has always paid in London at the time ours was, which I thought the safest way as it might perhaps have been neglected at Oxford; I have now acquainted the Collector that the Tax will this year and in future be paid at Malpas where he is entered as your inmate.

Richard to his aunt, Elizabeth Heber
Boulogne-sur-Mer, 2 December 1802

With an English heart and in the English vulgar tongue, tho' on French ground,[2] I send my love to you and tell you that we slept at Sittingbourne the night we left you — that we break-fasted the next morning at Canterbury and took a late dinner and slept at Dover. The next day, Wednesday, we crossed the water with fine weather and a favourable wind for Boulogne, but not for Calais. However, tho' the fine weather lasted, the wind did not, we were becalmed, and after many doubts on the part of the Captain whether we should make Calais or Boulogne, we at last reached the former about half past two in the morning (or rather later) after a passage of nearly twelve hours, the same distance is frequently accomplished in three. We found, as we have uniformly found, civil treatment and comfortable ac-commodation. I was almost the only person in the vessel not sick. John France was very much so, Eyre a little, and some sick unto death. We enjoyed a supper of French dishes and French wine and did not get to bed till six this morning, consequently we

---

[1] The hair powder tax: one of the extraordinary methods by which revenue was raised during the period of the war. All those who used hair powder of whatever sort were required to register with their local commissioner of taxes; a person who had more than one residence was required to register in all, but paid wherever he chose; the tax was £1 1s. a year. (41 Geo 3 cap 69).

[2] It is reported that 16,000 people visited France during the Peace of Amiens.

did not rise early. When we did, however, we got an English breakfast with much better butter than we had either at Dover or Canterbury, and after looking about us at Calais journeyed hither twenty-six miles. We have had a charming day, and I now write to you from the parlour of the Hotel d'Angleterre kept by an Englishman, Parker by name, a Lincolnshire man, with good coal fire, no small comfort I assure you, for at Calais we were nearly blinded by the smoke of green wood.

The carriage was very comfortable and roomy and we got on fast, the roads being good.

Richard to his aunt, Elizabeth Heber
Hotel de Paris, Rue de la loi, Paris
Wednesday, 8 December 1802

The dear little Ladies will not be sorry to learn that our journey which they know already commenced very favourably, continued equally so till we reached Paris on Sunday night. The weather was more like October than December, the roads good, the Inns comfortable, the beds and fare unexceptionable, in short, everything we have met with since we reached the land of wonders has given us a favourable impression. We are lodged at a good hotel kept by a pretty English widow, and I have met with several English acquaintances. We have delivered our passports to Lord Whitworth[1] as well as our private letters, but have not yet seen either him or the Duchess, except at the Opera, from which we have just come. The music is but ordinary but the dancing beyond all praise; the decorum, too, preserved at the French theatres is to an Englishman very striking, not a whisper to be heard and everybody in a crowded house attentive only to the performance; no rioting in the lobbies or, in short, any impropriety of behaviour. Yesterday night we saw a French play and entertainment at the chief French theatre (for you must know there are about fourteen of one sort or another), I thought the acting very capital.

[1] Lord Whitworth (1752-1825), Ambassador to France, had married the widowed Duchess of Dorset in 1801.

We made great haste to get here before Monday as we had been informed by a courier we saw at Calais that on that day Bonaparte was to hold his monthly review in honour of Lord Whitworth's presentation; but lo ! and behold ! when we got to Paris we had the mortification to find that it was just over, having been altered to Sunday morning very unexpectedly. We have not yet seen the Chief Consul who resides almost [entirely?] at St. Cloud, his Palace out of Paris.

There were [several?] parties tonight, one at Madame Recamier's[1] and one at Helen Maria Williams'[2] and elsewhere but we have not yet begun; neither have we yet entered the galleries and the National Library. The latter is only to be seen twice a week but we live handy for it, being exactly opposite. Poet Rogers[3] with whom we breakfast tomorrow is to take us to the former.

The general appearance of Paris is not at all equal to London, the streets being close and dirty with no foot-pavement and the houses high. But the public buildings surpass everything I have ever seen. The Palace and Gardens of the Tuilleries especially is truly magnificent and royal. Indeed every spot one looks at acquires an interest, tho' often of a melancholy nature, from the late great events which have been passing in the Metropolis for the last ten years.

The only remarkable sights on the road (between Calais and Paris) were the Cathedral of Amiens — which we walked through while the service was performing and which is one of the most beautiful Gothic structures I ever beheld, built in the 13th century by the English, ornamented with very rich and elegant painted glass and having a slender spire four hundred and four feet high, probably over topping St. Paul's — and the stables, gardens and ruins of the Chateau of Chantilly, about thirty miles from Paris, once the paradise of the Prince of Condé, but now the property of the nation, the remains of the house offered for sale, and the stables converted into barracks. We went over the

---

[1] Madame Recamier (b. 1779, m. 1794, d. 1834).
[2] Helen Maria Williams (1762-1827). Poetess, and ardent supporter of the Revolution.
[3] Samuel Rogers (1763-1855).

premises with the old game-keeper who seemed to bemoan the change. In fact, it was quite a heart-breaking sight, whatever ones politics might be, to see one of the grandest palaces and domains in France, with every decoration which architecture and gardening could supply, torn to pieces and made almost a wilderness.

Richard to his aunt, Elizabeth Heber
28 December 1802

The only inconvenience I at present endure is from a swelled face and gumbile, my old enemy, which I hope will not continue long. We have been going on much in the same style since I wrote last, sight seeing all morning and frequenting the courts and balls in the evenings, among others Mme. Recamier's and tomorrow I was to have gone to Madame Cabarrus[1] (*alias* Tallien) but my face will not allow me. Many English are here, among other the Duchess of Gordon and Lady Georgina,[2] the Duke and Duchess of Somerset, Smith (and family) the new member for Norwich, William Hill accompanied by Johnson a Brasenose man and Salopian and many more. We have dined with Lord Whitworth, a great favour it should seem, as hardly any have as yet been invited, for which the Duchess got the blame. We met there with Colonel Villiers[3] (Lord Clarendon's brother) and his wife whom I had met before at the Duke of Athol's, also Mr. Charles Blagden, Secretary to the Royal Society and Mr. Merry and Wm. Hill, the dinner was splendid and the reception agreeable.

Reginald to his brother, Richard
29 December 1802

There is no news in Shropshire except that Mr. Neville, the new Vicar of Prees, is a character likely to afford much amusement and no small wonder to the neighbourhood. John Hill

---

[1] Madame Thérèse Cabarrus (1779-1849). Her first husband Jean Tallien divorced her in 1802.
[2] Lady Georgina Gordon, later Duchess of Bedford.
[3] George Villiers (1759-1827), third son of first Lord Clarendon.

introduced him to the Shrewsbury Hunt which he greatly
astonished by handing round Proposals for a Volume of Poetry,
Heroic, Lyrical and Moral with which he is at present pregnant.
He sung and said divers specimens and concluded by expressing
a wish that the literary members of the Hunt would favour him
with any additions and communications they might think fit.
He is a person of spare form and solemn manner, very silent,
communing (as he himself says) only with the Muses, except
when overflowing with the God which generally happens before
you have sate long in his company.

Elizabeth Heber to Rev. Reginald Heber
10 March 1803

By His Majesty's message to His Parliament we appear to be
on the eve of another war.[1] The restless spirit of Bonaparte will
not long suffer the nations to be at peace till he has subdued them
all or perished in the attempt, which I trust will be his fate before
Old England becomes one of his conquered provinces.

Rev. Reginald Heber to his son, Richard
29 March 1803

Your friend Eyre acted wisely in bringing back your carriage
from the hostile realms of France or you would never have seen
it more. I know not what notions you travellers entertain, but I,
John Bull, ever have been and ever shall be an antigallican till
my dying day. Cobbet is right, the sooner you check their
insolence the better. Do them over while you have the right end
of the Staff in your hands. NOW OR NEVER.

---

[1] ' His Majesty thinks it necessary to acquaint the House of Commons, that, as very
considerable military preparations are carrying on in the ports of France and Holland,
he has judged it expedient to adopt additional measures of precaution for the security
of his dominions . . .' 8 March 1803.

Elizabeth Heber to Rev. Reginald Heber
30 *April* 1803

Dear Richard is at present at Oxford. He accompanied his friend Walter Scott[1] hither on Tuesday being desirous of conducting him to the seat of the Muses and introducing him to his poetical friends there.

Elizabeth Heber to Rev. Reginald Heber
7 *May* 1803

The uncertainty of Peace or War keeps the travellers in suspense at present, it must soon be determined one way of the other. Peace is the word to-day.

Rev. Reginald Heber to his sister, Elizabeth Heber
10 *May* 1803

Charles Cholmondeley was very successful last week at Chester Races, his famous horse *Cheshire Cheese* won everything he started for.

Rev. Reginald Heber to his sister, Elizabeth Heber
Oxford, June 1803

I deferred writing till we arrived here which we accomplished in two days from Hodnet. We could not visit the seat of the Muses on a more agreeable occasion than to see and hear our youthful poet in the rostrum where he acquitted himself much to the satisfaction of a crowded audience in the theatre and met with uncommon applause.[2]

---

[1] Sir Walter Scott (1771-1832), was two years older than Richard Heber. Their close friendship began in 1800.
[2] *Palestine* was the Newdigate Prize Poem at Oxford won by Reginald Heber aged twenty.

Rev. Reginald Heber to his sister, Elizabeth Heber
1 *August* 1803

Our heroic trio are going this morning to Hodnet to meet Sir Corbet Corbet[1] to confer with him about raising a regiment of Volunteers, I believe they want Richard to accept a commission of which I think he is not ambitious. And I trust Reginald and Thomas being *bona fide* resident members and students of the University are and ought to be excused and exempt. Perilous times these.

Elizabeth Heber to Rev. Reginald Heber
4 *August* 1803

What has dear Richard done at Hodnet ? accept or declined entering into the Shropshire Regiment of Volunteers ? I trust he will not engage in any corps in which he will be liable to be sent out of England. We are full of military preparations[2] in London and Westminster, our Major Commandant has begun to train all his men belonging to the Brewery,[3] the dray men are drilled, morning and evening. They have strong beer given them when they have done their duty but the man who refuses to learn is turned away. Mr. Elliot has requested that my two servants may learn their exercises at the same time, if convenient, to which I can have no objection as it is now deemed necessary to oppose this daring invader by a Nation in Arms.

Rev. Reginald Heber to his sister, Elizabeth Heber
8 *August* 1803

Captain Heber has I hope entertained you with a detail of his proceedings and rapid success in raising a Company of Hodnet Volunteers. I hope he will be as expeditious in drilling as he was

---

[1] Sir Corbet Corbet, Bt., of Adderley, Shropshire.
[2] 300,000 volunteers were enrolled within a few months of the outbreak of war.
[3] Miss Heber's house in Pimlico was in a Brewery yard which belonged to Mr. Elliot who was her next-door neighbour. The usual postal address was to ' Mr. Elliott's Brewery' or ' the Stag Brewery '.

in enrolling them: though I trust he will have no occasion of marching them beyond the precincts of North Bradford Hundred.[1]

Elizabeth Heber to Rev. Reginald Heber
18 August 1803

Richard is very diligently practicing the military exercise
morning and evening in our little garden under the direction of
a drill sergeant in the Guards.

Elizabeth Heber to Rev. Reginald Heber
1 November 1803

Mrs. Vaughan is under great apprehensions of the enemy
making an attempt to effect a landing on the Suffolk coast.
Many of her acquaintances at Woodbridge are gone or going and
blame her for not removing now, as should any alarm happen a
Post Chaise would not be to be had.

Rev. Reginald Heber to his sister, Elizabeth Heber
12 November 1803

Dear Richard is this moment return'd from his visit to Vale
Royal and the neighbourhood where many of the gentry were
assembled to pay their respects to Prince William of Gloucester,[2]
who, with his retinue, were sumptuously entertained at Oulton,
Ashton Grange, Delamere Lodge, as well as Vale Royal. He
says everything went off very agreeably.

Rev. Reginald Heber to his sister, Elizabeth Heber
18 November 1803

Lord Kenyon is very active in raising four hundred Volunteers at his own expense, and is very assiduous in drilling them
but I trust if Bonaparte's myrmydons venture to put to sea they
will sup with Neptune.

[1] North Bradford Hundred comprises about 30 parishes in the immediate vicinity of
Hodnet.
[2] William Frederick, second Duke of Gloucester (1776-1834), son of William, first
Duke and younger brother of George III.

V

THE HODNET VOLUNTEERS

1804

THE REV. REGINALD HEBER, died at Malpas on 10 January 1804. The widow and children moved to Hodnet Hall — a long low black-and-white house — which had been unoccupied for fifty years. It and the Marton estate in Yorkshire, which fell to this branch of the family in 1803, now belonged to Richard.

All the letters in this chapter were written by Reginald Heber to his brother Richard. They concern two periods of volunteer training, during September and October 1804. At this time the French army of invasion was assembled at Boulogne, waiting for the favourable moment when a French fleet should have secured command of the Channel. The period, as all Englishmen realized, was one of crisis.

We saw Richard in the summer of 1802 taking a commission in the Shropshire Volunteers. As Captain Heber he commanded the Hodnet Company; but in his capacity as landowner at Marton in Yorkshire he was also appointed Colonel of the Craven Legion, and was therefore compelled to delegate his duties in Shropshire to Reginald. It was therefore Reginald who led the Company to the battalion muster at Market Drayton in September and to the regimental muster at Shrewsbury in October. The letters which he wrote to his nominal commander about these operations are full of interest for the light they throw on the working of what can only be described as a rather haphazard and not very efficient organization.

Without knowing Reginald's military standards it is impossible to visualize with certainty the regiment's state of training and discipline. The men certainly seem to have been keen, and the officers not dilettante. One notes, however, the distinction in Mess between gentlemen and ' raff ' ; and the last letter describes a riot.

Although at Shrewsbury the regiment was under martial law, it appears very clearly that the personal relationship between officers and men was still more important than any super-imposed system of discipline. All depended therefore on the quality of the officers; we observe that some did not know their drill, but on the other hand many seem to have been thoroughly efficient; we know that Richard had been drilled privately by a regular sergeant and that the officers drilled separately from the men in the morning. The regiment apparently had its full establishment of muskets and was able to fire ball without casualties.

*   *   *

Reginald to his brother, Richard
Monday morning, September 1804

We had a very thin muster on Sunday, and only sixty-two privates came with me to Drayton, and of these many very un-willingly. We are very much the thinnest company here, the Adderley is complete and the two Draytons between eighty and ninety each. Quarme has at length made up his mind to join us and is expected on Tuesday. The men were easily pacified about your not coming when they were told you were prevented by business, but your having given leave to several to stay away has caused much grumbling. Cotton is expected to-day. The In-spection day is not till Friday, so that the men are kept a whole week. This has also caused discontent. Several were inattentive this morning and two drunk, as I was told, though I do not know whether it was not mere stupidity. They grew restive at my scolding them and fell out and ran off but have since humbled themselves. I hope we shall do better this evening, though the thinness of our Muster is very discouraging to them. They have heard about Quarme and have been puzzling themselves about him, though as Cotton is senior I think they will not be much afraid of him. My Mother, Mary and Tom leave Hodnet for Gayton to-day. Sir C. is well but not in high feather. The morning is given up entirely to drill and the officers are drilled by themselves in an adjoining field. In fact, both Sergeants and Officers will I think derive much benefit from this jaunt and be indeed the only people who will derive any.

While I was writing the above eight of our men passed by who are named for guard, a pretty figure we shall cut in the evening with the remainder ! To add to our misfortunes, Drayton is such a perfect brothel every night, that the men will lose I fear, their morals and civility as well as their discipline. I shall I think almost entirely give up the point of attendance till the day of inspection, when a fine of half a crown shall be imposed on all non-attendants, and I shall take no excuses at all. Such is the state of our military affairs, all that holds us together is the ten shillings pay and the arrears which I intend to give out on the Thursday evening. If any alteration takes place for the better and ᵗ cannot conceive anything worse, you shall hear in town.

Reginald to his brother, Richard
Friday, September 1804

I have a better account to give of the Company and of Quarme than I thought myself likely to give when I wrote my last letter. The first three days the men left me so fast, that on the Tuesday evening we had only nineteen file. Sir C. and the others pretended to condole with me, but I believe were really not at all sorry to see the crack Company in this miserable plight. Wearied out at length with the pity of our friends, the forebodings and long faces of Cotton,[1] the grumbling of the men and the laughter of the children in the streets, I sent over Sergeant Hughes to desire that all who valued the credit of the Hodnet Company would

[1] Probably Lynch Cotton, eldest son of Dean Cotton, Major in Cheshire Militia, d. 1813.

immediately join, and if the hay was got in, that Cartwright would send as many of your servants as could be spared for the two days. They came accordingly like the sand of the sea or the flood of the mountain or whatever simile may be preferred, and Drayton was exceedingly surprised at our next march to the parade, being ninety strong. On the day of inspection all the remainder, who had not very good excuses came, so that we recovered our credit entirely.

The men went home on Friday very orderly and steady, though they had got a good deal of drink at different places; first at Spoonley where they had some bread and cheese and ale, sent them by the Draytonians together with a Vote of Thanks, which was presented by Mr. Judson on parade; secondly, Mr. Essex gave them a pint each at Tern hill, and, thirdly, I had ordered them some at the 'Bear'. I went with them as far as Styche and then returned to dine at Adderley with Colonel Chaytor, and the Miss Shipleys,[1] Miss Cotton, etc.

The whole business has gone off pretty well, though there have been two or three foolish tricks played by our little Colonel, such as drumming a man out of Morcop's Company, placing sentries round the Town on the Thursday night to prevent people from going home, besides his making some speeches which did no good. Our greatest plague was drunkenness which was sometimes very bad indeed; the Hodnet Company behaved, I think, the best particularly in this respect. The first evening they were many of them in liquor, but I scarcely afterwards saw an instance, except in one case where I was obliged to drag the offender by the collar to the guard house, as he refused to down his musket and when Cotton had snatched it from him, attempted to wrest it back again. When sober however he was very penitent and was released the same evening.

Sir C. had a sad piece of work with the Adderleys, he had put their pioneer into the roundhouse and the whole party assembled tumultuously to demand his liberty. Owen was scared out of his wits, but Sir C. was firm enough and they dispersed immediately. The Adderley Company march I fear quite as well

---

[1] The Miss Shipleys were the daughters of Rev. William Shipley, Dean of St. Asaph.

as yours now, but are in every other point very careless and ill-managed, your men I heard two or three times calling them the Cheshire Hogs.

Reginald to his brother, Richard
Gayton, Friday 17 September 1804

I have seen yesterday Mr. Adjutant Lawrence who is at Park-gate, he has almost thunderstruck me with the account that the whole Regiment is going out again on permanent duty to Shrewsbury in October at the desire of Government. This was proposed to the Sundorn Division last Sunday Se'nnight and agreed to unanimously and I shall probably find a whole bundle of papers relative to it when we get back to Hodnet. This is really enough to put one out of patience, it were better to be in the Militia at once. I don't know that I am quite tired yet, but I think it will go near to tire all the men except indeed Francis Adams.

Reginald to his brother, Richard
Sunday, 30 September 1804

With regard to your other questions — Quarme has been so little with the men that it is difficult to judge, but he has a remarkably good manner of speaking to them and is going the right way to work to get influence and authority, as he is taking a great deal of pains to know their faces and names. Harvest has lamed some and made several slovenly, and the pieces in particular have suffered by it. This morning they were shamefully dirty. They have promised to have them in high order in the evening when we are to fire ten rounds, and I shall communicate to them the march to Shrewsbury, which though they all know, they have not yet heard officially, as I wished if you had been able to come down this week that you should do it. The day fixed for the going is Monday the 8th to stay seven days. If you can possibly manage to go with them to Shrewsbury, though you only stay three days, it will be I think of great importance. If not, Quarme is very anxious that I should go for the three first days at least. We have had very thin musters, till this morning's which has been remarkably strong, not above twelve absentees, band and such included. The band go alternately to the different companies in the Division so as to be always together for the sake of practice. We are to go to Shrewsbury in waggons fitted with seats, etc., according to the regulations, I am rather afraid this will be a riotous business.

Quarme is staying at the Hall, he has not been able to get lodgings. Ashley of Woolerton has a handsome niece and is perhaps afraid of letting in a strange officer into his family. Perhaps you will be able to persuade him as they are much the best lodgings in the neighbourhood. I have just proposed the march to Shrewsbury to the men, who cheered very heartily, they asked if you went with them, I said I did not know for certain but hoped so. Do come for God's sake.

Reginald to his brother, Richard
October, 1804

I got down on Sunday night and yesterday marched here on a very fine day, and not too hot, we mustered eighty-eight rank and file, the men clean and orderly. Pye, Gosling and Sam Roden refused positively to come, but Pye sent his submissions and declared that he was hindered by his Master but will join us this evening. As he had given in a very sufficient notice before he resigned, we have therefore no hold upon him, I have promised him forgiveness. The others I shall send a file of men for to-morrow, who will bring them as deserters by a warrant from Kynaston. Kynaston himself is in very high feather and spirits, as is his wife who has favoured us with some new plans for ornaments, tassels and the like. Lord Clive[1] has given us two field-pieces with mouths carved like tygers and 'la illah ul Allah' written from one end to the other. They were in the service of the Typpoo, and are very beautiful. Dymock, Anderson,

---

[1] Edward, second Lord Clive (1754-1839) was Governor of Madras in 1799 when Tippoo Sahib was defeated and killed. These guns are still at Powis Castle.

Hinksman and the other songsters are in full voice. Pelham has been wanting to get Boult as sergeant-major, but Sir Corbet prevented it at once as he very rightly concluded it would not be very agreeable to our wishes.

I had almost forgot to tell you that on our march yesterday, a very fine strapping fellow came running after us quite out of breath and in his shirt sleeves, and as soon as he could speak, prayed admission into the Company. He had heard the drum in the morning as he was riddling in a barn, a little on the Hodnet side of Northwood and at once by a sudden start of patriotism, and without stopping to put on his clothes, followed us till he overtook us, which as we had near two miles start, did not occur till we were nearby Shrewsbury. So ardent and robust an adventurer was not of course refused, he was sent with Kay to get fitted at the Hall, and in his new uniform looks very respectable and seems extremely docile. His name is Ridgeway, he is about eighteen as I should guess, and about five feet ten inches high.

We have been much pestered by quarrels between the Wem, Ellesmere and Drayton bands, who are all impudent and all play detestably. The men today were very attentive but really could not keep time to the music.

Reginald to his brother, Richard
Tuesday, October 1804

I deferred writing in the hopes of seeing you. The men fully expected you to the last and though they wondered and grumbled in their own hearts, yet kept exceedingly hearty and were at last completely reconciled by my assurance that you had always intended to join them and were, I supposed, only prevented by indispensable business.

I gave them breakfast at five on Monday morning and about quarter before seven we were joined by the Adderley and both the Drayton Companies. Our men mustered ninety-five rank and file, three sergeants and two drummers, they behaved remarkably well the whole march. They had another half pint of ale at Shawbury towards which Sir Corbet gave two guineas, half a guinea per company. This contented them very well, though we could not keep them from running to a well and drinking, and they were only driven away by my declaring if they did not go I would give you a list of the refractory. The thirst was however very natural, for the heat was intense and the dust suffocating. I marched with them the whole way and was delighted with their general conduct and their marching. T. Hulson however seemed likely to give some trouble, he had a hat slung behind his haversack and somebody (Lawton I think) put a clod into it. Hulson turned round and struck Hooley and threw down his musket and wanted to strip to fight. I collared him and shook him for four or five minutes heartily and threatening him with the Black Hole at Shrewsbury, he begg'd pardon and harmony was restored, at the same time I scolded Lawton for putting in the clod.

The Regiment met us at a place about three miles from Salop, the distance from Hodnet about fourteen miles and by Sir Corbet's guide being mistaken we made it above seventeen, the consequence was that some of his own Company were ready to drop down, and the Draytons were not much better off. They however took more liberty with regard to the alehouses that we past than the Hodnet, who I believe did not once enter any, though they often wished and longed. The Draytons were many of them quite drunk.

The men seem to have lost their apprehensions of Sir C. who commands the second grand division and seems likely to be a very useful field officer, at least to judge by his marching us on Monday as he was very temperate and steady and did not fidget in the least. I saw Colonels Kynaston and Corbet and Mrs. Corbet on the field. Quarme has not been heard of. At five we sate down to dinner. I have seldom seen a greater number of raffs collected in one room, about twenty-four or twenty-five had the appearance of gentlemen, the rest very bad indeed, and their language a dialect between Shropshire and Welch. Soon after dinner Cotton and self went round to the different quarters and found all the men comfortable and satisfied.

Wednesday. I was obliged to leave off yesterday and now resume my narration or if you please commentaries. Our system is now settled thus, half past six in the morning exactly we muster then drill till eleven, then muster again with side arms at half past one. Dine at six. Yesterday I drank tea with Mrs. Owen where I met Mr. Owen of Woodhouse and his wife[1] whom I remembered at Bath as Miss Cummyns, and her sister who is going to be married to Mr. Sparling who was also there as well as Richard Hill of Berwick. Coming away from thence I met Mr. Roberts who persuaded me to return to the Mess to hear some of the Wem Band who sang beautifully, I accordingly went with him and found a small party with Mr. Dymock at one end of the table and Worrall at the other, the rest were Kenyon, Oakley, Adjutant Lawrence and three more. We sate till about eleven, towards the end your health was proposed by Mr. Roberts and drank.

This morning and yesterday the men have behaved admirably in the field, all the field officers rode up to thank them and all the Companies were told to imitate their example. The file marching the Colonel declared was quite as good as any regulars he had ever seen. We have had a little battle about the Pioneer. Pace of Stoke Heath who performs that honourable duty refused to march so that I sent him to the Black Hole, but on his repentance and submission he was discharged. Everybody praises the Hodnet Company so much that I am afraid they will become petted and careless. They are not at all attentive at private muster this morning, and I, as Cotton was not there, was obliged to make them recover six times before they did it properly.

Reginald to his brother, Richard
Wednesday, October 1804

Thank you for your letter which the men have just done by three cheers. If you could possibly be here on Monday when our colours are presented pray come, even to be present at the evening part of the business (if the morning is impossible) would

[1] William Mostyn Owen of Woodhouse. His wife was Miss Harriet Gordon-Cumming.

be taken kindly by gentle and simple. I think they seem to expect that you should at least make the attempt to join them on or near that day. Our system has sustained some alterations since I wrote last and I have found this party more pleasant than I at first expected. You have compared your mess to the B.N.C. club, I think ours resembles the Brasenose Hall as the set is excessively good or infamously bad according to ones good or bad fortune in getting a seat. There are two favourable circumstances which destroy the resemblance, one that the dinners are excellent, the other that the raffs are all sober and leave as soon as they have finished their pint, which they do with all speed. The set which remains is generally very good.

Dymock is our grand champion in everything, after him comes Pelham and Kenyon and Woollaston, and Cotton bears a very distinguished part. Dymock is an admirable soldier and is at work without cease, he drills the Light Company and all the officers, conducts the management of the mess and sings as often as called on from seven o'clock till one. I was agreeably surprised in Pelham, from whom I had expected very little and whom I find a very gentlemanlike agreeable man and who is certainly one of the pillars of the concern. I cannot say much for your friend Oakley. Sparling nobody sees much of and not many know him, I never saw deeper marks of dejection and misery in any countenance. I met him at Mrs. Owen's when I was introduced to him and talked with him a little, but as he seemed inclined to cut me the next morning I endeavoured to prevent him by cutting first, and turned my eyes another way. He seldom appears in the mess, or if he is there, has generally sate very silent and left immediately.

I have not heard of any of our men enlisting. If they offered it, I believe they would cool their heels in the Black Hole, if they belonged to some of the Companies. Cotton makes a very good officer but though the men like him very well, he has not much influence. The men have on the whole behaved well, but there have been some instances of carelessness and obstinacy, which I fear they have learnt from the other Companies. In sobriety and cleanliness and adroitness at the lockstep and manual they are without fault. Our plan of exercise is now from half past six till a little after ten, and from half past one till five. The morning is generally drill, the evening given up to marching in review and the maneuvres.

Sir C. makes a very good officer and knows more of his business than any. Pelham is tolerable though he is frequently wrong. Plowden and Corbet of Sundorn are as bad as bad can be. Boult, I am sorry to say, is execrable at the maneuvres, so that Cotton has a great disadvantage. Tomorrow we begin firing with ball cartridge at which I can see some of the men are a little startled. As a fourth sergeant was necessary, I have appointed Percy Pace.

Even if you cannot come in time for Monday, try for Tuesday, since that would at least prove you had made the attempt, and the men are really very anxious. The other day a tall man in black was seen at the other end of the field and they all cried out, ' The Captain! the Captain!'

Reginald to his brother, Richard
October 1804.

As I do not know any means of information more intelligible to the logbook system of arrangement, I shall give you a short journal of our most important gests. On the day I wrote last we sent a corporal and a file of men for Pye, Gosling and Timothy Roden, who made a virtue of necessity and returned with a good grace, professed sincere repentance and have in truth behaved uniformly well. Nothing remarkable occurred after this till Sunday, which being rainy and idle, several men ran home, they were however brought back as deserters and confined in the Black Hole, though as they were really half way on their road back to Quarters when the patrol met them, I released them in less than an hour's time with a suitable admonition.

Monday we had also terrible plague with the arms, as we were to fire ball on Tuesday. It must be observed by the way that we have also had a good deal of trouble about silence and steadiness, in which I think the regiment in general is by no means improved, any more than they are in morals and sobriety, and though to do *our* men justice I have had but little reason to complain.

Tuesday was a day to which I looked forwards with some anxiety, Kynaston was ill and underwent a cupping, the two Batallions were to fire in the same field, that field by no means a safe one; besides we were under the eye of General Williams who looked after our faults with tolerable minuteness. I was however agreeably disappointed. The whole Regiment behaved admirably, both in their march and the steadiness of their firing, and the Hodnet Company was such as I could not possibly wish better. There was scarcely a word spoken or a motion done amiss. Colonel Chaytor himself, with whom we are not at present quite in charity, would not have been able to find fault. And the next morning their pieces were as clean as possible. . . . . .

But these private griefs were driven out of all our heads by the events of last night. We have seen ' The Broadsword with bayonet clashing, seen through the mud the Colonels dashing ' etc. In short we really might have seen not only this but much more than this, had it not been for the immediate exertions of the officers and the most gallant and steady conduct of the privates. Dymock had confined one of his men; in the evening about twenty of the Light Company with a numerous mob of townsmen came to rescue him. Heanage was Capt. on Guard, Cotton one of the subalterns. Cotton and myself were enjoying female conversation on sofas at Mr. Wingfield's at the Old Hall, when we were summoned by news of a dreadful riot, we ran to the Guard immediately and all the Officers almost, with the Colonel assembled in the orderly room and nearly besieged by a numerous and very noisy mob. The Guard however were turned out, and notwithstanding that they had to attack their brother volunteers and comrades, were as determined and as orderly as the oldest troops.

At last the bugles were blown, a vast quantity of lights struck, ' the officers' powdered hair was reddened by the torches' glare ', the remaining volunteers flocked down with their arms and shewed the utmost zeal for their officers, the streets were soon cleared, and about a dozen ringleaders, mostly townsmen, were thrown into divers dungeons and blackholes, in which service Kenyon was particularly active and resolute, and at length we concluded the evening by a supper in the Guard room given by Sir Corbet Corbet, be doubling the Guard, and about two o'clock leaving Cotton with his associates to their benches and great-coats, we who were not on Guard retired to bed. *Unum pro multis dabitur caput.* Dymock's Company have certainly misbehaved, but I can forgive them for the opportunity they afforded for displaying the steadiness of the other men. I went along the line of the guard of one outpost when we were told that the Light Company had got their pieces and were going to fire on us, I never saw more steadiness or can conceive greater willingness to stand by their leaders than was evident in their firmness and orderly behaviour.

VI Letters to
RICHARD HEBER
1791-1804

W E TURN NOW to Richard Heber. In 1791 he was
seventeen years old ; by 1804, when his father died, he
was recognized as a bibliophile and man of letters and
was surrounded by a circle of friends who, while not men in the
front rank of public affairs, were influential in their sphere. In
the present chapter we see the growth of this circle.

John Richardson (1771-1841) of University College, Oxford,
was called to the bar and followed a prosperous career as barrister
and judge; he was knighted in 1819. John Stonard of Brasenose
College (1769-1849) did not attain fame ; he was tutor in the
families of Stanhope and Lowther, and was rector of Aldingham
in Lancashire. Henry Hobhouse (1776-1854), like Richardson,
made his mark in the civil service; he graduated from Brasenose,
was called to the bar, and served as solicitor first to the customs
and then to the treasury; he became permanent under-secretary of
state in the home department and keeper of the state papers ; in
the latter capacity he superintended the editing of the state papers
of Henry VIII.

Hugh Cholmondeley (1772-1815), although he was contemporary with Richard at Brasenose, had also other claims to his
friendship : he was the third son of Thomas Cholmondeley of
Vale Royal and therefore a neighbour. He entered the church
(in what spirit plainly appears from his letters) and became Dean
of Chester (again, by methods of which the letters fully inform
us). Thomas Smyth, also of Brasenose, became vicar of St. Austell
in Cornwall and was prebendary of Exeter until he died in 1854.

Richardson, Stonard, Hobhouse, Cholmondeley and Smyth were all about the same age as Richard. They were university friends, the sort of group that one might expect to find round a wealthy, intelligent man; a group in which some afterwards attained worldly distinction and some did not. Circumstances threw them together and there was something automatic and unpremeditated about the friendships which were formed. But some of Richard's other friendships had not this character : those for instance with Sydney Smith, John Leyden and Walter Scott.

Sydney Smith (1771-1845) became a fellow of New College the year after Richard matriculated. He was not much older than Richard but he was more brilliant; we may imagine that his acquaintance with Richard was more deliberate than the others; certainly it was worth cultivating. Smith's strong personality had led him to Normandy during the French Revolution, where he joined the Jacobin Club for safety, and to Edinburgh, where he made friends with Walter Scott and Dugald Stewart; in 1802 he started the *Edinburgh Review*; he was a firm whig and had strong connections with Holland House; he believed in Catholic emancipation; he was not far removed from politics and he played his part in shaping the future of England.

In the first of Smith's letters here printed he writes about a common friend, John Leyden. The character of Leyden (1775-1811), like Smith's, was rich and powerful. In everything an enthusiast, he cultivated a defiant and flamboyant manner. He was a Scot educated in Edinburgh University; he met Richard in 1799 when Richard was visiting Edinburgh; Richard introduced him to Walter Scott, with whom he collaborated; in order to pursue his oriental studies he went as a physician in the East India Company's employ to India and Malaya — a project in which Richard again helped him, and he stayed with him in London for some months before sailing. His letters to Richard from the East show us an indomitable spirit in full pursuit of his objective. He was tamed in the end by death, when he caught a fever by entering (it was said) an unventilated library in Java.

There could hardly be a greater compliment to the personality of Richard Heber than the friendship of these two men.

Frodsham Hodson (1770-1822), who was a fellow of Brasenose when he wrote to Richard in 1801, became Principal, Vice-Chancellor of the University and regius professor of divinity. He was a tutor of great reputation, a man of high quality and standing in the academic world. He guided Richard through the toils of an election when Richard stood for the University.

Robert Southey (1774-1843) needs no introduction. We find him in 1802 asking the loan of Richard Heber's copy of *Amadis of Gaul*, a version of which he shortly after published. Leyden, Scott and Southey were the friends of Richard's maturity, made in his travels. James Boswell (1778-1822) also entered this circle; he became a fellow of Brasenose, a barrister and a member of the Roxburghe Club.

George Eyre (1772-1837), was the friend with whom Richard visited Paris during the Peace of Amiens. He was a graduate of Oriel College; he became high sheriff in his county and verderer of the New Forest. Richard and Eyre had been school-fellows under Dr. Glasse. Eyre wanted to go with Richard to Italy in 1803, but the war breaking out again prevented it.

That was Richard's intimate circle so far as it revealed in letters to him up to 1804. What can we say of it in general terms? Undoubtedly, that it was made up of lively and liberal men. They were young; but it is also true that they had grown up in a time when ideas were unusually active. We catch them off their guard, with the pen running freely, generally in a mood of gaiety. They seem to be of altogether a different world from that in which Richard's father moved, and one understands that the father's occasionally-recorded distress over Richard's wine, music and book-collecting were not merely incidental to parental responsibility. The father, like the son, was physically energetic, but in matters of mind there was a gulf between them.

Richard's tutor at Brasenose had been Ralph Churton (1754-1831). Churton was born in Malpas parish, educated at the grammar school there, and sent to Oxford under the patronage of Dr. Townson. He took a fellowship and became rector of Middleton Cheney in Northamptonshire and archdeacon of St. David's. From Middleton he sends Richard advice on how to conduct himself in Italy, in a letter remarkable for its pomposity.

Another of the older generation who writes to Richard in these years is William Roscoe (1753-1831) the historian. He was engaged at that time on a history of Pope Leo X, published in 1805, and wanted Richard to perform a commission for him in Italy. This is a formal letter and cannot fairly be compared with the more personal communications of Richard's contemporaries. Nevertheless the style and thought of it are so reminiscent of the Rev. Reginald Heber — and this in spite of Roscoe's whiggery, sympathy for the Revolution and belief in Catholic emancipation — that the parallel cannot be avoided. Roscoe's principles were the reverse of the elder Heber's. Roscoe was Heber upside down. But they give the impression of being cast in the same mould. The spirit of both seems to be equally removed from that which pervaded Richard's circle.

*   *   *

Rev. Ralph Churton to Richard Heber
Malpas, 21 July 1791

The riots in Birmingham,[1] bad as they were, seem however to have been less outrageous and formidable, except to the dissenting party, than the papers have in general represented them. So I collected from accounts on the road and from a gentleman who was present and saw much of their proceedings. None perished but some who were buried in the ruins; they dispersed without being fired upon. Several inflammatory papers spread by the presbyterians had exasperated them. I have a copy of one, violent and abusive beyond expression. ' Church and King ' was written on every house and shop in the town.

[1] The house of Dr. Priestley and other houses and buildings associated with Dissent and republicanism were burnt on 14 and 15 July 1791 by a mob provoked by the defiant behaviour of members of the Birmingham Revolution Society assembled to commemorate the first acts of the French Revolution.

11

John Richardson to Richard Heber
Welshpool, 6 August 1792

I am living a life approaching to the vegetable. Nothing to rouze the mind, all tranquility, no agitations. When I first saw this country, when I walked thro romantic vallies tenanted by rosy-cheeked healthy girls, simple unaffected and good humoured, I became an enthusiast for an Arcadian life: I formed a pretty theory of domestic happiness with a companion, uninformed indeed but possessing every good propensity and sound natural capacity; whom you might with vast satisfaction instruct in all the fortuitous advantages of more extended knowledge which a better education had enabled you to obtain. This I confess is still a very agreeable subject for private contemplation: but it is a theory not to be realised by a man who possesses no irriguous vallies, no shady streams; or if he did, whose shepherd-happiness would often be discomposed by the pricks of ambition.

John Richardson to Richard Heber
Oxford, 27 October 1792

In this invigorating air, a man's mind relaxed and unstrung by habits of long indolence and the contagion of female imbecillity soon recovers its tone. Stonard has already reason to lament *crassos transisse dies*. The gout has invaded his toes and he thinks it expedient to confine the enemy to the extremities by copious potations of cordial port. The fact was that he spent the vacation at a bathing place on the Southern Coast, where he rioted five times a week on delicious soles.

John Richardson to Richard Heber
Oxford, 18 November 1792

You have heard no doubt of our exertions on behalf of the exiled Clergy.[1] The University in convocation voted a donation

---

[1] The united committees of subscribers for the relief of the suffering clergy of France, refugees in the British dominions, arranged on 15 October 1792 that all in need of charity should apply to the Bishop of St. Pol de Léon at 10 Queen Street, Bloomsbury Square, whose duty it was to examine applications. Advertisements and long subscription lists were published in the newspapers. A rival subscription list for laity and clergy was also opened.

of £100. The Chapter of Christ Church contributed 50, to which
the members added so much — particularly the Commoners
nearly 60 — that the College subscription amounted to about
200. Magdalen gave from the public fund 100, the President
added 20 and the members something more. Brasenose distinguished itself, the College voted 30, the Principal gave 20
and the contributions of individuals amounted to 50 more.
Stonard was particularly active. We collected at University
nearly 50. Oriel makes a shabby figure. The Vice-Chancellor
has transmitted to town already £500, he will be able to send I
should conceive half as much more.

It is said that Richards will be a candidate for the Poetry
Professorship. Hale of Christ Church is mentioned as an opponent.
Pierrepoint is gone to perform military duties in Nottingham-
shire. Smyth is here and by his Father's particular desire is
attempting to *draw*; an art of which he will be no adept or I am
no prophet. Old Langton croaks about the progress of democratic
vulgarity and the re-approach of night and barbarism. Stonard
eats with unusual voracity.

John Richardson to Richard Heber
Oxford, 1 December 1792

Your frigid panegyric on our Academic Charity raises my
scorn rather than my thanks. Never before did I hear surprise
expressed because the principles of Whiggism were united
with the feelings of humanity. On one subject I will join with you
in condolences, because grievous has been my disappointment.
I pictured to myself that the downfall of Toryism[1] would be the
revival or at least promotion of Oxford Arts, Literature and
Poetry. Alas ! Things still go forward in their dull unimproved
unprogressive round. The subjects for the honours of next year
have made their appearance and to the great chagrin of me and I
believe of all well-wishers to the glory of the Isis, the Prizes are
two only in number. The temper of the public mind, the peculiar

---

[1] The whig Duke of Portland succeeded the tory Lord North as Chancellor of Oxford
University in 1792.

circumstances of the Whig Duke's election, the splendour of his inauguration, all concur to enforce the striking propriety of the present moment for additional patronage to the cause of literary merit. However the spice, I suppose, of the old leaven, which so pertinaciously sanctifies against improvement all venerable abuses at this place, has protested against this innovation.

Holmes'[1] office expires after enjoyment, I believe, of ten years. He has a muzziness of intellect which his successor will not easily rival.

Rev. Ralph Churton to Richard Heber
Williamscot, 1 August 1793

If you have not carefully read Herodotus, Thucydides, and Xenophon's *Hellenica*, you cannot in the present period of your academic studies, do better than to read them and in the order mentioned. You will of course take with you the collateral aids of geography and chronology. As to the latter subject, Hebricus's tables are useful and that at the end of Bentham's *Orationes Funebres* etc.[2] It is also very expedient to make short abstracts of the history for yourself especially in reading Herodotus whose work is in a degree a miscellaneous or general history, and this justly celebrated Father of History is a very pleasing and honest writer who gives you his authorities fairly, whether they rest on his own knowledge or were told him by Egyptian priests or others.

John Richardson to Richard Heber
Oxford, 17 August 1793

There are two great subjects on which a wise man may reasonably exercise his thoughts: his happiness in this world and the next, Politics and Religion. The first ought to be banished from the drawing-room since women always descend from

[1] Robert Holmes (1748-1805), Professor of Poetry from 1783.
[2] Edward Bentham (1707-76), *Funeral Eulogies in Greek*.

principles to persons and the discussion ends with idle expression
of their hopes or their fears. On the other, some good practical
hints may be derived from the conduct of a well-educated
woman; but enquiries and examinations they are taught to
tremble at. From all this it follows that books and men are the
only rational companions. Wherefore I have partly resolved to
absent myself from all Balls and public Breakfasts next week.

John Richardson to Richard Heber
31 March 1794

I see one principle beginning to be adopted with which I am
highly pleased. I mean that of multiplying the means of internal
defense beyond what establishments merely military can effect,
by putting arms into the hands of respectable classes of the community, by teaching us to look upon ourselves and our neighbours for our protection, by inspiring us with confidence and
courage, and giving us a centre of union to which, with our
muskets taken down from our chimney-pieces, we may on the
press of danger in a moment repair.[1]

Rev. John Stonard to Richard Heber
Chipstead, Chevening, Kent, 17 August 1794

Glad the famous Robespierre is gone at last: gone to Hell as
sure as he's born: and Barrère and all the tribe of them. I only
wish that all the French Convention were gone with 'em. Aye,
and the French nation, too. It would be a signal service to the
human race. Hope we shall drive the Ragamuffins back now.
Pray do you think the late events in Paris will lead to a Peace.[2]

[1] The militia had already been considerably expanded. In 1794 a number of volunteer
corps were raised. These measures to supplement the armed force of the kingdom are
open to the criticism that they hindered recruitment to the regular army without creating
a force sufficiently efficient to take its place.
[2] The *coup d'état* of Thermidor (1794), which overthrew Robespierre and the Jacobin
party, was a reaction from revolutionary puritanism and the Terror; but it did not lead
to any change in the foreign policy of the French government.

Rev. John Stonard to Richard Heber
Chipstead, Sevenoaks, 26 February 1795

The fact is this, that people cannot afford to pay more taxes: therefore any new tax will either diminish the consumption as you yourself acknowledge or else entirely prohibit the use of the article on which it is laid and therefore the revenue will not nor can be increased by additional taxes. I declare to you that I think a national insolvency is to be speedily apprehended unless the war very quickly comes to an end. The necessaries of life will bear no further taxation. I see a good deal of the poor and I know they can hardly live. It is with them a life of starving to death.

I am ashamed the M.P.'s have not entirely abolished franking; the King ought to give up some part of his revenue. If he does not and the taxes go on accumulating, he'll lose it all. Much as I hate all popular tumult and piously as I deprecate all popular government, I should not wonder and I declare I could hardly blame the lower class of people if they were to make, which God forbid, some desperate and dreadful effort to better their condition. It is not the romantic and absurd notion of French liberty that will entice them to such an attempt; the desire of life and the hard struggle which men make to pursue it, it is this alone will impel them to rise against their Governors.

But I declare that I cannot regard the present scene or look forward to what is coming without the most awful feelings. I do on my conscience believe that the Divine Wrath is manifesting itself against the sinful nations of Europe. Whether the Vengeance of God, now that it is aimed against our transgressions will be appeased by anything short of our destruction as an Independent Nation, is among the secret things of Omniscience. But let us not run into the evils we may justly dread.

Henry Hobhouse to Richard Heber
Brasenose, 10 May, 1795

Though you do not mention it, I conclude that you were present in the Upper House on Friday at the Debate I have just been reading in the *Sun*. Lord F's speech,[1] as it is there given, goes I think to prove him a weak man, and almost wholly actuated by an inordinate love of popularity.

Rev. John Stonard to Richard Heber
Chipstead, 15 May 1795

Mr. Flickerfly,

I have just received your very stupid shabby and impertinent letter; and I write this to say that I don't believe a word of it. You are a silly ape and don't know one moment where you will be the next. I should not wonder if instead of going to Oxford you were to remain in Town and indeed I don't at all believe that you were under the least necessity of going to Oxford: for I see by the Almanac there's plenty of time for keeping term yet. I should not direct to Oxford only that I believe you will remain in Town and then if they send it after you, you will have double postage to pay which will be some comfort to me. You call this silly trick an alteration in plan. What the Devil do you mean by that ? Your new plan will cost me a couple of guineas for besides that I had something for dinner which I shall not eat, I intended to have gone up in a chaise with you on Monday and so have neglected taking a place in the Coach; and therefore shall be obliged to go up in a chaise by myself. I never heard of such planning and counter-planning. If you had but followed my plan and my prudent directions and come yesterday, all would have been right, but you are too wise I suppose to accept of advice from anybody but your own plan-mad pate. Indeed, when I found that my own wise scheme was rejected, I had some little presentiment that all would not succeed, and so it has happened; which is nothing more than common for I never knew anything finally succeed that was done contrary to my opinion. But some people are so daringly obstinate and head-strong and withal so variable and giddy that they will reject any counsels that don't originate in their own folly and even in what

[1] *See* footnote on page 91.

their own ignorance and stupidity suggests, they will keep no steadiness but excuse themselves for breaking their own monkeyish resolutions by alledging an alteration in plan. An alteration in plan ! An alteration in your backside ! I should like much to produce a good useful alteration in it by the means of a stout rod or a cat-o'-nine-tails. An alteration in plan ! as if that were any reason for disappointing people, and as if the reason for the alteration ought not to be given. But one may look long'ere that be found. For it's then said ' Don't inquire particulars '. Oh, dear Sir, by no means, for the Devil a bit do I believe there are any particulars to enquire about.

What do you tell me of your 8 shillings for, Mr. Nincompoop ? Who cares a —— about your 8 shillings ? Oh ! but I beg your pardon for not having mentioned before that it was a most unfortunate alteration in plan, prodigously unfortunate indeed ! And I daresay you will lament your own and my misfortunes with great glee and violent gusts of laughter that very evening in College. But don't suppose you shall enjoy your impertinence with impunity. Whenever I see you ὥρα σε αελλοποδων ἱππων σθενερωτερον φυγᾳ ποδα νωμαν.[1]

Pemberton shall give you an imposition, the subject to be the above Greek sentence. No ! that shan't be the subject, it shall be *Quid primum deserta querar.* No ! that won't do: it must be something in Greek. But it must do for I can't think of anything in Greek that will do. I don't think the Greeks ever heard of anything so foolish and impertinent. It must be something poetical, and Ode or an Epic Poem. I won't write any more or I shall write myself into a good humour, a temper of mind that I am determined not to be in at present. So make haste and send your imposition which is the only way of obtaining forgiveness for your confoundedness.

From your injured affronted impudentized follyized and therefore angry

John Stonard

---

[1] '. . . you had better run like the wind ' is the sort of translation intended by Stonard for this line from the Œdipus Tyrannus of Sophocles.

Rev. John Stonard to Richard Heber
23 December 1795

What a fool our republican Peer[1] has made himself again. I detest and despise him with all my heart. We cut him out tho' in the Kentish address. Ours was subscribed by 17,000 names, while his democratical Lordship had no so many, altho' he boasted of having 20,000. Beside our folks could all write their names; a great deal more than can be said of his ignorant ragged brutal swinish crew.

Henry Hobhouse to Richard Heber
Oxford, 13 May 1796

What says Billy to the desertion of the King of Sardinia,[2] that Pattern of Fidelity ? Will not this protract the life of the Parliament ?

Hugh Cholmondeley to Richard Heber
St. James's Hotel, Jermyn Street, 27 March 1797

I suppose the *Sun* of this evening will inform you of what the guns have just been firing for: the capture of the Island of Trinidad[3] without the loss of a man by Admiral Hervey[4] : the *San Domaso* a 74 is taken. One 84 the *San Vincente* ,two 74 and a 36 gun frigate were burnt by the Spaniards before they capitulated. I really am quite vexed to find people so disponding. I hope however there is but little chance of a change of Ministry.

---

[1] Charles Stanhope (1753-1816), third Earl Stanhope, scientist, politician; President of Revolution Society; withdrew from Parliament in 1795, having failed to find any support for his proposition that the form of government in France ought to be no bar to normal Anglo-French relations. On 5 December 1795 a meeting under his chairmanship at Maidstone approved a petition which drew attention to the present scarcity and distress and entreated the King ' immediately to set on foot a negotiation in order to procure for this country a speedy, honourable and lasting peace '. The wording was impeccable, but the spirit behind it, though genuine and liberal, was extremely dangerous in a time of war.

[2] Armistice of Cherasco, 28 April 1796. Bonaparte in a vigorous campaign in north Italy succeeded by this armistice and the peace which followed it in neutralizing the King of Sardinia. He was then able to go on to the second and more important phase of the campaign — the attack on and defeat of the Austrian army in Italy.

[3] General Abercromby captured Trinidad, a Spanish possession, in February 1797.

[4] Sir Henry Harvey (1737-1810), rear-admiral in command of the naval forces.

John Richardson to Richard Heber
Inkburgh, Alcester, 20 October 1797

I wish you joy most heartily of our victory over foes not beaten by us since the days of de Ruyter and Van Tromp.[1]

Hugh Cholmondeley to Richard Heber
Vale Royal, 21 October 1797

We shall hear no doubt in the King's Speech at the opening of Parliament of the heartfelt satisfaction with which he congratulates on the late glorious Victory etc., etc.[2] This is not the first instance of Pitt's Luck this War.

I recollected a circumstance the other day that you once mentioned to me about some fields that you and your Father wanted to purchase and could not agree about the price with old Forester of Willey.[3] Cecil Forester is his next heir and most likely to have his fortune at his death, though the old gentleman will not assist him in his present distress, but says he will never undress himself till he goes to bed.

I think there is but little chance of our putting into execution another projected expedition of ours to the Continent while the War continues which there now appears but little chance of an end to. Everybody here is in an alarm about the talked of buying up of the Land Tax.

Hugh Cholmondeley to Richard Heber
Stanmore, 15 May 1798

After much consideration I have almost resolved to take Orders next Trinity Sunday. It is an object to me to get settled

---

[1] Battle of Camperdown, 11 October.

[2] ' The public spirit of my people has been eminently displayed; my troops of every description, have acquired fresh claims to the esteem and admiration of their country, and the repeated successes of my navy over all our different enemies, have been recently crowned by the decisive victory with which Providence has rewarded the exertions of my fleet under the command of Admiral lord Duncan. No event could be attended with more important and beneficial consequences, or form a more brilliant addition to the numerous and heroic exploits which, in the course of the present war, have raised to a pitch hitherto unequalled the naval glory of the country.' Extract from the King's speech of 2 November 1797.

[3] George Forester of Willey, Shropshire (1735-1811) eventually left his estates to his cousin Cecil Forester who was cr. Lord Forester in 1821.

upon some Curacy or other, for living this wandering kind of life will not do for me. And one is more likely by being in Orders to meet with anything than otherwise. I shall then, too, be able to take Priest's Orders at Christmas and get it all over. I am not particularly anxious to go into the Church, but as it must be my profession the sooner I take it up the better.

I have heard nothing but what your letter informs me of the military proceedings at Oxford. I think I shall do as little as possible. The idea of an invasion, I think, may now be given up. The French will find employment for the Army of England on the Continent and will never be able to transport them here.

A gallant business this has been with the old Invalids at St. Marcou.[1] What a pity our frigates could not come up to destroy everyone of the gun-boats. The Cheshire Militia have been marched from Glasgow and are to be quartered at Wolverhampton, Kidderminster, Bromsgrove, etc. Parker and my sister are to be at the latter place. They are I fancy by this time at Astle, where they intend to stay ten days or a fortnight. They regret leaving Scotland.

Hugh Cholmondeley to Richard Heber
Oxford, 20 May 1798

I came here with an intention of going into Orders by the advice of Drummond and my sister, but I don't know whether I shall change my mind.

There are here nothing but soldiers now. They get up and are at Prayers at six. Immediately afterwards go to Exercise till $\frac{1}{2}$ past eight. They begin again at a $\frac{1}{4}$ before two and continue it till $\frac{1}{2}$ past three and dine at four and Chapel at six. This all the Fellows except Parsons, Farington and Halliwell join in. I fancy I must fag at it myself this Vacation to come up with them. I do not think they will be able nor will it be quite fair to keep the men to their duty during the Long Vacation. They say they must have 120 gentlemen (and they have got above 500 names set

---

[1] Saint Marcouf, an island a few miles off the French coast, occupied by a garrison of British invalids, was attacked unsuccessfully by the French in May 1798.

down by the different Colleges and given into the Vice-Chancellor) to be in Oxford during the Vacation. This will be a bore to many.

Harper dissuades me very much from taking Orders and what astonished me very much, the Bishop did the same, when I called on him this morning. I think I shall defer it and become Military.

John Richardson to Richard Heber
Glasgow, 23 September 1798

We saw the Speddings, John[1] and Anthony and their beautiful sister Margaret at Keswick, but saw little of them, being pressed for time and devoted to the ladies of our own party, Mrs. Park and one of her sisters. These said ladies did not climb Skiddaw, so that I escaped the peril that once overwhelmed you, of fracturing my small-clothes in assisting them to ascend.

Rev. Hugh Cholmondeley to Richard Heber
B.N.C., 26 May 1799

I was ordained last Sunday, so you may direct to the Rev. H.C. This and other business has completely occupied my time.

A few days after you left us I had my bureau broke open and $29\frac{1}{2}$ guineas of Common Room money stolen. Charles the hall boy is now in the Castle for it and will be convicted next Assizes. The money except one guinea I recovered very luckily. There were others concerned whom I took infinite pains to bring the charge home to, but the Vice-Chancellor is very stupid and cautious.

Dr. Martin Routh[2] to Richard Heber
Oxford, 28 May 1799

As you have so obligingly interested yourself in the collection of the MS. in the British Museum, I ought not to omit informing

[1] John Spedding, of Mirehouse in Cumberland; the father of James Spedding who edited the works of Francis Bacon.

[2] Dr. Martin Joseph Routh (1755-1854), fellow of Magdalen College, Oxford; president 1791 till death.

you that the Board has agreed to give Mr. Porson[1] 50 guineas for his trouble, which sum, it was understood, his friend Dr. Burney[2] had been prevailed on to mention.

Rev. Thomas Smyth to Richard Heber
Oxford, 3 July 1799

I have been fagging very hard for Oriel and have just finished the *Persae* of Aeschylus. College is thinning very fast. Harper is very busy arranging the Library, Halliwell is inventing methods to make the men attend prayers more regularly, Boswell[3] is haranguing against College discipline, Palmer and Popham in bathing and fishing, and your humble servant in poring over Greek and writing Prose Latin.

Rev. Sydney Smith to Richard Heber
19, Queen St., 7 March 1800

Leyden sent a message about curious books which I have forgot. I met him at supper at Stodarts where we spent a very pleasant evening with much punch and pleasantry and beguiled life admirably well for a few hours. Campbell[4] the bard was there who has more metre than politeness or elegance in his mind.

Rev. Thomas Smyth to Richard Heber
Macclesfield, 15 March 1800

I tremble at the thought of the examination, though I have certainly read more than I could possibly have expected and in compliance with your advice, have frequently composed in my

---

[1] Richard Porson (1759-1808), Greek scholar, was at this time transcribing the Harleian manuscript of the Odyssey for the Grenville Homer, published in 1801.

[2] Charles Burney (1757-1817), classical scholar.

[3] James Boswell the younger (1778-1822), lawyer; Brasenose College, Oxford; Vinerian fellow; called to the bar at the Inner Temple in 1805; completed second edition of Malone's Shakespeare; Roxburghe Club: edited third variorum Shakespeare 1821. He was a good friend of Richard Heber and Walter Scott, and reappears many times in these pages.

[4] Thomas Campbell (1777-1844), poet. On the point of starting on a tour of Denmark and Germany.

leisure hours. Before I leave this, which will be next Wednesday but one, I shall have read all Aeschylus except the *Choruses* 3 times over, all Sophocles as often, and five or six plays in Euripides, the greater part of Demosthenes, all Juvenal, the 1st book of Thucydides and all the speeches 3 times over. So that I really in some happy moments think that if I have any luck. I may pass a decent examination.

John Leyden[1] to Richard Heber
Edinburgh, 24 April 1800

I have held consultation with Scott about the possible anticipation of his *Eve of St. John*, the result of which was that he determined to print a very limited edition of his *opera omnia* at Kelso by Ballantine an excellent typographer, solely for the use of his friends. The Border Ballads are to be printed *on the Border* at Kelso and I hope will not be long delayed.[2] Scott wishes exceedingly to have the original airs of Liddisdale etc. so that it is not impossible but they may remain in *status quo* till we make our tour of Liddisdale. I have agreed to compose one or two Ballads for the occasion in order to introduce legendary histories and apprehend I shall write one professedly on Ld. Soulis, besides Keeldar in which he is one of the actors and another on Merlin or rather Michael Scott who in reality seems to have been the Roger Bacon of Scotland. Scott is to compose one on Thomas the Rhymer and the enchanted men of Gildon.

Keeldar seems increasing immeasurably; it is not yet finished though it now consists of about 70 verses. I have been long tired of it and have betaken myself to the composition of sermons in the way of my profession as your friend Sydney Smith

---

[1] Richard Heber found Leyden in Archibald Constable's little bookshop, in High Street, Edinburgh, and introduced him to Scott, to whom he became an invaluable lieutenant. Leyden was a scholar, which Scott was not. (Buchan's *Life of Scott*.)

[2] 'The Eve of St. John' was written in 1799 for Matthew Lewis's collection of romantic verse, *Tales of Wonder*, in which it later (see page 176) duly appeared. The publication of this work being delayed, Scott published a limited edition of some of his works from the press of Ballantyne at Kelso. The success of this co-operation encouraged Scott to proceed with the *Minstrelsy of the Scottish Border*, the first two volumes of which were published by Ballantyne in 1802, and to which Leyden contributed the Cout of Keeldar, Lord Soulis, The Mermaid, and the Ode on Visiting Flodden.

says in his preface. I suppose that gentleman has informed you
that he has just published a volume of sermons. When I saw him
last, he was expressing his design of sending you a copy to make
you sleep o' nights when disturbed by insomnia. ' Hereby shall
all men know ', says your friend the divine, ' that we are his
disciples, since we wake that others may sleep, i.e. we compose
sermons in the night watches to lull others to sleep even in the
broad day '. All of which confirms me more and more in my
meditated apostasy to Braminism, so that if I can procure an
appointment in the Company's service in due time I will renounce
the black for any other colour under heaven, make a present of
all my theological MS. and sermons to Sydney Smith and betake
myself furiously to the study of the Vedas and Shastras.

Henry Hobhouse to Richard Heber
21 July 1800

I do not know whether you have heard that Sidebottom has
taken to wife one of the Miss Holmes whom we saw at Chis-
wick. N.B. — The one with two eyes.

John Leyden to Richard Heber
Laswade Cottage, 4 November 1800

I heard of you several times in the course of my Northern Tour
which lasted about three months during which time I walked
about 600 miles, sailed 400 and rode 300. This with my expedition
to the Lakes of Cumberland, of which I think I gave you some
account, gives a walk of 1,200 miles this summer. You perceive
I have rambled nearly as much as yourself.

Mrs. Scott begs you would either procure a little better ink
or allow her to send you a bottle of her own making, that
everybody may not be obliged to sit gaping round Scott who
pauses stamps and swears every three words that your handwriting is little better to read than a runic inscription or a weather-
beaten whinstone.

Rev. Sydney Smith to Richard Heber
Cheam, Epsom, Mrs. Pybus, Saturday, 6 January 1801

I am sorry that our mutual efforts have not produced a meeting but this we will endeavour to accomplish after the 20th of this month. I am charged with all sorts of affections for you, from longing widows, from chloratic virgins, from ponderous professors, from tottering senility, from airy vigorous youth, from every stage and vicissitude of human life, such as it is found North of the Tweed.

Professor Andrew Dalzel to Richard Heber
Edinburgh, 31 *January* 1801

Leyden, or as you used to call him, the Cloud King, now the Elfin King, and Walter Scott are both mad at Lewis for such a paltry imposition on the public as the *Tales of Wonder*.[1]

Dr. Frodsham Hodson to Richard Heber
Liverpool, 2 *February* 1801

The papers talk of Mr. Pitt's resignation.[2] I hope and believe there exists no such signal cause for a national mourning. The King may well order a general fast if he has parted with the ablest Minister in Europe and perhaps another crown besides Paul's may be suspected to cover insanity.

Dr. Frodsham Hodson to Richard Heber
Liverpool, 21 *March* 1801

Pray, too, give me fairly the general opinion on the late change of administration. My spirits were never so low ! The great man at the head of the Admiralty is a compensation for Lord Spencer[3]

[1] Matthew Gregory Lewis (1775-1818) was a well-established poet when Walter Scott and Leyden were unknown. Both were much flattered to be invited to contribute to his *Tales of Wonder*, which was published in 1801 with deservedly little success.

[2] Pitt resigned 14 March 1801.

[3] Lord St. Vincent went to the Admiralty in Addington's administration, replacing Lord Spencer.

but he is none for Pitt. His loss is irreparable and the tongue of faction has confessed the truth.

Rev. John Stonard to Richard Heber
Sandridge, 15 April 1801

Rare news indeed from the Northern Lights.[1] Old Hamlet's ghost must have been roused from the grave to revisit once more the glimpses of the Moon or scan much greater light. They have a letter at Combe Bank that mentions Lord Nelson saying he never saw (such) firing before, so a pretty affair it must have been. Who is it has slain the Russian bear ? I suppose Bonaparte will bag his skin to cover his coach-box by way of hammer cloth; unless expecting to go shortly the same journey, he makes it into a couch.

Dr. Frodsham Hodson to Richard Heber
Liverpool, 16 April 1801

I am going to dine with Mr. Case and we shall not forget Lord Nelson's health and still less that of the great man whose last official act was to despatch the fleet to the Baltic. Tho' *manus haec inimica tyrannis* there is something so barbarous in the thought that I believe we must omit the Emperor of Russia's physician.

John Leyden to Richard Heber
21 April 1801

It is not impossible but you may see me in London in the course of this year as having been unsuccessful in my application for an Indian appointment, *medical civil* or *military*, I am hesitating whether to take a walk through Africa to Timbuktoo or to settle a godly parson in Scotland and publish ' romances and other Tales of Bawdrie '.

---

[1] Battle of Copenhagen (April) and assassination of the Tsar Paul (March).

Dr. Thomas Dampier[1] to Richard Heber
Rochester, 9 June 1801

I am glad you saw everything so well at Cambridge. Tho'
you do not mention it, I presume that you were amazed and en-
raptured by King's College Chapel. Mr. Wyatt[2] has given a
design for filling up the two vacant sides of the Quadrangle in
the same stile which if ever executed will but set off the superior
elegance of the original building.

Dr. Matthew Raine[3] to Richard Heber
Charterhouse, 11 August 1801

At present I have no opening in my own house and circumstanced as I am at present I really cannot fix any time before
August 1802 when I can positively promise. This is much too
distant a date, the age of your friend's son considered and I
must therefore intreat his permission to engage a place for him
in our other boarding house. In any case I trust there will be no
objection to confide him to me as a boarder with Mr. Stewart.
If a single bed be necessary, I must know it, and it must be understood as adding five guineas annually to the board.

My vacations are three in the year, at Whitsuntide three
weeks and $\frac{1}{2}$, and at Bartholomew-tide and Christmas four
weeks and half each. I do not mention Easter because we have then
only the Calendar holidays. Wearing apparel is to consist of
two suits of clothes, eight shirts and the same number of etcas.
with shoes in proportion.

Dr. Martin Routh to Richard Heber
Oxford, 13 August 1801

I received this morning a present for the College Library,
Milton's Poetical Works in 6 vols. 8vo. It came from the Editor,

---

[1] Thomas Dampier (1748-1812), in 1801 Dean of Rochester; then successively Bishop
of Rochester and of Ely; was, like Richard Heber, a noted collector of books.
[2] James Wyatt (1746-1813), architect.
[3] Dr. Raine, Headmaster of Charterhouse.

Mr. Todd of Canterbury, who appears to have spared no pains in the work, which I hope will do him credit as he is a worthy and respectable man.

Rev. Thomas Smyth to Richard Heber
Mrs. Angelo's, Eton, 12 November 1801

Keate[1] I have reason to think has received your letter and I write to thank you for having so soon attended to my request. Bayley mentioned to me the importance of being well introduced to Keate and it was on this account I wrote to you for the letter which you had promised me when in Oxford. He called on me immediately upon my arrival here but as he only staid a few minutes with me, I could not form any opinion of him. Dr. Goodall[2] sat long enough with me to convince me that he was one of the most agreeable men I ever met with. Dr. G. speaking of Wm. Way mentioned to me that he had shown him a copy of verses by a Mr. Heber of Brasenose which ' perfectly astonished him '. I believe these were his exact words. A compliment from such a man ceases to be a compliment and I felt pleasure which my regard for Reginald will ever make me feel in anything that reflects honour upon him.

Eton I think I shall find very pleasant. Those whose chief pleasure is in cards and routs must find it a perfect Paradise and even to the few that have no pleasure in either, Eton has its attractions.

With my visit to Ireland I was upon the whole very well pleased and seriously advise you to take the first opportunity of seeing Dublin which in splendour of its public Buildings is almost equal to London. The people I found generous and open-hearted, yet the vile custom of duelling is as much in vogue amongst them as ever and a stranger cannot go into a gunsmith's shop without receiving a printed card to inform him that he can be accommodated with ' Duelling pistols warranted to hit point-blank at a distance of a certain number of yards ' or into a bookseller's shop

---

[1] Dr. Keate (1773-1852), Headmaster of Eton.
[2] Dr. Goodall (1760-1840), Provost of Eton.

without seeing 'Instructions to Principals and Seconds in Duels by an Officer in the Army'.

John Leyden to Richard Heber
Edinburgh, 14 February 1802

I will give you only one hint concerning Ritson[1] and it is this, I am by no means afraid of him after having seen him. You sent down to Scotland your old lion, Walter Scott and I pared his claws and drew his teeth and returned him upon your hands a perfectly trained and domestic animal.

But what I write to you now concerning is of infinitely greater importance to me than ever any literary question and if by any horrid chance you be absent from town when you receive this, I may as well be *dead damned and straughted* (you understand Scottish) as the living man I am. I have procured an appointment as assistant surgeon in the Madras Establishment but unluckily so much sooner than I had expected that it is almost impossible if not utterly so to disengage myself here within the specified time as I am ordered to be ready to sail on the 24th March. The appointment is from Mr. William Dundas[2] and delicacy therefore forbids either Scott or me from applying to that quarter to have my departure postponed for six months, a thing which is done sometimes when the matter is supported by any person of influence at the India Board. But various applications have been made by my friends among the rest to Sir Stephen Lushington[3] which I have reason to think may be successful in securing his influence. But there are certain forms at the India Board of which I am entirely ignorant, such as those that relate to the regular form of the Petition which I believe must be drawn up at the India House, the mode of presenting it etc. Now what I most earnestly request of you is — immediately on receipt of this to call at the India House, enquire into these forms and see that they are accurately observed.

[1] Joseph Ritson (1752-1803), eccentric antiquary and author.
[2] Rt. Hon. Wm. Dundas (1762-1845), Secretary at War, 1804.
[3] Sir Stephen Lushington (died 1807), chairman of the Board of Directors of the East India Company.

I have written to Mr. Meheux, the Assistant Secretary, stating that such an application would be made and assigning as grounds of the petition for postponing my departure to the East till the first ships of next season, the difficulty of disengaging myself from my engagements here in so short a period, the impossibility of arranging everything for the successful pursuit of my Oriental studies, such as books, etc., and the necessity that there would be of leaving a historical work on Africa, Ancient and Modern, imperfect as the first volume is nearly printed off and I am certain no use could be made of my rough manuscript of the remainder. If you are in town I have no doubt you will be able to manage the matter extremely well. But I must beg to let me know immediately the aspect of the matter for I shall remain in a most horrible state of suspense till I hear. If you are out of town I am at my wits' end. In this cursed hurry I wish I have written intelligibly.

John Leyden to Richard Heber
(received) 23 *March* 1802

I often wonder how it happens that the persons for whom we entertain the sincerest friendship and esteem and to whom it is the greatest pleasure to write are precisely those with whom we use the greatest negligence in correspondence. Can it be that indolence always reckons upon real friendship being least apt to take offence at these our irregularities ? and being most easily pacified when real offence is given ? Are you ever subject to this whimsical humour which has often made me wonder at my conduct ? For instance in the present case, since the fourth of March on which I received my *furlough* from Mr. Meheux till this 15th day of it, I have postponed writing you though I have despatched a great many letters of ceremony to persons to whom I had by no means the same obligations as to you; and of the extent of these obligations which I owe to you I have been perfectly well informed by Mr. Mackenzie and others. But my regard for you is not the less though divested only too much of formality. I wish for my own sake I were a more punctual correspondent, since nothing gives me greater pleasure than to hear from you and I am not the only person in Edinburgh of the same sentiment. When have you written to Scott?

I received Mr. Meheux's letter just as I returned from the College of Surgeons with a Diploma in my pocket which I thought proper to take at all events in order to secure myself against any unlucky accident that might occur, if I had after all been obliged to sail immediately for Madras, but since I have procured leave of absence, I shall fortify it with a medical degree or M.D. But as our University only confers these degrees twice in the year, in June and in September, I must again request you to procure me information whether I am to be allowed to reside in Europe till August or December. If the latter, it will be most convenient for me to graduate in September. I am unwilling so harass Mr. Meheux on this subject after the trouble he has to politely taken already.

You are perfectly accurate in supposing my views on India to be chiefly literary and I confess I think it is the finest literary field in the world and if my situation allows me time to prosecute Oriental learning, and affords me any favourable opportunities for this purpose, I do not despair of supplying some of the *desiderata* of Sir William Jones.[1]

The fame of that Orientalist is absolutely discouraging: for who can adventure to rival him in either extent or accuracy of information: but the Devil will be in it if he have known everything better than any other person. In my opinion he has only shown us how much is still to do. It is true Bengal would have been preferred by me, had it been practicable to procure an appointment in that presidency, but I shall find much to learn at Madras; and tho' Sanscrit is my object, yet it is not my only object, for I intend to study Canara, Telinga, Mahratta and Malabar languages as well as Hindustani, Bengalee and Sanscrit. I do not mention Persian and Arabic, these I have some knowledge of and have begun to work at them with vigour. I likewise intend to learn Turkish, Armenian and Mantchiu Tartar. Of

---

[1] Sir William Jones (1746-94), orientalist and jurist, was the recognized authority on eastern languages and, especially, the father of Sanskrit studies.

Ethiopic and Coptic I have some knowledge but am woefully deficient in books which you know are not to be procured in Scotland on any terms. Moreover I think I shall contrive to compare the languages of Africa with those in the East and shall soon commence that after my arrival in India, examining the traces of Sanscrit etc., in Coptic.

Sir Wm. Jones neglected Armenian because he could not hear of any original works in that language, but I cannot persuade myself of this and at all events think the traditions, traditional poetry etc. of a nation placed like the Armenians in the vicinity of various ancient civilized nations ought to be neglected. The affinities of the language with the Persic have never been discussed to my knowledge.

I understand the Presidency of Madras is accustomed to send deputations or embassies to the native princes of India frequently. I am ignorant how such appointments are regulated, but am not devoid of hope to be found a proper person for accompanying some of these after some residence in India.

Robert Southey to Richard Heber
35 Strand, 7 May 1802

Will you trust me with your *Amadis de Gaul* till I can procure one or till I can abridge it — that is till the end of autumn ? Longman and Rees had thought of translating Tresson's *Romances*. I advised them not to do it — because tho' he was an able man, his books are too modern and what is worse too French. I have engaged to abridge *Amadis* myself from the English translation and as nearly as possible into the language of that translation, omitting as little of importance as possible and adding nothing.[1] This is a mere trial — if it succeeds the whole army of *Romances* will be proceeded upon in order. To the *Amadis* I prefix a Dissertation on the *Romance* in general — my name is not to appear — and I trust it to you my reason for asking so long a loan of a book which the bookseller has vainly tried to procure. The book

---

[1] Southey published his *Amadis* in 1803.

ll not be injured. I use books too much ever to abuse them; —
if you want the work or fear to send it travelling, say so as
freely as I have asked it.

John Leyden to Richard Heber
(received) 16 July 1802

It has been suggested to me that the most convenient mode of
going out to India is with an extra ship on its return. These extra
ships are built in India and proceed to England without any
surgeon, but are commonly very happy to carry one with them
on their return. Consequently the advantage of going out in this
manner, besides the medical practice on the voyage and a saving
of £120 or £130 for passage, is the sole and undisturbed possession of a cabin for the purpose of study etc.; not to mention the
chance of a glorious fracas or an opportunity of having your
throat cut should the Lascars mutiny.

George Eyre to Richard Heber
Clapham, 16 August 1802

Some hopes were entertained of seeing you on Friday. Not
knowing exactly when I shall meet you, I must in a note make you
acquainted with the arrangements already settled. Ede of Stratton
St. has orders for the post-chaise to be finished by the 14th of
October. It will have two small imperials, two seats under the
body, two trunks and all the necessary appointments with a box
behind capable of holding one or two servants. Schweitzer &
Davidson are to make me one uniform coat with two white
cloth waistcoats and breeches which will be full dress throughout
Europe. I shall have in addition three common English with such
a supply of shoes and Hussar boots as will carry me through the
year. I think 14 shirts will be sufficient. You will do well to get
your clothes in a forward state as some of your tradesmen are
probably like mine very dilatory. Do not forget to collect such

letters as you can. They must be so written that we may present them or not as we deem advisable.

I have it in contemplation to go to the Isle of Wight early in September for sea bathing.

William Roscoe to Richard Heber
Allerton, 14 November 1802

I am sorry to find that you have postponed your Italian trip and in this I fear I am not without some selfish feelings as I am well sure I should have derived assistance from your kindness. You are however right in seizing the present moment for a trip to Paris which seems likely to be soon closed against the English. Pray can you tell me what madness has seized upon the news-paper writers of almost all descriptions who in defiance of their former principles are endeavouring like so many devils to blow up the flames of war in Europe ? It is surely a most extraordinary circumstance that these incendiaries by their atrocious attacks upon the *character*, the *authority* and the *life* of the First Consul[1] (who whether good or bad is the idol of the French native) should have been allowed to drive the Country without any hostile act by either Government to the very verge of war. I trust the common-sense of the Country will soon return and crush these reptiles who seem to have found out that their craft does not flourish in times of peace and are therefore desirous of another conflagration.

Rev. Ralph Churton to Richard Heber
Middleton, 29 December 1802

I was lately informed that you were gone on a trip to Paris, were to return to spend the holidays with your friends, and then meant to shape your course for Italy, so I trust this will find you somewhere in ' the land we live in ' and I heartily wish you a prosperous journey and many happy returns of this best of seasons.

---

[1] Virulent attacks on Napoleon in the English press, mainly the work of *emigrés* helped to provoke the war which other causes made inevitable.

I shall not pretend to give you any directions on the occasion which I am sure you do not want. You will not sally forth an inexperienced boy, but possessed of many advantages which will enable you, with His blessing who I trust will ' go along in all the way ', to reap the fullest benefit from your travels, as besides a stock of general knowledge and experience. You have visited, I believe, most parts of this island and being master of the French and Italian languages and intimate with the best writers of ancient and modern Italy, you can readily compare places times and men.

The late Lord Bagot[1] having been admitted to the honorary degree of M.A. set out upon the tour you are about to make in the year 1749; and Dr. Townson, who had been his tutor, in his Procuratial speech adverting as usual to the transactions of the year, said — he was viewing the scenes which his favourite Milton had viewed before — ' ingenio vix impari, melior certe civis rediturus ' — if I quote the words as I know I do the sense correctly from memory; and having mentioned our ever dear friend, I recollect another anecdote. He saw Bishop Wilcocks,[2] I think, twice only and at an interval of some years; and his Lordship each time mentioned an epitaph (at Christ Church I believe) on someone ' cui, post Romam bis aditam, nec patria displicuit nec fides '. Perhaps the writer of the epitaph had in mind an old English proverb ' He that goes to Rome once, sees a wicked man; he that goes thither twice, learns to know him; he that goes the third time, brings him back with him '. I have certainly no fear lest you should import this ' man of sin ', if you were thrice three times to visit the city so well worth visiting; but we live in a momentous age, have seen many strange events and may possibly see others equally unexpected and not less wonderful. I do not expect the final overthrow of Rome (perhaps by an earthquake or volcano. Rev. XVII. 8.21[3]) before the

---

[1] William first Lord Bagot (1725-98).

[2] Joseph Wilcocks (1673-1756), fellow of Merton College and Bishop of Gloucester and of Rochester.

[3] ' Therefore shall her plagues come in one day, death, and mourning, and famine; and she shall be utterly burned with fire.

And a mighty angel took up a stone like a great mill stone, and cast it into the sea, saying Thus with violence shall that great city Babylon be thrown down, and shall be found no more at all.'

year 1866 which you may live to see but I shall not; but it is evident from prophecy that days of great distress are to precede that fatal period; and though the ultimate predominance of iniquity is limited in God's mercy to three years and a half, yet it is I believe nowhere said by what previous conflicts nor in what length of time that ascendancy may be gained. When such things are impending and therefore left uncertain that we may be on our guard, it behoves every man, especially such as are not void of talents and interest to prepare and conduct himself ' as on his single arm the moment lay of Victory ', of that best Victory by which he may adorn and defend his country and religion and both in life and death, save himself.

I am sorry I do not know your fellow traveller, Mr. Eyre; nor even whether he is a clergyman or not. When our dear Dr. Townson travelled with Mr. Drake and Mr. Maxwell, he stipulated that he should read the Service of the Church of England with them every Sunday. When the poet Collins[1] went abroad, he had only one book with him but that, as he emphatically said, was the best — an English New Testament. You, who will travel with better accommodations and I hope better auspices than the unfortunate Collins, will have room for two small volumes, the Common Prayer of the Church of England (only not inspired), and the Book of our Salvation in Greek; and your Sundays and all your days will be those of a true son of the Church of England, always sincere, never ostentatious, praying to God through Christ every morning and evening; and giving to the first day of the seven the priority of esteem and reverence in the house of God wherever it is practicable and where it is really otherwise, in the closet.

Forgive me, dear Sir, that I have deviated with this needless topic. I make no apology for it, as I am sure you well know how natural it is to give superabundant caution where one feels true esteem and affection.

I have had letters from Rome when Dr. Chandler was there and if you favour me with one, it will probably find its way, as one lately did from the Bishop of Peterborough, via Bombay!

---

[1] William Collins (1721-59), poet.

George Eyre to Richard Heber
Hotel de Paris, 22 January 1803

What think you of making a complete tour through the South of France — then Switzerland taking a peep at Milan, then the Tyrol, the great cities of the Rhine and Holland so as to return to England about next November? This will suit our time perfectly, we shall pass through and have time to enjoy the finest country in Europe and we need not quit Paris till April. We must in this tour become tolerable Frenchmen without mixing Italian. The inconveniences attendant upon my former plan are hurry and above all being at Naples and indeed perhaps at Rome at an unpleasant if not dangerous season. Turn these points in your thoughts.

I smile at our opinion of Ley's great proficiency in the parley-vouing. Worse than anything I have met with. Finding difficulties, full of prejudices, in short Winchester saturated with New College. But he as he has taken my Master into pay, a French woman into keeping and has quitted the Cercle in the hopes of finding a table perfectly French, we may expect great things.

I have been confined by a severe and unprovoked cold. It is better. But it lost me the Duchess of Gordon's Ball, a pleasant dinner with Scott and his friend and still keeps me a prisoner.

Madame Recamier has shut her door and Madame Cabarrus. I should be in Madame d'Oyen's if I were able this evening, but I have taken the powder of Jaques and must remain in my room.

Many of my acquaintances complain of want of comforts in their lodgings. Since writing the postscript, Wickham has called. He found his sheets last night very damp. I asked him why he did not throw them aside. He said he wished to do so, but on examination he had no blankets!

James Boswell to Richard Heber
Mrs. Cumings, Dryden, Lasswade, Edinburgh (undated)

You required me when I left London to write to you when I had been two days in Edinburgh and had seen Hugh Mackenzie

and young Leyden. Now I have been upward of a week in
Edinburgh and have seen neither. I paid a visit to Walter Scott at
Lasswade College (q: who was it read the word so ?) and was
invited by Mrs. Scott to eat hăm-pŭf. I dined with him a few
days afterwards and had some very good slang. I told him I had
met in London a little man whom I believed he knew something
of, one Masquerier,[1] but alas our expectations were miserably
disappointed: he did not turn up his nose and call him a hop-my-
thumb little fellow as you and I confidently and fondly hoped.

I dined the other day in company with Thompson the correspondent of Burns,[2] who after dinner favoured the company with
two of Burns' unpublishables.

John Leyden to Richard Heber
(probably) Thursday, 10 February 1803

I have delayed writing you till I could ascertain whether a
visit would be absolutely impossible, and as the plot thickens,
matters now begin to assume that decisive aspect that I feel it
would be highly imprudent to risk anything. Conceive what a
ridiculous figure I should cut to be left ' down among the
Hottentots, capering ashore ', after having paid my passage and
sent part of my luggage on board.

The spirit of hesitation doubt and dubiety seems to have taken
compleat possession of the conscript fathers of Leadenhall Street,
since you left us, our departure has been twice changed and the
' Hugh Inglis ' is finally ordered to Portsmouth instead of Deal
so you see that the laws of our Indian Consuls are quite unlike
those of the Medes and Persians, and yet in no degree whatever
more philosophical. Descartes, as we all know, found strong
profound confirmation in doubting ' Dubito ergo sum ' which is
nearly as good as his ' cogito ', but our Senators on the contrary
like so many weather cocks, the more they change become the
more changeable.

[1] John James Masquerier (1778-1855), a painter of some note in England in the first
years of the nineteenth century.
[2] Robert Burns (1759-96). With Scott, Byron and others he contributed songs to a
collection of airs made by one George Thomson (1757-1851),

Ritson has just been with me in a great fury at the whole world, particularly at God Almighty and the absurd custom of printing his name in capitals, just as if the old gentleman above were to look down in a great passion and to say 'Damn you, why don't you print my name with proper respect in capitals'. He is however very nearly convinced of the existence of ghosts, and admits that some damned malicious being pesters his chamber by knocking at his inner door in such a frightful stile all the night over for the mere purpose of preventing him from sleeping, and then staring at him with such ghastly faces.

John Leyden to Richard Heber
Portsmouth. (probably) 1 April 1803

Here I am arrived in Portsmouth and for the first time in my life have acquired an accurate idea of a garrison town, Gibraltar, for instance, though probably Bergen-op-Zoom would have been a better example, for here are neither rocks nor precipices nor hills nor vallies, except trenches and ramparts, besides which there is a great abundance of half-moon ravelins, hornworks and covered ways.

Apropos of horn works and covered ways, the men are all rogues and the women whores and the town itself is only an immense turn-pike gate pitched down on the boundaries of sea and land to take toll of all nations on the face of the earth, particularly adventurers to India. They scream out for ever like so many cormorants, for half of the prize money in the whole world is swallowed up between Portsmouth and the coast of Wapping. Pray do you know any Grecian authority for Charon having ever resided in Portsmouth, I cannot say I recollect any, but I cannot look in the face of any of the inhabitants without recollecting Lucian's dialogue between Charon and Manippus. You see the old fellow's exclamation 'pay me my fare, you scoundrel' so legibly written in every countenance. Nature writes a good bold hand here.

John Leyden to Richard Heber
Ryde, 7 April 1803

We have been on board the greater part of the day, hove early from our moorings, and from the uncertainty of the wind have been forced to bring to again. Smith and the greater part of us have returned to Ryde. We shall be aboard again at daybreak in order to pass the Needles if possible early. I fear your Strabo and Plutarch will be too late — n'importe. I have discovered today that (of) four passengers, one speaks Telinga, another Malabar, and a third Moors or Hindustani. You may congratulate me.

John Leyden to Richard Heber
12 *April* 1803

After beating up and down between the Needles and St. Helens without being able to get out to sea, we have now got a fair breeze and are just opposite Undercliffe in Wight. The pilot is just leaving us and I have only time to say that he has brought me on board the parcel with Strabo and Plutarch. I have only time to bid you adieu for he is off.

George Eyre to Richard Heber
Lyndhurst, 9 *May* 1803

Bonoparte seems like necessity and knows no law. Delays are dangerous. We may be disappointed in our object. Per contra, a sudden commencement of hostilities might involve us in peculiar difficulties. So I will conclude with Dr. Pangloss that all is for the best. A week may unfold some mysteries.[1]

Rev. John Stonard to Richard Heber
Brasted, 12 *May* 1803

I can hardly believe my eyes. I now see you talk of leaving Old England next week. I before read next month. This comes

[1] Our Ambassador left Paris on 11 May.

of your shapeless pothooks and hangers. Suppose there is Peace,
War will nab you on your journey home. Yes, you may have
the pleasure and favour, such as they are, of being introduced to
the ' petit Corse' once more, by the hands of a republican
soldier instead of a British Ambassador. It will be a righteous
retribution for your first folly.

Dr. Frodsham Hodson to Richard Heber
B.N.C. 22 May 1803

How fortunate it would be for Lords Whitworth and Hawkesbury if we could forget the ability with which Lord Grenville
instructed and Lord Malmesbury negotiated.[1] I should like to
see the patchwork pulled to pieces! But most of all I long to see
an administration whose talents and whose courage will afford
grounds for confidence.[2]

Thomas Thompson[3] to Richard Heber
Edinburgh, 17 August 1803

Scott is living at his cottage but I suspect is handling the
sword oftener than the pen.

---

[1] Lord Whitworth was British Ambassador at Paris and Lord Hawkesbury (later
Lord Liverpool) Foreign Secretary. Lord Malmesbury and Lord Grenville were in the
same position during the abortive negotiations for peace in 1796.

[2] The ministry of Addington was one of no talent. Pitt refrained from attacking, and
it operated in some degree under his tutelage. It was impossible that ministers should
remain in power with such personalities as Pitt, Fox and Grenville available. Addington
resigned in April, and Pitt was invited to form a ministry. He proposed a coalition; but
such a course proved impossible. There was no alternative but to gather round him the
nonentities of his own and Addington's group.

[3] ? Thomas Thomson (1768-1852), a close friend of Walter Scott; jurist and legal
antiquary.

A T THIS POINT it seems desirable to restate the positions of the members of the Heber family and to carry on their personal history for a few years.

Richard, now a man of thirty, was well known in the literary and academic world. He was for ever travelling, London, Yorkshire, Scotland, Shropshire, Oxford being his focal points.

At the General Election of 1806, a vacancy occurred for Oxford University. The Dean of Christ Church nominated Mr. Abbott and Richard contested the election as an independent. The influence of Christ Church and that of the government as a whole was too much for him and he was defeated but honourably so.

In the literary world his chief activity was as an enthusiastic supporter and contributor to the *Quarterley Review*. But politics and literature were as nothing compared with his passion for book collecting. Though this was the mainspring of his life, only small reference to it can appear here, mainly because mere lists of books and prices make dull reading now. But purchases of books were taking place all the time, although the war caused them to be modest compared with those that he made later in life.

Reginald was twenty-one and had just taken his degree. He spent a year in 1805-6 travelling in Scandinavia and Russia. On his return to England he was ordained and was appointed Rector of Hodnet in 1807. In 1809 he married Amelia, daughter

13

of Rev. William Shipley, Dean of St. Asaph. In 1812 he rebuilt Hodnet Rectory.

The youngest brother, Thomas Cuthbert, was only nineteen when his father died. He became a fellow of Brasenose, Oxford, and later Rector of Marton in Yorkshire and died in 1816, a bachelor, aged thirty-one. His hobbies were genealogy, heraldry, and the study of ancient church brasses.

Mary Heber and her mother lived at Hodnet Hall to begin with; later — was it due to the influx of books ? — they moved to the Vicarage at Moreton Saye, which now is a separate Parish but was then a Chapel of Ease attached to Hodnet.

*   *   *

Robert Southey to Richard Heber
Keswick, 20 February 1804

You have had so much to do with Ellis's *Specimens*[1] that there would be some propriety in my writing to you upon this subject — even if I were not disposed to do so from other motives. I think of publishing *Specimens of Modern English Poetry*[2] as a companion work to his, beginning where he leaves off and including all Poets who are dead down to the present day, that is literally dead, for those gentlemen who are only dead in the literary sense of the word must wait till they are buried before such Resurrection Men as you and I do them the honour to look after them. I shall follow his plan as closely as possible and copy the size and mode of printing. In the Preface only I must trespass over the frontier by investigating the effects produced upon our literature by the Restoration.

I have of late been very unfortunate in my books, having lost two cargos on their way from Lisbon. The one went with the *Diamond*, the other had been landed from the same packet on its last arrival, but the Captain received his mortal wound in the

---

[1] George Ellis (1753-1815), *Specimens of the Early English Poets*, first edition 1790, followed by later editions much expanded.

[2] Southey, *Specimens of the Later English Poets*, 1807.

action and I have not been able to trace them. Some were very costly books — others very scarce — and all very necessary for my immediate and main pursuit.

James Boswell to Richard Heber
London, 11 May 1804

Malone[1] told me some little time ago that the Duke of Roxburgh's library was certain to be sold and that absolute beggary would be the consequence to you, Lord Spencer and himself. It will be a mighty good sight to behold you seeking your substance chaunting your black letter ballads about the streets with dildo's and fadings, jump her and thump her like old Autolycus, but for the present you escape, as I understand the will is contested.

Nothing is talked of in this town but politics and every man stares at his neighbour and asks how this is to end. Not all the eloquence of Folkestone[2] will be sufficient to vindicate the conduct of the Grenville party[3] in my opinion. Their present attempt to annihilate the undoubted prestige of the town is grossly unconstitutional and I think will completely fail. What say you to all this in Yorkshire ?

James Boswell to Richard Heber
Undated

Late last night I received your pithy and well ordered epistle enjoining me to set off at seven o'clock and upon awakening at nine, found it impossible to comply with the request therein contained. But I have another reason for writing to you of high and various import. Mr. William Shakespeare, a famous poet of

[1] Dr. Edmund Malone (1741-1812), Editor of Shakespeare.
[2] William Pleydell-Bouverie (1779-1869), Viscount Folkestone, sixth Earl of Radnor 1828; whig politician.
[3] William Wyndham Grenville (1759-1834), Baron Grenville; politician; of Christ Church, Oxford; foreign secretary in Pitt's first ministry; refused office without Fox in Pitt's second ministry, 1804; chief minister, 1806-7, and abolished the slave trade; resigned because the King would not accept his advice to open commissions in the army and navy to Roman Catholics; chancellor of Oxford University 1809.

our country, and who has been styled the divine and the match-less in sundry playhouse bills as Mr. Pope a writer of consider-able credit relates, hath right wittily observed that :—

> ' He that filches from me my good name
> Robs me of that which not enriches him
> But makes me poor indeed.'

To which purpose a pleasant conceit is delivered to us of a certain Quaker who being wroth at catching a dog in his pantry, made this apt and pregnant speech, ' I will not hang thee, I will not drown thee, but I will give thee a bad name.' Whereupon calling him mad, the poor dumb beast being persecuted by the younger fry, perished in extreme dolour. Now, O Jehoshophat, does not your heart smite for you deliberately writing (*litera scripta manet*) that my sentiments were now so vitiated that I was anxious to appear like a gentleman. I do most pointedly and positively deny the charge. I appeal to the whole tenor of my life and conversation to disprove the fact. Once indeed I did suffer that principle to operate when you persuaded me to dine with the shabbiest pack of Christians I ever met with. I do confess that a yellow coat or anything which would have distinguished me from my com-panions would have been very acceptable. But is this one instance to mar at once all the fair texture of my better days ?

How long stayest thou at Oxford ? When you come to town again let me know where and when we can meet, but don't let it be at seven in the morning.

Rev. John Stonard to Richard Heber
Chelsea, 18 June 1804

You do not seem to have been yet informed that in addition to young Lowther,[1] I have at the request of Mr. Pitt taken James Stanhope,[2] the youngest son of my old *friend*, Lord Stanhope, under my roof. Mr. Pitt has entirely supported him since he quitted his father's.

---

[1] ? William Lowther (1787-1872), second Earl of Lonsdale of the second creation.
[2] James Hamilton Stanhope (1788-1825).

William Herbert to Richard Heber
7 February 1805

What the Devil makes Walter Scott publish all his books at such exorbitant prices. Who is to give 25 shillings for his *Lay*[1] which I suppose is not many hundred lines ? or is there a large appendix of notes ? The advertisement gives no such hint.

Rev. Sydney Smith to Richard Heber
30 June 1805

I shall be most sincerely happy if you succeed. I will contribute my mite towards it[2] tho' these are occasions in which I sincerely regret that my mite is not a talent. I know no reason why you should not succeed except that you are fit for the office in all respects: a circumstance which furnishes a strong analogy against you; or as the Scotch have it, an*ai*logy.

Rev. John Stonard to Richard Heber
Chertsey, 25 July 1805

I cannot give you so good an account as I would wish of my canvass. I conversed with Lady Hester[3] almost two hours. She says Mr. Pitt has been so much engaged, she has not spoke to him these 5 or 6 days except at dinner in parties. Canning came in while I was there.[4] Lady Hester introduced me and my suit.

He said, 'Why canvass when you don't know there will be a vacancy ?' I observed that Windham etc. were going on as fast as possible. He did not make any reply of consequence but I think from his manner he is in our favour.

---

[1] *The Lay of the Last Minstrel* published in January.
[2] The canvass for Richard for the forthcoming election.
[3] Lady Hester Stanhope (1776-1839), niece of Pitt's and mistress of No. 10 Downing Street, 1804-6. She left England in 1810 and after much travelling settled in Lebanon.
[4] George Canning (1770-1827), statesman; treasurer of the navy in Pitt's second ministry.

Rev. Hugh Cholmondeley to Richard Heber
High Legh, 28 July 1805

After all however, is there any chance of a vacancy ? If C. Williams is to be believed Sir William Scott[1] will not get the peerage he is so anxious about. He wants to be made a Viscount to get place above his brother Lord Eldon and Government sees no occasion to give him any title at all.

Rev. Ralph Churton to Richard Heber
Middleton, 31 July 1805

The Bishop of St. Davids has given me the Archd. of St. Davids and I must go down V.D. to be instituted as soon as Mrs. Churton is about again, perhaps about the middle of September. The income is not great, about £50 per ann. and a corpse which I suppose yields a fine now and then by death or otherwise.

Rev. Hugh Cholmondeley to Richard Heber
7 September 1805

My brother sent me a note to Lady Hester Stanhope who lives you know with Mr. Pitt mentioning this business. The answer he got from her was that Mr. Pitt might be seen at such a time, but that she knew there was no thought of giving a peerage to Sir W. Scott. Cholmondeley that morning was at Lord Chatham's when Mr. Pitt came in and accordingly he mentioned the matter to him, when he expressed his astonishment that such an idea should ever have existed, that Sir W. Scott could not be spared out of the House of Commons. He at the same time gave his usual answer to such applications that he made it a rule never to interfere in any Election whatever. This was exactly the answer my Brother received from him when he communicated his intentions of standing for Cheshire, and

---

[1] Sir William Scott (1745-1836) M.P. for Oxford University : did not get a Peerage till 1821. His younger brother John (1751-1838), cr. Lord Eldon in 1799 and Earl of Eldon in 1821 : Lord Chancellor, 1801-6 and 1807-27.

Cholmondeley will not believe he is friendly to you, but that if he were to incline to anyone, it would be to Dickinson.

Archdeacon Ralph Churton to Richard Heber
Middleton, 12 September 1805

I am glad you had a peep at Boulogne and the camp before the Gasconaders trooped off.[1] They will never touch our shore, I ween, nor attempt it, but it is well and necessary to be prepared.

James Boswell to Richard Heber
16 September 1805

You make a mighty good story of your excursion but it won't do, by the Lord. I know you. When a man becomes a Captain in Shropshire and a Colonel in Yorkshire at the same time for reasons sufficiently obvious we know very well he would scarcely go to see Boulogne before the encampment broke up, excepting at Spring Gardens.

I met Sir J. B. Burgess at Lewes. He and Cumberland are writing in concert an Epic Poem ! ! ![2] In order not to take the publick in, they are to publish it by degrees, one book at a time. Could O'Keefe[3] go beyond all this ?

Dr. Frodsham Hodson to Richard Heber
Liverpool, 12 October 1805

I need not tell you how happy I always am to see you when we meet but as *matters now are*, I would much rather forego the pleasure of seeing you at all than see you in Oxford. Every man has his incorrigible point and this seems to be yours. And yet you cannot be ignorant what a handle has been made of your lingering

---

[1] Napoleon broke up the Boulogne encampment on 29 August.
[2] Sir James Bland Burges (1752-1834), politician, under-secretary of state; in collaboration with the dramatist Cumberland, wrote *The Exodiad*, 1807-8.
[3] John O'Keeffe (1747-1842), a prolific dramatist whose *Wild Oats* is still performed.

in Oxford after Commemoration. Even the underlings have got hold of it and affect to shake their heads and regret it. The fact certainly is that it has given real offense to some, and that others pretend to share the same feelings. You must therefore keep away !

Dr. Frodshaw Hodson to Richard Heber
Liverpool, 19 October 1805

You don't suppose that I subscribe to the propriety of your banishment from the University — far otherwise. I think it is a damnable doctrine and position, but private opinion must yield to established custom and sometimes to unreasonable prejudice. But when Cooke the Bookseller could assert here that Mr. Heber had injured his cause by continuing in College, it must convince you that now at least no caution is superfluous.

Prenez garde donc ! Amen.

John Leyden to Richard Heber
Pooloo Penang, 24 October 1805

About a month ago I was snug in Travancore, whither I had descended from Mysore after having been fairly driven out of that strong country by four very powerful foes, liver, spleen, bloody flux and jungle fever which all the world knows is cousin-germain to the Egyptian and Yellow fever. I was not so fortunate as to obtain much respite in Malabar for which reason I broke up (to use a martial phrase) from before Quilon and getting aboard a Massilla brig, the horrors of which greatly surpass those of Charon's skiff, after a most tedious voyage arrived in Penang so feeble and exhausted that if I had not naturally a great deal of life in me, I should be strongly tempted to despair. You cannot conceive in what a horrible bilious exhausted and lethargic state I write. I was given up for the 5th time three weeks before leaving Malabar.

If I but live a few years longer even with the liver, I dare now say boldly that in Orientals I shall be *nemini secundus*. Make my respects kindly to Drs. Parr[1] and White,[2] Winstanley[3] and Ford[4] and assure them how happy I shall be to aid them in any of their enquiries in any branch of Orientals. I forgot however that all the while you may not have learned with what languages I can claim acquaintance. I shall just say that before my last attack of fever in August, I had offered the Madras Government to furnish them with a grammar and dictionary in 2 vols. 4to. in the course of a year in any of their 4 languages, viz. Tamul, Malayalam, Talinga or Canara. I specified particularly the last of which there are not 3 individuals in the country that have the least knowledge and I offered to see these 2 vols. through the press without charging Government a single favour for composition or correction, only declining to take the risk of publication on my own shoulders. To this I received no answer — never expect any.

Lord Cornwallis is dead of the dropsy in the chest on the 5th of this month. The Wynand is totally reduced as is Travancore which was the most formidable rebellion in the Peninsular and expecting a French co-operation too, but defeated by the abilities of the Resident.

We shall have no Mahratta peace without hard fighting, indeed it is dubious whether the recall of Wellesley[5] which has given new life to all the native princes will not ruin us utterly in India.

I was very nearly taken by the French in my voyage from Malabar to Penang.

I constructed during my voyage a pretty curious vocabulary of the Maldivian languages which has hitherto escaped all investigation.

[1] Samuel Parr (1747-1825), scholar, authority in the Latin language; book-collector; whig; a Cambridge man.
[2] Joseph White (1745-1814), Wadham College, Laudian Professor of Arabic 1775-1814.
[3] Thomas Winstanley (1749-1823), Brasenose College, Laudian Professor of Arabic from 1814.
[4] James Ford (1779-1850), Trinity College, Oxford.
[5] Richard Wellesley (1760-1842), first Marquis Wellesley, resigned from the governor-generalship of India in 1805. He had made the British an imperial power, and in so doing had incurred the hostility of his masters the East India company. Lord Cornwallis (1738-1805) replaced him, but died the same year.

The danger of French intervention in India was at this time as seriously regarded as that of Russian later, and it was partly this consideration that induced the wars and disturbance which marked the governorship of Wellesley.

John Leyden to Walter Scott
Pooloo Penang, 24 November 1805

My dear Friend,

I conjure you by the Great God who stood 260 million years
between heaven and earth and whose body is as resplendent as a
diamond, by the most holy and powerful Devil who performed
penance for ten millions of years in the furnace of fire-sacrifice
standing on the crown of his head on the point of a spear till his
soul was as white as a skinned potato, by the self-moving quoit
which administers justice by cutting of the head of all offenders
and by the prayers of the enchanted saw which of its own accord
divides the ribs from the backbone of those who are devoid of
pity and compassion and by what I dread infinitely more than
all these put together, I conjure you by the liver and the spleen
and the flux and the fever who have embraced me most fraternally
these fifteen months, in short I conjure you by all things dead or
alive to write to me if it were only to tell me how you are and
what you are doing.

I have written so often and sent such parcels to you and Heber
that I have now given up all hope and prepared myself a bath
of lime-juice. If I die of this bout, I have ordered myself to be
scalped and the scalp to be sent to be hung up in your cottage as
proof positive that you have brought down my grizzled head
with sorrow to the grave. You shall not want for a ghost, depend
on it, to grace your Gothics and I am devilish likely to make my
debut some evening at your writing table with a spring that would
do credit to Gilpin Horner himself to the utter astonishment of
Camp[1] and you.

When you see Pooloo Penang I make no doubt you will be
ready to stare your eyes out and enquire like the Captain in
Billie Taylor what wind has blown me here. Why, really, the
story is too long to tell, if I am to tell you it from the beginning,
which I shall be happy to do provided that I could only learn
what letters you have received from me. My friend Mr. Erskine
writes me from Bombay that no letters have ever been received

---

[1] Walter Scott's dog, Camp.

from me in Scotland at all. This has filled me with vexation in
the very idea. It is true there were about seven months during
which I was totally unable to sit at a table or to hold a pen and
may therefore be supposed to have held a very limited correspondence, but I have despatched numerous packets for the coast
both before and after. To be sure I have no means of ascertaining
that any of them were ever embarked.

With respect to the Cr side of the question be it known that
I have not seen the trace of a pen from Europe except a letter
which I only received about three months ago from Mr. Erskine
before he left Edinburgh, which letter being possessed of a
wandering and evil spirit performed the tour of the remotest
and unfrequented districts of Hindustan and Dekkan before
visiting me in Malabar. As I am now getting stout and able to
write which I have scarcely been for these fifteen months, I shall
set about preparing a little digest from my journals from my
arrival down to the present for the use of you and those of my
Scottish friends that recollect at this distance of time that there
ever was such a person.

I am ashamed to have written so far without enquiring for the
good the kind the sweet the dear Mrs. Scott. I am ready to cry
when I think of her. Good God what would I give — I would
swim the Annan though I don't swim any more than a stone to
have the pleasure of drinking tea with her again and astonishing
her teapot.

Apropos of swimming, I have had some little adventures in
that line, which are in my opinion very little inferior to those
of the Witch of Endor or any witch of all of them that ever
crossed the sea in an eggshell or a sieve. I was one day sent to a
great distance to take charge of a sick officer who had been seized
with jungle fever in the depths of one of the vast forests and
wildernesses of Mysore: after travelling for two days as fast as
horse and men could carry me, I arrived at one o'clock in the
morning at the bank of a large river in the midst of a forest.
The river was in flood and roared out terribly and seemed very
rapid. I sent in a palinquin boy that could swim and he presently
got out of his depth. At a little distance stood a village within

these three years notorious for being a nest of robbers. I with great difficulty knocked up some of the villagers who were nearly as much afraid as Christie's Will at the visit of a Sirdar. After a great deal of discussion in Canara and Hindustani, in order to induce them to show me a ford or make a raft to cross the water on, three of them at last undertook to convey me over alone. I got into a large brass kettle with three ears and sat down in the bottom of it, balancing myself with great accuracy; each of the three swimmers laid hold of one of the ears and then we swam round and round in a series of circles till we reached the opposite bank. Had it been light I should have been quite giddy. Now did you ever hear a more apocryphal story in your life ? and yet it is merely fact. I have only to add that after crossing the river, I found myself in a wilder jungle than ever and was dogged by a monstrous large tiger for nearly three miles. He seemed as large as an ass.

But pray my dear Mrs. Scott lay aside that pretty unbelieving face of yours, there are other swimmers in these lands besides your humble servant. What do you think for instance of your brother as a swimmer ? I am obliged to speak of him from hearsay, having never been able to get within a hundred miles of him, though I have had many invitations and a good deal of correspondence. I sent him the Minstrelsy soon after my arrival. Now with respect to your brother, he is a great swimmer in Tanks and all that and I find in my medical pocket book a little bit of a memorandum in these words. Mem. It is not everybody's skull that a crocodile can crack. Charles Carpenter Esq. Salem is accommodated with one these head pieces of proof. The fact is that Mr. Carpenter is probably the only person alive whose noddle escaped scot-free from the lanthorn jaws of an alligator and that after being dragged by it to the bottom of a pond. I wrote to congratulate him on his marriage just before I left Malabar.

And now my dear Madam after I have told you all these wonders tell me in return how Earl Walter is and the young lady who did not use to think me quite a raw hind, head and bloody bones, as all children great and small have resolved to do. I can tell you the imps of India will not come near me, one of them. In short, they are very little better than their brothers, poor dears, the Terrestial Celestials here who have neither got legs nor arms for any useful purpose as you have in Scotland.

I could run on long enough, but you see Camp insists on being taken notice and is determined in shaking hands with me. Well God bless you all, I wish I could pay you a morning visit for I have no idea of leaving India this long and many a day.

Besides I must tell you of the collection of Indian arms and armour that I have made to illustrate the Cottage with, and which I am greatly distressed how to have sent, for there are paper shields and wicker shields and shields of tortoiseshell and a polygar spear 18 feet long and a Nair bow eight feet high which might have served Robin Hood himself and there is an immense sword six feet long which when once set a-going, goes like a sword-mill and cuts you out a line through the enemy fourteen feet broad over which you may drive a corn waggon, but the management of it requires such skipping and so much agility that there will be no fun at all except I were present to show you the performance of it at which I was very dextrous before I had the liver. N.B. — This sword is cross-barred in the handle. Besides there are Creeses waved and plain and poisoned, and polygar daggers for forward foining: and Nair knives that form an intermediate breed between a coal-axe and a tomahawk and a sword which belonged to Jungle Moottoo the invulnerable Massilla chief who cut his way through a battalion of Sepoys single-handed after being half roasted in a house which was burnt over his head. Moreover there is the skin of a very bloody minded royal tiger and that of a leopard.

I am quite delighted with India and if I could fairly recover my health which is no easy (matter) after fifteen months during which I have been five times given up for good and all by the physicians, I should have very little inclination to revisit Europe in a hurry. When I left Mysore and when I departed from Malabar for the purpose of making a voyage by sea, I had been thoroughly well assured by the most experienced of our physicians that I had not the least chance of recovering on any land in India and when I left Malabar for Pooloo Penang I was again strongly urged to visit Europe, but this I positively refused and since my arrival in the island three weeks ago I have recovered vastly.

I found Mr. Dundas and the new establishment among whom I discovered a brother of the peerless blade. I have met with the utmost attention from Mr. Dundas and all of them who form a little Scottish colony here. Mr. Dundas, whose books are not arrived, told me of your welfare but was unable to furnish me either with the 3rd vol of the *Minstrelsy* or with *Sir Tristram*,[1] but fortunately Miss Wedderburne had got the *Lay of the Last Minstrel* and ten numbers of the *Edinburgh Review*, perilous combustible stuff all of it. I descried your hand in an instant and am particularly delighted with the review of Thornton's *Sporting Tour*. I am quite pleased with the *Lay of the Last Minstrel* and have no doubt it will prove a very general favourite. The *Review* I must tell you has filled all India with horror and stifled in embryo more publications than you can readily guess. We are astonished here that the authors have not long ago been formally confuted by rapier and pistol. For my own part, as it betrayed symptoms of hostility in the review of the *Minstrelsy* when I was yet in London, I have sworn on a second attack to serve it as the Caliph Walid served the Koran by sticking it upon a Malay spear and riddling it full of holes with pistol bullets. ' Dost thou ' said the Caliph ' rebuke every rebellious perverse person ? Behold I am that rebellious perverse person. When thou appearest before thy Lord on the day of Resurrection say — O Lord, Al Walid has torn me thus.'

I forgot whether you call in the last volume of the *Minstrelsy* the passage of Froissart which mentions the Emperor of the Turks by the name of Lamorabaquyn, this strange term is Al-Ameer-Abka-Khan, the Emir Abka Khan. Abka Khan is an old Turkish or Tartar title which was afterwards assumed by the Sultan of Iconium. I likewise observe in Godwin's Chaucer which Mrs. Dundas has given me perusal of, an Oriental allusion:

' I am till God me better minde sende
At Dulcarnon, right at my wittes ende.'
— *Troilus* and *Cressida*.

[1] *Sir Tristram, an historical romance*, ed. Scott, 1804.

Dulcarnein the two horned is an Arabic title always given to
Alexander the Great and the circumstance of his being at his
wits' end forms a long chapter in Ferdasi.   It ought therefore to
be printed *as* Dulcarnon.

In spite of all my illness and jungle service, none of which are
remarkably convenient for study, I will yield to no person whatever in the acquisition of Indian languages during the same space
of time, not even to Sir William Jones himself. Were I to mention
to you the names of the languages in which I should not hesitate
to pass an examination, without suggesting that they are several
of them rather to be considered as dialects than as original languages, you would think (me) either mad or telling you more than
the fact. In short I am perfectly at home in all the languages of
the Peninsula and shall soon convince you and everybody else
thoroughly of this point, for as the Psalmist sings :
   ' Moab is my washpot, and my shoe I'll over Edom throw
   And o'er the land of Palestine I will in triumph go.'
Before leaving Malabar I was urged to communicate some
Alphabets and Vocabularies to Mr. Carey[1] the Sanscrit professor
(they were of the Uriya language which is spoken at Ganjam and
Cuttack and which is the only language in the Madras territories
that I have not formed a Grammar and Dictionary of). I told the
Bengal agent that the Uriya language was my own right and
property and that I would not yield it unless by force of arms
to any man of Christendom, much less to a missionary. I shall
soon be ready to attack Chinese having already made good progress in Sanscrit. 'Gilead is mine by right, Manasseh mine shall
be.' But I have acquired a superior knowledge of Indian literature
manners mythology religion and laws to any man in the Madras
Presidency very decidedly and by transcribing, (1st) the Lada
Lippee inscriptions of Mysore and Carnatic which are ancient
Tamal: (2nd) the Jaina inscriptions of Mavalipoorum which are
ancient Canara and (3rd) the famous brazen tablets of the Cochin
Jews which are ancient Malayalam, none of which had ever been
translated before, have established my reputation as an Orientalist

---

[1] William Carey (1761-1834), orientalist and missionary; professor of Sanskrit at
Fort William College.

beyond all contradiction. Before I set off for Bengal I shall have acquired the Malay which is childishly easy and made some progress in Pali Siami, and Birman and then there will not be a language from the point of the promontory of Malabar to that of Malacca, the dialect of Bengal itself excepted, of which I shall not possess a respectable knowledge. God grant me only a few years of health and none of my Scottish friends shall need to be ashamed of me.

If you meet any of Col. Malcolm's[1] friends and relations I shall be delighted if you can show them any attention. The Colonel came from Bengal to Mysore with General Wellesley[2] when I was confined there and hearing I was a Border man instantly came and called without ceremony and we were perfectly acquainted in the course of five minutes. He has always acted as a true and steady friend and my illness alone has prevented me from being able to avail myself of it hitherto.

Rev. Hugh Cholmondeley to Richard Heber
London, 14 December 1805

I find you have written to my brother whose letter of application was forwarded to Mr. Pitt at Bath by Lord Chatham last Monday accompanied by one in my favour to Pitt from Lord C. I dare not venture to hope though I certainly have a chance. Pitt will receive the letter the same day the Dean died.[3]

Rev. Hugh Cholmondeley to Richard Heber
B.N.C., 18 December 1805

Thank you heartily for all your exertions. Indeed my friends have been wonderfully zealous, and Cholmondeley has most fully done his duty. The Dean's death was known to Parker[4]

[1] John Malcolm (1769-1833), Indian administrator and diplomatist; K.C.B. 1815; vigorously pursued a policy of expansion in India.
[2] Sir Arthur Wellesley (1769-1852) the victor of Assaye, 1803 : later to become the Duke of Wellington.
[3] The Dean of Chester died on 10 December 1805.
[4] Thomas Parker of Astle, Cheshire (vide page 46).

in Chester on Friday last. He instantly sent off an Express to Cholmondeley which on Saturday afternoon found him just returned from a capital run at Belvoir. He instantly set out in a hack-chaise for town where about 12 o'clock on Sunday he arrived at Drummond's. After some consultation about 2 o'clock he started again for Bath from whence I this morning have received the following letter :—

Bath, Monday

My dear Hugh,

I have this moment left Mr. Pitt, he told me the Grosvenors,[1] J. R. Mill and Leycester had apply'd, but allowed no promise had as yet been given. I spoke to him like a man and a relation,[2] not as a petitioner and left him with an assurance that he would do all in his power to arrange matters so as to serve you and not affront them. I may be sanguine but my opinion is you have a good chance. Of this I am certain, had I not seen him, nothing would have been done.

Yrs affect
Thomas Cholmondeley

Rev. John Stonard to Richard Heber
Chertsey, 21 January 1806

Poor dear Pitt is I am afraid very bad, very bad indeed. They ought to have prevailed on him to resign when they found him not gaining ground at Bath. Anxiety is the most formidable enemy in the world to a gouty constitution. In the event of his decease, I apprehend the Grenvilles and Fox must come in. There does not seem to be anybody to whom the King can turn, but then the one doubtless will not come in without the other. Indeed the aspect of public (affairs) is extremely discouraging both at home and abroad. There is no conjecturing what is to

---

[1] The family of the first Earl Grosvenor (1731-1802) was of great authority in Chester and Cheshire.

[2] He was Pitt's second cousin.

come to pass. I am extremely grieved for the poor young Stanhopes[1] who will be left without a protector on Mr. Pitt's death. To Lady Hester in particular it will be a most dreadful blow. Instead of being mistress of the Prime Minister's house, she must become dependant on some cool-faced friend or relation for protection. Lord Mahon is dreadfully off at present, but he had some good prospects at a short distance while Mr. Pitt continued in office. Charles I think is the best off of the family. But poor James will have to encounter a sad reverse.

George Eyre to Richard Heber
Lyndhurst, 23 January 1806

· Who will touch the lyre now Pitt is gone ? ![2] O what a fall was there my countrymen ! He stood like the centre pillar in the old Chapter House, the whole edifice depending on it. That being broken down, the parts surrounding will crumble into dust. I feel anxious for the event. Will the opposition succeed at once — or will it be attempted to patch up a Ministry ?

Rev. John Stonard to Richard Heber
Chertsey, 3 February 1806

I ought to have answered your letter before but I have been waiting in the hope of hearing from Stanhope conceiving that

---

[1] Charles Stanhope, the third earl, had by his first wife three daughters of whom Lady Hester Stanhope was the eldest, and by his second wife three sons as follows: Philip Henry, Lord Mahon (1781-1855), the fourth earl; Charles (1785-1809), killed at Corunna; and James (1788-1825), the correspondent of Richard Heber and the pupil of Stonard.

[2] Pitt died 23 January.

> Hadst thou but lived, though stripp'd of power,
> A watchman on the lonely tower,
> Thy thrilling trump had roused the land.
>
>   o   o   o
>
> Now is the stately column broke,
> The beacon-light is quench'd in smoke,
> The trumpet's silver voice is still,
> The warder silent on the hill!
>   —Walter Scott, On the death of Pitt.

he might give me some further information on circumstances which would so much interest you. I saw him the day you left us having met him just set out on his way to town with Canning in his carriage. He got out, came to me and in my post-chaise, followed Canning's chariot to Egham. I remember less of his conversation than I could have imagined to be possible. But it was not very well connected on his part and tho' I was very attentive, yet my mind being full of so many things, some parts of what he said perhaps escaped my hearing and others made little impression on my memory. He certainly was more collected than I expected to find him and spoke tho with all feeling yet with proper firmness of the awful and distressing circumstances of the preceding days.

The physicians were I think blameably late in communicating to Mr. Pitt's friends their apprehensions of danger, especially as it does not appear that he entertained any such till told. He made a will as you have seen in the Papers and attempted at first to write it himself, but finding his strength insufficient, it was done by the Bishop of Lincoln. He did not, as the Papers have stated, receive the Sacrament. It was offered but he declined it, I forget with what expressions or for what reason exactly, but to the best of my recollection because he could not sufficiently abstract his thoughts from the political affairs on which they were so much employed. Neither did Lord Chatham as the Papers have said see him on Wednesday. He came but was not admitted, and there are reasons for thinking it as well that he was not, but that's all mum. Indeed it had been resolved that he should not see any of the family, but while the doctors were at dinner, Lady Hester stole out to him. She knelt down at his side and took his hand. He was sensible of it and spoke to her. She asked his Blessing which he gave her in the most affectionate and paternal manner, and then (I think) he advised her to leave him. He enquired for her afterwards, but recollecting her great affection for him, he thought it better that she should not undergo the trial of seeing him again. Stanhope saw him soon after Lady Hester had left him and Mr. Pitt knew and spoke to him, but I do not remember what he said: unless it was to him (for I cannot ac curatelyrecollect whether it was as speaking *to* him or afterwards *of* him) that he expressed the wish that he should return to me, a wish which you may be sure I never can forget. He was at several times and for a good while together delirious, talking of Dispatches and continental politics and expressing his thoughts tho' not irrationally aloud.

The following is an undated unaddressed fragment presumably written by Lady Hester Stanhope

Finding that I must send early tomorrow to my friend Townshend yr neighbour I have put off conveying the intelligence I promised you by the penny post.

Mr. Pitt left Town for Bath on 7th December and returned the 11th of January. He arrived at Putney the evening of that day accompanied by Charles and Sir Walter.

Tho' nothing hurts and enrages me so much as persons claiming Mr. P's friendship who neither possessed nor desired it, I am more than anxious that those he really loved should be known by the world to have enjoyed so great a happiness, as it ought to make them stand high in the estimation of every honest man. Might it not be as well to particularly mention the affectionate manner he received Lord Wellesley on his return from India (the Tuesday he saw Lord Chatham) and to add that the Marquis was one of his oldest and dearest friends. As this is really fact, for whenever I complained about the fools, he used to say, 'Have patience, Wellesley is coming home, in him you will (find) all the talent and spirit you can desire.'

If Canning is mentioned in the sheet you did not bring, it may be fairly said Mr. P. loved him as his own child, for when he first introduced him to me, he said, 'You must love him like a brother,' and I am sure I have obey'd.

Yrs sincerely

H. L. S.

Richard Heber to his step-mother, Mrs. Reginald Heber
1806

All the difficulties between the King and the new Ministry are at length said to be settled.[1] The last remaining was about the Duke of York who is now to be subject to the control of Government, very properly in my opinion.

Rev. Hugh Cholmondeley (now Dean of Chester) to Richard Heber
B.N.C., 16 March 1806

I never pass an afternoon in the Common Room without hearing something said about your promise of presenting a set of curtains. We are going to lay a new floor this summer and I really wish for your own credit that you would give the necessary orders for the curtains.

I have a party of 16 to dine with me tomorrow in the Common Room consisting of all the Resident fellows, Masters, etc. upon my arriving at the dignity of B.D. I shall give them as good a dinner as can be got and the best wines I have.

Dr. Frodsham Hodson to Richard Heber
Oxford, 26 October 1806

It is the decided opinion of your friends that you should be in Town infusing into your friends there all the activity which your presence will naturally give. But for God's sake don't come through Oxford ! Go from Chester or from Birmingham thro' country. So says your Committee and *obey*.

Dr. Frodsham Hodson to Richard Heber
B.N.C., 6 November 1806

Scott[2]	.. 651
Abbot[3]	.. 404
Heber	.. 275

[1] Attempts to form a new ministry showed again that personal animosities and party loyalties made impossible a broad-bottom administration. Grenville refused office. Again Portland was forced to take the lead, with Canning and Castlereagh under him. The cabinet itself was divided, and the ministry cannot be described as a happy or united one.

[2] Sir William Scott, see note on p. 198

[3] Charles Abbot (1757-1829), Speaker of the House and later Lord Colchester.

Your minority is glorious and if the numbers were dissected, I apprehend that in the University yours will be equal to Mr. Abbot's. As for the objection which was taken to his eligibility, Richardson seems to think there is nothing in it and if there were, you would not like to represent the University with only a minority of votes. I would have you in person or by letter, as you judge best, inform Mr. A. that you know not whether there be any force in the objection sufficient to give him any anxiety, but if there be, you are happy at once to remove it by assuring him that no petition shall as far as your influence intends be presented against his return.

Write me and tell me that you glory in the testimony thus given to the world of what personal influence can do.

Archdeacon Ralph Churton to Richard Heber
Middleton, 7 November 1806

You have hear of the glorious 275 a number that would have carried almost every election however hardly contested in any time till the present, when Royal Dukes and Dukes not Royal, Committees of the Treasury, E. India Company and that great body of Ch. Ch. overpowered us.

Dr. Edward Copleston[1] to Richard Heber
Oriel, 16 November 1806

It is a great consolation to me as well as to the rest of your friends to find that our endeavours have not been altogether fruitless. The numbers in the poll-book are no test of the feelings of this place. They are a powerful test of the activity the skill and the numerous and overbearing connections of our opponents.

Now with regard to your own appearance here. It is impossible

---

[1] Edward Copleston (1776-1849), fellow of Oriel College, professor of poetry; provost of Oriel 1814, bishop of Llandaff 1828. Known as a tory of the Pitt and Canning school — that is, as a liberal tory. Wrote on pauperism, the burning social question of the day, in the 1820s, when the declining value of money was reducing the value of real wages; he advocated a stable currency which he thought could best be attained by the resumption of cash payments. He favoured the admission of dissenters to universities and in the Lords, as a bishop, supported the bill for removing Roman Catholic disabilities.

that your desire of coming can be greater than ours to see you and I rejoice that the prospect is so near. But to speak freely with you, I conceive it would be highly improper for you to pay us a visit till the successful candidates have paid theirs. I am sure the habits and prejudices of the place would revolt at it.

Rev. John Stonard to Richard Heber
Chertsey, 17 November 1806

I am very angry with you for giving up to the nasty little lickspittle of the Duke of M.[1] I am sure you might have hoisted him out. You're just like the poor Emperor Francis when he made peace after losing the Battle of Austerlitz, just when he might have got the victory.

Rev. John Stonard to Richard Heber
Chertsey, 6 December 1806

I want very much to see the Vice-C's list of the voters for O.U. The numbers were lost by the villainy of the Dean of Ch. Ch. is prodigious. I wish I were a member of the Univ. I would certainly petition though you will not. All that I can say is that if Abbot is not expelled, the Univ. is turned into a dirty rotten Minister's borough. I hate to think of the little nasty stinking Imp, a mere cast-off tool of the Duke of M, the refuse of the offscourings of Woodstock.

Rev. Sydney Smith to Richard Heber
9 March 1807

I would have called upon the Bard but I understand you in general forbid morning visits, so pray set that to rights between Mr. Reginald and me, who by the way seems to be a very good fellow, a coarse appellative but means in my dictionary so many

[1] George Spencer (1766-1840), a graduate of Christ Church and from 1804 to 1806 a lord of the treasury, succeeded his father as fifth Duke of Marlborough in 1817 and governed the political activities of the family for many years before that time.

excellent things that I am sure neither you nor he would be affronted if I were to interpret it.

Rev. Sydney Smith to Richard Heber
No date

It occurs to me upon more mature deliberation and it did not occur to me at the time our rapid compact was formed, that to rush thus upon Stodart & Co. in consequence of this well meant and injudicious invitation of the former, will not be quite the thing and I believe you will think so too. It must have been a Bacchanal expansion of the heart and it is no bad rule in general to forget every invitation made after 10 o'clock as they are most commonly forgot by the inviter.

Robert Southey to Richard Heber
Keswick. 14 March 1807

You have had ere this my unhappy *Specimens*, hurried at last into the world after three years delay, in such haste that the sheets were never sent to me for revisal and so the cancels are to be made after the book is published. It is needless to say how much I am provoked with the printer for his intolerable blunders, how much with Bedford for his manifold offences, both of omission and commission and how much more with myself for trusting either the one or the other. If ever the book should reach a second edition (for which in my conscience I am afraid it is too bad) it shall assume a very different appearance. One half of the *Specimens* shall be omitted to make room for numberless authors now left out. I will insert what he has unaccountably thought proper to strike out and strike out what he has with as little propriety inserted. For if he had not undone much which I had done and done much which I designed to leave undone, the book would have been far better than it is. I never intended that he should be Inquisatorial Censor over me. This however is only said to you that you may not suppose me more in fault than is really the case. The book must take its chance in the world, as if all its sins

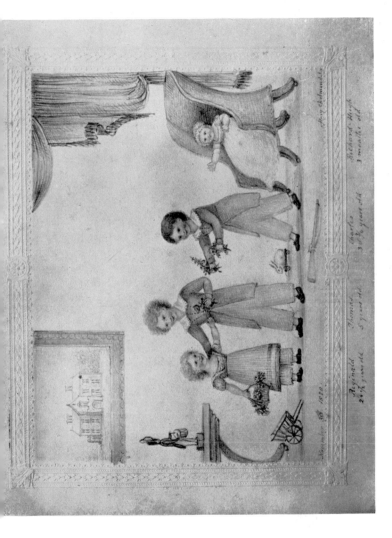

V THE CHOLMONDELEY CHILDREN IN 1828

This picture was drawn by their mother Mary (plate iv), and has a view of Hodnet Rectory, where they were living.

MARY HEBER—'MAMA'

HER HUSBAND—'PAPA'
REV. REGINALD HEBER

VI SILHOUETTES OF THE HEBER FAMILY
Artist unknown.

MARY, DAUGHTER OF

REV. REGINALD HEBER

HER HUSBAND

REV. CHARLES

CHOLMONDELEY

By courtesy of Brig. Heber-Percy of Hodnet.

VII RICHARD HEBER

of Hodnet and Marton

1774-1833.

The book collector, when middle-aged.

rested upon my head. I should not have written to you about this but having occasion to write the subject was uppermost and so out it came.

I have a strong desire to edit *Morte d'Arthur* one of these days. Will you secure a copy for me when one falls in your way, if the price be not beyond all reason.

My *Chronicle of the Cid* will extend to a quarto volume and supply the place of all introductory matter to the History of Portugal by giving a compleat picture of the heroic age of Spain — that is of the whole peninsula. A very curious work it will be and will I am confident please you well. It is wrongly announced as a translation, the *Chronica del Cid* is the basis but everything not relating to the subject is thrown out and everything which does relate to it and can be collected from other sound authority is put in.[1]

Archdeacon Ralph Churton to Richard Heber
Middleton. 28 October 1807

I'd found out the comet before we had heard of it; but it is not to be compared with one I saw when I was a schoolboy at Malpas near 40 years ago, with a tail of solid flame as long as my arm. This has only a vapoury tail and will probably not be better, as I cannot but think he is certainly going further from the sun, mounting higher eastward every night.

Robert Southey to Richard Heber
Keswick, 22 December 1807

Let me now tell you what I purpose doing to *Morte d'Arthur*. My preliminary matter will take in a wide range. I shall examine the old question of the origin of romance with the hope of saying something new about it — and I shall prove that it was in no instance intended to outrage probability, till it got into the hands

---

[1] Southey published a reprint of Malory's *Morte D'Arthur* in 1817, *The Cid* in 1808 and the *History of Brazil* (to which he refers in the next letter) in 1810-19.

of the Italian poets. With respect to its effects on society, a good many facts have fallen in my way, my reading lying in a track which has been little beaten.

Walter Scott's plan was to print a small 4to and give wooden cuts of costume. To this I wish to persuade the publishers, it is not likely they will object, but your opinion will have weight with them. No one knows the public taste better than Scott. I shall be able to make out the subject of Costume as it is part of my plan to enter with some minuteness into the subject of armour and all its varieties. To make the book really handsome, there should be a half-title with a vignette to every book. Engraving on copper is better than on wood and has the great advantage that it is more easily procurable, there being more artists.

I have many things on hand; the *Chronicle of the Cid* will be likely to please you — it is the most curious piece of chivalrous history in existence and I have rendered it to my own satisfaction. Next will come the *History of Brazil*.

Rev. Thomas Smyth to Richard Heber
20 January 1808

Marmion is finished. YOU will be very glad to see it, in seven or eight days it will be published.[1]

Rev. Thomas Smyth to Richard Heber
17 February 1808

Walter Scott has been very kind to me. He is in high spirits as a man who first touches land after a long voyage. *Marmion* is finished, lying on his table; on Friday it is to be published. I wish I were near you when you first open the book and could hear you roll out some of the lines which I could point out to your notice but I must say no more.

[1] The sixth Canto of *Marmion* was dedicated to Richard.

Archdeacon Ralph Churton to Richard Heber
Middleton, 17 March 1808

I saw Mr. R. and Mr. T. Heber at Oxford about a fortnight ago and was very glad of the opportunity to congratulate one as Rector of Hodnet and the other as Fellow of Brasenose.

Rev. Hugh Cholmondeley, Dean of Chester, to Richard Heber
16 April 1808

You may perhaps not object to a line conveying the information that Mr. Jacson died at Tarporley yesterday evening about five o'clock. You will not be sorry to hear that I think myself secure in succeeding him. I have not however omitted any step to ensure it. But as we know by experience of College Elections nothing can be reckoned upon till it's finally fixed. I expect next Thursday when a Chapter is to be held, will decide the business.

Rev. Hugh Cholmondeley, Dean of Chester, to Richard Heber
24 April 1808

I am happy to announce to you that on Thursday I was presented to the Living of Tarporley.

Rev. John Stonard to Richard Heber
Chertsey, 31 May 1808

I hope Purvis will not stand shilly-shallying at Cadiz; but close with what the Spaniards offer. The most generous we can give will be the most favourable. I have no doubt.[1]

---

[1] Napoleon had invaded Spain. The Spaniards had revolted. The provincial governments of Asturias and Seville had applied to the governor of Gibraltar for an alliance against the common enemy. There were French ships in the harbour of Cadiz and Purvis was there blockading them. He was not, however, by any means in charge of the negotiations; and it was difficult not to shilly-shally, because the Spaniards refused to allow British troops to land or ships to enter the harbour, lest Cadiz become another Gibraltar.—Peninsular War, 1808-14.

Archdeacon Ralph Churton to Richard Heber
Malpas, 15 July 1808

One thing I am very glad of, that I saw Mrs. Heber and Miss Heber on my way hither which eventually was the only opportunity. The gentlemen of the family more uncertain of their motions are however accessible in other places and London, Oxford or Middleton may I hope repair the disappointment of Hodnet.

I was glad to see you doubling your Library. The two rooms together will hold pretty many books — I mean what you, I suppose, would call pretty many, is perhaps more than any one house in Shropshire or any adjoining country contains. Two or three other things struck me forcilby. I hailed from far your lofty and spacious and very green fields, fringed with fine woods at the end of the promontory, a sort of landmark which told me I was going right. When I approached nearer, after eyeing the pigeon house on higher ground, the Hall with its fine trees on a bright morning, looked so delightful and so comfortable that I could not help saying to myself, ' One cannot wish it were in any other spot.'

I had no very long time in the Library, and my eyes from want of time to sleep on my journey, seemed to have ' no speculation in them '. Yet I saw a very fine work your sister is employed upon, copying a Holy Family by Reubens. And I observed a curious book ' De arte excerpendi ', which as excerping is a good deal of my employment, I tried if I could learn the art of doing what I have long done without art. But I hardly made myself master of the new method and my own plan suits my own purpose tolerably well.

Dr. Edward Copleston to Richard Heber
Beddgelert, 24 July 1808

It is but an ill return I make for the hospitality of Hodnet Hall in not giving you a line before now. But as we have been generally so hurried and tired as always to furnish me with an excuse for intending well instead of doing well.

I was much pleased with Reginald's flock on Sunday. In the evening we had the Volunteers parading before the house and had the singular advantage of seeing Thomas bearing quarterly a drawn sword looking if not speaking very fierce.

Since that, we have passed two days at Llangollen, a place which exemplifies every thing I had conceived from reading Marmontel's[1] description of his native village, especially if you stand on what they call the Green.

As we were breakfasting at Corwen, Woollcombe looked through the window with his knapsack on his back having come 13 miles that morning. In this stile he has generally travelled. We have not been so ambitious. Post-chaises and Welsh ponies have conveyed us to the wildest and most sequestered spots.

Our ascent of Snowdon rewarded us for the perseverance we displayed. Before we had been ascending half-an-hour, it began raining and during the last hour, the rain was violent and incessant, but as we approached the peak, it suddenly cleared off. The thunder was heard round and round below us and the mists driven in to the hollow side towards Capel Curig were whirled about, exhibiting a hurly-burly not unlike what one can fancy of a volcano. The immense depth of the Cauldron being marked by points of rock seen dimly in the Gulph. On the whole this agitated state of the weather, which gave us at intervals a view of every part near and distant, produced more striking scenery than a brighter day could have shewn.

Yesterday we arrived at this place and today have been hearing a Welsh sermon. After Church the majority of the Congregation with many other repaired to the brewhouse of the Inn, where a Methodist, a Wesleian as our host called him, led the way, in singing and afterwards prayed and preached. The praying was enough for us, we did not wait for the preaching. I never beheld a more melancholy sight. A decent well-dressed young man continued bellowing in the most frightful manner what they call extempore prayers, accompanied with horrid contortions of countenance, loud sobbing and violent gestures of hands and arms. And this, our host says, is the *moderate* Methodist meeting.

[1] Jean Francois Marmontel (1723-99) French novelist and dramatist.

A society of Jumpers meet at a house below near the bridge, but they do not gain much ground. For the Minister of the Parish is a very good *nice* man and indeed he seemed to us to go through the service with great decency and to preach with proper animation and even fervour. Yet all this will not do, so rapid is the progress of enthusiasm in this country. The brew-house was quite full and people were collected round the windows in deep attention.

Hitherto we have been highly gratified by the scenery of Wales. It has exceeded my expectations. Reginald or any great traveller would perhaps laught at me, but I cannot well imagine a more imposing solitude than the mountainous district round Snowdon presents. Even the Valley of Diamonds in the Arabian Nights never affected my imagination more. Still as you descend into the vallies, you find it is not absolute solitude but such is the vastness of the features of nature that the works of art shrink into insignificance and if one could check that execrable progress of improvement which has already deformed the finest counties of England, I should not despair of seeing Carnarvonshire always poor and always sublime. Audi hospes continuera opes. Now that Adam Smith[1] is so generally read, a real patriot ought to do something to counteract him.

Robert Southey to Richard Heber
Keswick. 13 *March* 1809

I know nothing of the Valencian Mariana. They edit their old historians incomparably well in Spain, but they are apt to promise more than they perform and to announce notes, dissertations and appendices which never make their appearance. This is sometimes the author's fault for dying sooner than he ought, but I am afraid it is more frequently the fault of the public. It is melancholy to observe the many excellent and important historical works of which we have only the first part, the second remaining unprinted because the first did not remunerate the publisher.

[1] Adam Smith (1723-90), author of *The Wealth of Nations*, 1776.

You will have heard that I have nearly compleated a long poem which was begun eight years ago. In all likelihood it would never have been compleated, had I not fallen in, in the course of my last year's journey, with Savage Landor.[1] He stung me to the resolution of executing those plans which I had long lain aside. I publish this poem as a last experiment; if it produce me as much ' sweet remuneration ' as the same portion of time would have earned if employed upon the lowest species of literary trade, I will then devote more time to poetry, and publish what I write. If on the contrary and as I fully and entirely expect, it merely pays the expenses of publication for the first two or three years, I shall then, as I am doing now, give only the early morning hours to this occupation, execute as many of my intended poems as that time will allow me to do and reserve them for post-humous publication. By converting them to post-obits they will at least enable me to evade the unjust laws of copy-right which will take from my family all property in my published works just when they begin to be worth anything.[2]

G. Mitford to Richard Heber
No date

Gertrude of Wyoming[3] in my opinion is a poor creature, and her whole body is not worth Marmion's little finger; and yet the famed Song of the Chiefs is very good and a few of the cantos as ' El Dorado ' for instance, but what Campbell has done with his poetic Δαιμων, I can't imagine, and oh and alas ! over the 5th and 6th cantos of the Battle of the Baltic ' and make sub-mission meet, to our King ' is like the last couplet of a poem written by one of our Suffolk weavers in imitation of Collins' *Ode to Evening* :—

> ' and in their hearts Content
> Each Man takes his Lass
> To Haverhill Fair.'

[1] Walter Savage Landor (1775-1864), author.

[2] Copyright was originally secured by Letters Patent from the Crown, or registration at the Stationers' Company. Authors first received statutory protection in 1709. Unpub-lished works were protected by Common Law. The Copyright Act of 1842 founded the modern Law, codified in 1911.

[3] Thomas Campbell (1777-1844) published *Gertrude of Wyoming* in 1809.

Edmund Malone to Richard Heber
Foley Place, 4 May 1809

The first edition of the first part of *Henry IV*, 1598, is one of the scarcest of our Shakespeare quartos; No collection possesses it but Capell's[1] and Garrick's;[2] and Garrick obtained it very latterly by a gift from a gentleman in the country. We have therefore in general been obliged to take up with the Second Edition, 1599, which however I collated with the first. That Edition also is sufficiently scarce. I was long without it but obtained it a few years ago after a short combat at Leigh's in Covent Garden at the enormous price of £10. Kimble I think was the contester. After that Steven's copy of the same edition (for he never had the other) came for sale and I believe but am not sure was bought by Kimble at a very high price in consequence of competition by the Duke of Roxburgh. If this latter statement be correct, you will not have any very powerful opponent and I conceive £7 . 9 . 6 (half-a-crown beyond seven guineas) may overtop any of the little sharking speculative booksellers who in consequence of the former high prices will hardly let it go for less. However as only the above-mentioned two copies have appeared in 30 years, you will judge for yourself how much further you would go.

The *Henry V* is of little value being the 3rd Edition, half-a guinea I should say. *Richard II* and *III* are both of them *second* editions but the first editions of each of these plays being extraordinarily rare (I have never been able to procure the Richard III 1597), I fear you will be forced to pay a good price for them, from £2 . 10 . 0 to three guineas for *Richard III* and £1 . 10 . 0 for the other as imperf. *Richard II*, 1608, it is also necessary to have because it contains the parliament scene which was suppressed in all preceding editions and as both Kimble and I have it, I imagine you will get it for 18 or 20 shillings. Nothing now remains I think but *Mid. N. Dream* and the *M. of Venice* They are printed by Roberts in 1600 and occur oftener than any others of the quartos. They are not near so valuable as the other

[1] Edward Capell (1713-81), Shakespearean commentator, bequeathed part of his library to Trinity College, Cambridge.
[2] David Garrick (1717-79), actor, poet, dramatist.

Edn of the same year, *M.N.D.* by Fisher and *M. of V.* by Heyes. I bought them many years ago for half-a-guinea each and then thought a great price; but I fear you must now give £2.2.0 or perhaps £2.10.0 for each of them.

James H. Stanhope to Richard Heber
Swansea. 27 August 1809

How splendid but how dearly bought a victory was that of Talavera.[1] I have no hopes whatever of taking Antwerp[2] and if we do it is not worth the money. When the Austrians were compelled to sign that most helot-like armistice, the ulterior object of the expedition, co-operation on the Continent was out of the question: then, had the expedition been (sent) to Bayonne to occupy the passes of the Pyrannees in the rear and Sir John Stuart's[3] force brought to a co-operate in the South, while Wellesley, Cuesta and Venegas advanced in front, we should have forced the French army to have laid down their arms before the arrival of any reinforcements, the effect of which would be much diminished by our occupying the passes. But now having 90,000 men abroad, Wellesley is in extreme distress for want of assistance and our blood is shed in vain; Stuart is compromising our honour on the coast of Baia, while the great rival of Hannibal is beseiging old hulks in the Shelt and thus a force competent to defeat any hostile army is (thrown) away and scarcely makes a paragraph in the Journals of the Continent.

[1] The battle of Talavera, 27 and 28 July 1809, was an extremely costly and much criticized action, capping a campaign sometimes described as unnecessary and rash. It was at all events a victory.
[2] The expedition to Walcheren, on the other hand, was both costly and a defeat. The object, as Stanhope says, was to invigorate the Austrians and perhaps to influence also the policy of Prussia. Embarkation began in the second week of July; on 22 July came the news of the battle of Wagram, followed by that of an armistice between the French and Austrians. The first troops landed on the 30th; it was found impossible to proceed against Antwerp; Walcheren was finally evacuated in December. There was much force in Stanhope's general criticism that the expedition was too late, but in any case the tactical difficulties of the operation are considered to have been insurmountable.
[3] Sir John Stuart commanded a small British force in Sicily, and was engaged in sideshows which carried little credit. Wellesley and the two Spanish generals were in no condition to undertake the plan lightly put forward by Stanhope.

Rev. John Stonard to Richard Heber
Staines. 25 September 1809

In what a cloud of terrific gloom is our political sky enveloped. There is no one man in the Kingdom who can stand forward as a Leader. Parliamentary influence not talent and political wisdom will perhaps predominate in the appointments and we shall have a Ministry without a head, without one whose acknowledged authority can crush their sordid dissentions and hush the jarring elements to peace[1]; like Lord Chatham[2] at a Council of War, not knowing how to decide when the military doctors disagreed.

Robert Grant to Richard Heber
Avondale, Ireland. 11 October 1809

Various are the adventures which I have met in this same island, but on the whole I am far as yet from repenting of my tour. I know not that I am the worse for having danced a jig after a fasting walk of a whole day, or for having found a pig at my bedside the next morning.

Dr. Edward Copleston to Richard Heber
Oriel. 12 November 1809

I believe I never answered a short and hasty epistle I had from you in the summer relative to the *Quarterly Review*.[3] I have read through Whitaker's *History*[4] and think it a very review-able book. But I shall never think of communicating an article to that *Review* after the treatment Kidd[5] experienced and the unmannerly rejection of Penrose's[6] article. I call it rejection, because the

---

[1] An administration under Perceval emerged in October 1809.

[2] John Pitt (1756-1835), second Earl of Chatham; commander of the land forces in the Walcheren expedition.

[3] Dr. Copleston and Heber were of the many contributors to the new *Quarterly Review* started under the editorship of Gifford (after Scott had declined it) to counteract the influence of the *Edinburgh Review*.

[4] ? John Whitaker (1735-1808), historian; the reference might be to any of several works of this author.

[5] Presumably Thomas Kidd (1770-1850), Greek scholar.

[6] Presumably John Penrose (1778-1859), clergyman and theologian.

proposal to admit it was clogged with such conditions as he would naturally refuse with disdain. Is this the way Messrs. Gifford[1] and Ireland[2] mean to procure the co-operation of Oxford ? Sooner than risk such treatment I would throw my labours into the fire or send them to the rival work notwithstanding its base calumnies against Oxford.

Dr. Edward Copleston to Richard Heber
Oriel. 23 November 1809

You are I see warmly interested in the success of the *Quarterly Review*. My anti-*Edinburgh* feelings are as strong as yours can be but I cannot say I am a great admirer of the *Quarterly*. It has many of its rival's faults — hasty and imperfect view of the book reviewed — political prejudices of a narrow kind continually interfering — and a mongeration to the false taste of the public in order that it may be a selling article. Many sheets dedicated to the review of an Austrian manifesto as a literary work are rather more than my loyalty and anti-gallicism can swallow. Upon the whole I am not over fond of their politics. As to terms I can say without any affectation that they would not have the slightest influence upon me. If I ever write, it shall not be for profit. If I review Whitaker's book, I shall give him the highest praise, but I shall point out many errors in the Latinity. At present I have other things in hand.

I believe you are wrong as to the writer of the Strabo article. I hear from more than one quarter that it is one Pillans[3] a Scotch private tutor at Eton who reviewed Hodgson's *Juvenal*.[4] I think Payne Knight[5] must be more of a gentleman than to write such trash. If you can learn anything respecting the author, particularly

---

[1] William Gifford (1756-1826), first editor of the *Quarterly Review;* critic and editor.

[2] John Ireland (1761-1842), friend and supporter of Gifford of the *Quarterly*, dean of Westminster 1815, rector of Islip 1816-1835.

[3] James Pillans (1778-1864), Scottish educational reformer ; professor of ' humanity and laws ' in Edinburgh University 1820-63.

[4] Francis Hodgson (1781-1852), fellow of King's College, Cambridge ; later provost of Eton ; *The Satires of Juvenal*, 1807.

[5] Richard Payne Knight (1750-1824), authority on ancient art, vice-president of the Society of Antiquaries.

whether Jeffrey[1] himself had any hand in it, I should be glad to be informed. I feel a strong interest in the promised flagellation of the scurrilous foul-mouthed calumniator.

Dr. Edward Copleston to Richard Heber
Oriel. 28 November 1809

That Penrose's treatment is very discouraging I still think and I cannot agree with you that Oxford has shewn itself indifferent to the *Quarterly Review*. So indignant did I feel that I had determined thro' Ward[2] to send some communications to the *Edinburgh*. But the infamous libel in the last number restrained me and I think we must declare open war against them.

The vindication of Oxford[3] will run out to a greater length than I at first proposed. The world ought to be set right in a serious way as to the nature and system of our studies. I am convinced that as things are now managed, Oxford is the most efficient University in the world.

Archdeacon Ralph Churton to Richard Heber
Middleton. 21 December 1809

Two reports in Oxford gave me much concern on your account. A gentleman said ' I am told Mr. Heber is an illumine, (perhaps I mis-spell the execrable word) is it true ? ' This, though I was sorry to hear the surmise of such a thing, I could readily repel with a prompt denial that there was any foundation at all for the charge. The other was an alleged fact of which I was totally ignorant; but it was said you attended and assisted Lord Grenville's committee in town.[4] If this was so ' infectum fieri nequit ', but if it was not so, I shall be very glad to be able to

---

1 Francis Jeffrey (1773-1850), Lord Jeffrey ; Scottish judge and critic ; helped to found the *Edinburgh Review* in 1802, edited it 1803-29, and made it decidedly whig. ' An impartial and acute critic '.

2 Presumably John William Ward (1781-1833), first Earl of Dudley and fourth Viscount Dudley and Ward; of Oriel College; politician, scholar; contributor to the *Quarterly*, friend of Copleston.

3 Copleston, *A reply [and a second and third reply] to the calumnies of the* Edinburgh Review *against Oxford*.

4 Lord Grenville was elected Chancellor of Oxford University on 14 November.

contradict it, if I should hear it again, as the report may be of disservice to you. But indeed — that most portentious election has so staggered and confounded all hopes and prospects, that there is no knowing what may be for and what against any man; only our duty, thank God is the same as ever, to adorn and defend the University, the Church and State by honourable and prudent Christian conduct.

After a full week of increasing distress, such as I never before felt in all my life, I am beginning D.G. and only beginning to recover a very small degree of tranquility. From our public enemies, we have V.D. nothing to fear. From ourselves, there is I fear everything to dread; this disastrous election may very probably be the beginning of mischief and I shall not wonder if you and even I, if we are permitted to live the usual term, live to see the day when there may be no University no Church and no State in this envied land. Do not fancy my fears Utopian: Heaven grant they may be so! but Rev. xi 7[1] etc. whatever may be the true import or time of it, must be accomplished; and assured as I am that we have the pure truth of the Gospel pre-eminently among us, I hardly dare hope that we shall not be the chief sufferers; and deserting our own cause and our ancient principles, we invite and aggravate our ruin.

These evils however D.G. are not yet come; and oh ! that they may never come ! But whatever may be the result of this most marvellous election, as it regards Lord G., I can see it in no other light than others do, that in presuming to be a candidate, he in effect said, ' I well know that by the repeated and recent acts of the University you are all against me; but I will crush you and subdue you if I can,' and by overwhelming interest he has done it, twenty of the Heads of Houses, being, as I was told, decidedly against him, I verily believe the wishes of threefourths of the University being also on the same side. This at least is certain, that I scarcely met with a voter for Lord G. who did not lament that he was compelled to vote for him and in all appearances, heartily wish well to his opponents.

---

[1] " the beast that ascended out of the bottomless pit shall make war against them and shall overcome them and kill them."

I have not seen or heard of a single argument in support of the cause, except that one gentleman of Brasenose used the term ' union ' or ' uniting ', that is uniting light and darkness, one subject to King George alone and one subject to the pope and the pope to Bonaparte.

A republican or worse than republican argument they tell me has been used and they say, I hope not truly, that it came from Brasenose: ' The late petitions and other acts of the University are nothing to me because I did not assent to them.' Precisely on the same ground every member of Parliament who happens not to be present when a Bill passes, may say, ' It is nothing to me, I am not bound by it, because I did not assent to it.'

I have no personal antipathy to Lord G. To his virtues and his talents I can give just praise. But his judgement, in many instances besides Astlett's business, when a Bank Director said he ought to be hanged, I have been unable to approve; and his principles as to the Roman Catholics and breaking down the ancient barriers of the Constitution, if they prevail, cannot but be the ruin of the country.

P.S. — I have touched perhaps some of the greatest evils with which this unexampled election is pregnant, but not half of them. It is strange and unprecedented that our College should set up an *alien*, one rejected by his own college ! Three Heads just elected espouse the candidate whom all the seniores and discretiores steadily oppose ! The Princess of Wales and the Royal Dukes canvass for the avowed opponent of the wishes and principles of the King their Father ! The Chancellor of Cambridge a Socinian ! The Chancellor of Oxford the advocate of the pope's vassals ! So is the purest Church on earth protected ! !

Dr. Edward Copleston to Richard Heber
Oriel. 19 January 1810

The article on Strabo has detained me longer than I expected. Upon a closer inspection I found the whole of the reviewer's Latinity unsound. The dry rot was in every timber and the sentences crumbled to pieces as I took them in hand. Here at least I am victorious but I scorn the praise of victory over such an ungainly antagonist.

James H. Stanhope to Richard Heber
Southsea Hotel, Portsmouth. 30 January 1810

You doubtless think that by this time I have passed the straight ' where Calpe's armed steep '[1] thus to *unreginaldize* myself. I have approached Morgibello but instead of meeting the wild gales of these climates, I have been boxed up with my sister here in a damp, cold house under the accumulated grievances of cold, disappointment and the Lords Commissioners of the Admiralty.

The misconduct of the latter has become more irksome as all our injuries have been accompanied with the highest assurances of regard.

When I last dined with you at the Alfred, I told you that the Admiralty had recommended us to give up the *Unité* and go on board the *Manilla* as being more comfortable from my ship-mate Seymour being the Captain. When I arrived here (my sister being left in London) I saw all the comforts that he was kindly preparing for her accommodation. The hour of sailing was drawing near and the Admiralty were urging my sister to leave London, the very day *after* they sent down an order to embark on board the ship 2 Generals, their staff and divers military doctors. You will hardly believe that Ward signed this order first on the Tuesday and on the Wednesday at 2 o'clock wrote to my sister saying that he had just then heard for the first time that Government had found it necessary to turn us out of the *Manilla*, and still will you credit me when you hear that Lord Mulgrave[2] after this declares most solemnly how grieved he is at the event but that the Admiralty never knew of my sister's intention to embark on board the *Manilla* and confesses that he had other ships wherein to send them. We did not want their assistance but merely the civility commonly paid to a woman, that we have not rec'd and I should feel highly indignant if I

---

[1] A quotation from Reginald Heber's "Europe," published 1809.
[2] Henry Phipps (1755–1831), third Baron Mulgrave; friend and supporter of Pitt, in whose second ministry he was secretary for foreign affairs; first lord of the admiralty, 1807–10.

did not feel convinced that the whole of our mortifications have proceeded more from a bad system than from any other cause. I cannot disguise the ill effects of it, as my sister is much disimproved since she arrived here. God grant us enemies and save us from the friends of Mr. Pitt.

I have so nearly finished my paper that I cannot tell you all that I wish about Gd's Life of him.[1] The account of the last illness is *almost wholly false* and the work has a strong and marked bias to the Bishop and Lord C. Still I like it. The political part appears (to one who is and can be no judge) admirably done and the causes as well as the effects minutely and clearly detailed. Gifford under such tuition cannot be blamed, *in such society*, God knows *how much he is to be pitied* ! !

We go now as we advance near to the Spring strait to Messina. We sail tomorrow in the *Jason* frigate for Gibraltar from whence you shall hear again.

James H. Stanhope to Richard Heber
Gibraltar. 17 March 1810

I fear that from my long absence you will either believe that some accident has befallen us or that I have neglected the promise I made to you over our last bottle. We were detained at Portsmouth some days after I wrote last to you and finally weighed the 14th ulto. Baffling and light winds lengthened our passage considerably and when we at length made Cape Trafalgar, the violent gale in which the Cadiz Squadron has so much suffered, placed us on a lee shore and dispersed the whole of the convoy. We passed the shoals in 14 fathom, but the gales continuing we were obliged to run through the Gut and take refuge under Ceuta, where we have repeatedly drove with 2 anchors ahead; when the gale moderated, we came in here and I landed my sister (I think rather the better for her adventures) on the 10th. The Governer, Colin Campbell, has given us apartments in his house and we are waiting, in patience, for a return chaise to

---

[1] John Gifford (1758-1818), a vigorous tory pamphleteer and strongly attached to government, published a *Political Life of Pitt* in 1809, and was rewarded with a London magistrate's appointment.

Messina. So much for ourselves and I am almost ashamed to find 3 pages so employed.

What does Reginald now say to his :—

'Go cast thy fetters on the troublous sea
But Spain, the brave the patriot shall be free '[1]

Had I left England with even Anti-Jacobin ideas on the hopes of Spain, I should by now have changed them; and if Mr. Frere[2] had been my idol, the recital of his deeds I every day hear would have inspired me with deep contempt which he deserves. The Junta have perfected their work of folly or treachery by wishing to give Cadiz to the French and had it not been for a rapid and judicious movement of the Duke of Albuquerque, they would have succeeded. As the French had no heavy artillery in Spain and without it any attack on Cadiz would be futile, it became of great importance to save the Spanish Arsenal at Seville, and we offered to remove to Cadiz for their own use the whole of it, which was peremptorily rejected and 150 mortars 300 battering pieces of brass artillery with clothing for 30,000 men furnished by England, fell into their hands at this same moment when the Spanish troops are without every necessary a soldier requires.[3]

Yesterday we received a total return of all the French troops on this side of the Sierra Morena — which on its way to Soult was intercepted — and it only amounts (exclusive of 16,000 in Cadiz) to merely 25,000 men. With this force have they over-run and plundered every part of Andalusia, Algesciras, St. Roque, Tarifa and other places near here have been laid under contribution by the smallest detachments, the former by 200 men of whom only 16 entered the town, which by the way contains no less than 5,000 patriots who next morning threw up their greasy caps and screamed for independance.

Neither my time nor paper will allow me to pursue the nauseating details of weakness and wickedness which darken Spain. Of Frere I have much to tell you but I must leave it till we meet

[1] Closing lines of Reginald Heber's "Europe."
[2] John Hookham Frere (1769-1846) was minister to the Spanish Junta. In the opinion of many he was by his interference considered to be responsible for the retreat to Corunna and the death of Sir John Moore.
[3] Seville fell to Soult on 1 February 1810.

as I cannot commit such infamy to paper. I believe it would blot the whole.

Lord Wellington's army is recovering gradually. The remaining at Badajos has been defended by no one. No less than 5,000 men have been buried in that ill-omened plain. On this you may depend, indeed I have carefully compared everything I have heard of on both sides and I have not allowed my hatred of Spain to outweigh the truth. An officer who came from the army told me they always buried a brigade a month. Indeed I have no reason to change my opinion that Sir John Moore[1] fought for England and Wellesley for himself. These wretched officers who have deluded themselves and their country, these important military diplomats are augmenting in presumption as their prospects diminish and Doyle,[2] Roach, etc. I understand vie with each other in falsehood and folly.

We are not very active here and though I do not wish to libel my host whilst the taste of his wine is on my lips, I think he might by now have secured the occupation of Ceuta to our troops. We have been waiting for nearly a month for the order of the Junta at Cadiz to admit us, it came yesterday, when on being presented, the principal persons of Ceuta have assembled a council of war to decide on the propriety of their obeying it. This is an 'imperium in imperio' to a vengeance. Promptitude and energy may yet succeed but I scarcely know whether to hope or fear.

I wrote the numbers of the French on a report given me from high authority but having now obtained the despatches myself I am enabled to give you a correct account of this 1st Corps.

Near Cadiz	18,992
Cavalry round the County	2,395
Total in Andalusia or on this side of the Sierra Morena	21,992[3]
Detached and on the route	5,619
Total ..	27,006

[1] Sir John Moore (1761-1809), killed at Corunna.

[2] Colonel Charles Doyle was military agent attached to the Spanish army. He was grossly optimistic of the effectiveness of the Spanish war effort.

[3] Stanhope seems to have transcribed the third figure incorrectly; it should presumably be 21,387.

James H. Stanhope to Richard Heber
Undaunted, off Cadiz. 22 April 1810

After I wrote last, we remained till the 7th when we obtained a passage on board the *Cerberus*, but finding that my battalion was arrived at Cadiz I was (most unwillingly) obliged to abandon my Mediterranean prospects and witness her sailing alone. I think she is ere this arrived at her journey's end as the same strong Western blast that has detained us till this time must have expedited her.

The last fortnight has been passed by me in the society of a most agreeable, well-informed and (what is more surprizing) a very modest Spanish female who with her brother-in-law Genl. Mendozo are also passengers to Cadiz with my old friend Maling. The wind being foul we have passed from Gibraltar to Algesiras, Tarifa, Ceuta, Tetuan and finally Tangier so you can conceive what with society on board and riding and shooting on shore the time has passed rapidly and pleasingly away.

General Graham[1] in the handsomest manner has appointed me as his extra A.D.C. He could not do more as I am still on Sir D.D.'s[2] staff. Fine work here.

The only good news is the occupation of Ceuta by our troops, the 14th regiment occupies the Citadel and as there are no other troops in it with them, I conceive our interests are well secured in that quarter.

Dr. Edward Copleston to Richard Heber
Oriel. 12 June 1810

How do you relish the distribution of the Prizes ? For my own part, independently of my partial interests, I am glad they are divided among several colleges. Coleridge's[3] verses are upon the

---

[1] Thomas Graham (1748-1843), Baron Lynedoch, general; served with distinction under Wellington and Moore.

[2] Presumably Sir David Dundas (1735-1820).

[3] Sir John Taylor Coleridge (1790-1876), when at Corpus Christi College, Oxford, won the Chancellor's prize for Latin verse. He was the nephew of the poet.

whole a fine copy — his plan is admirable and the versification pure and flowing. Whateley's[1] essay is philosophical but rather dry.

Dr. Edward Copleston to Richard Heber
Oriel. 24 July 1810

Nott[2] is staying here and is almost my only walking companion, but he is too fond of contemplating in church-yards for me. When I walk out, it is to stretch my limbs and refresh my spirit. Hervey[3] I can read at home.

James H. Stanhope to Richard Heber
15 August 1810

How melancholy is the fate of poor Lady Sarah Napier[4] and that family at the moment; she escapes a severe loss in one son, to lose another in a stupid manoeuvre of Crawford's and to have a daughter given over in a decline. I fear she will not be able to support such heavy and accumulated misfortunes.

The last accounts I had from Hester were from Malta 25th June whence she was going to Constantinople and the Greek Islands, having given up Sicily from the existing state of affairs in that country which from letters I have had from Catania is dreadful. The Queen is seen betraying us by everyone but the English Ambassador and General. I believe the threatened invasion is nothing more than a feint to keep our troops there, 10,000 of them would do much and 5,000 would keep the Citadel.

---

[1] Richard Whately (1787-1863) of Oriel College owed much to Copleston. He became professor of political economy and later bishop of Dublin.

[2] George Frederick Nott (1767-1841), divine, fellow of All Souls.

[3] James Hervey (1714-58) of Lincoln College, wrote religious works which had a great vogue throughout the century, and among them *Meditations and Contemplations*, containing ' Meditations upon the tombs '. It is said of him that ' if he had condescended to write plain English many of his descriptions would have been pleasing.'

[4] Lady Sarah Napier, d. 1826, on whom George III had cast sheep's eyes as a young man, had three sons who all became generals. The eldest was made prisoner in this campaign but was exchanged in 1811.

Richard Heber to his sister, Mary
25 *December* 1810

With respect to your drum, if you and Emily[1] have a violent desire for it, I have no objection, only remember, it is your concern not mine, for I cannot possibly get down in time and if I could, should never think of giving a fête in such an old ragamuffin mansion as mine is at present.

The part of your scheme which I like the least is making the library a partaker of your festivities. Consider what a vile bad approach there is to it, and what moving of tables and sorting of papers must be previously encountered. Remember also what a rascally little fireplace it contains, unless indeed you propose making the farther room into your supper apartment, in which case the servants will share your conversation. If however you have fixed your heart on one or other of these poor unfortunate chambers, I do hereby most strictly insist that you neither clear nor sort any of the books on the shelves or change their position in the slightest degree or put candles or lamps or bottles or glasses or oysters or butter boats on or near any of the shelves or prop up the feet of tables with books however mean to counteract the unevenness of the floor. I should also wish my new writing tables to be put out of the reach of spruce-beer and bottled ale and not to exhibit the impression of the glutinous bottom of goblets and decanters. The carpet will want beating I suppose and the room sweeping, but allow me to crave mercy for the books themselves. As to dancing, you may dance as long as you like in the dining parlour, which is in fact the only room fit for it. With respect to inviting neighbours, you must please yourself, tho' I think you will find it difficult to draw the line without offence. Indeed 24 will be as many as you can accommodate comfortably with chairs or anything else.

If you are determined to be kissed under a bunch of mistletoe, let it be suspended anywhere but in the library and do not ornament the shelves by sticking holly and laurel all over them.

A merry Xmas and much good foolery to you all.

---

[1] Reginald, now Rector of Hodnet had married Amelia (Emily) Shipley in 1809.

Robert Southey to William Gifford
Keswick. 14 January 1811

If you are not provided with a review of Capt. Pasley's[1] book upon our military policy, will you entrust to my hands for your next number and I will promise you an article in a right English spirit. I should like also in the compass of about two pages to counteract the mischief which such a rascally work as Lewis Goldsmith's[2] is calculated and, as I believe, designed to do by its absurd and palpable falsehoods.

If I understand my own manner of writing, the style always grows out of the subject. I know no other rule or system than that of always expressing myself (1) as perspicuously as possible, (2) as impressively as possible, (3) as concisely as possible.

Dr. Edward Copleston to Richard Heber
Oriel. 2 March 1811

Let me now say a few words freely to you about our friend Gifford. They must be taken in perfect confidence — for nothing offends so much as strictures through the medium of a third person. There is no man who possesses or deserves to possess so great an influence over him as yourself, so that your advice may sink deep and be well received. He does not appear to me to feel the nature of the situation in which he is placed. He seems to rely on the zeal and the co-operation of others, without recollecting that he alone is the responsible person — that he ought to be regarded as the mainspring — as the living soul that animates the mass which is set in motion. He can write an excellent letter and it is his business to cultivate a correspondence with those

[1] Charles William Pasley (1780-1861) had a most useful and distinguished military career. After serving as a staff officer in the Peninsula he went on the Walcheren expedition and was wounded. While convalescing he wrote an *Essay on the Military Policy and Institutions of the British Empire*, 1810. The work attracted great attention and ran immediately into several editions, and was favourably reviewed in the *Quarterly* of May 1811; by Canning, as has been supposed.

[2] Lewis Goldsmith (1763?-1846) had spent the last few years in France, acting — unwillingly, as he claimed — in the employ of the French government. He came to England in 1809 and at once attacked Napoleon and the French in print. He published in 1811 a *Secret History of the Cabinet of Bonaparte*.

who are *well disposed* and *inclined* to help him, But he now and
then talks as if these writers must take an interest on their own
accord — that they will be turning in their heads what they can
do to serve him. All this is a pure mistake — at least as far as
Oxford is concerned. Nobody here will write unless he is roused
or entreated or flattered into it. G. must think of work and
propose it to them. Why does he not endeavour to establish a
correspondence with those whose names have been introduced
to him and lay a list of two or three new publications before
them out of which they may make their choice ?

He is too, I fear, rather apt to reckon upon his friends and well-
wishers as *engaged* to give him regular assistance. One or two
phrases of his last letter to me imply as much and I am anxious
to undeceive him. I cannot look upon myself as a *writer in the
Quarterly Review*. Everything of that kind which I may do will
be done in consequence of a painful effort and it will cost me the
sacrifice, for the time, of other pursuits more pleasing and more
important to myself. I am afraid therefore he interprets my
language and endeavours wrong. Nothing can be kinder or
handsomer than his way of speaking on all occasions, but I can
never look upon myself otherwise than as an occasional contributor when I have nothing else very pressing upon my attention.
The same I believe may be said of Davison[1] and of everyone
here whose assistance is worth having. Surely he ought to see
this. He is at the Headquarters of intelligence. He knows what
works are published and it is easy to guess what parts are likely
to suit certain performers. When the thing is undertaken, would
it not be as well to send or offer a copy of the book thro' Murray ?
All this is sacred to your ear. Something of the same kind I have
heard from yourself.

Robert Southey to Richard Heber
Keswick. 9 April 1811

Longman's new *Review*, so far as it succeeds, will interfere
with the sale of the *Quarterly* but I doubt if there will be sufficient

[1] John Davison (1777-1834), fellow of Oriel College; theological writer.

sea-room for the two sailing upon the same tack and in that case the *British* will sink.

I have missed an opportunity of tomahawking Jeffrey. I would have exposed the abominations of the Scotch *Review* in morals and politics and their utter ignorance of the first principles of taste as clearly as Copleston has done their lack of Greek — and upon the score of honesty I would as they deserve have whipt them like common rogues.

Richard Heber to his sister, Mary
Westminster, May 1811

I have given up my intention of going to Cambridge as Tom Smyth cannot be of the party and the weather seems unpropitious and the conveyance precarious. You will however have Reginald whom Murray tells me he has just left, imbedded in a heavy stage coach among children, Professor Xtian and other live lumber. Dr. Raine is also at Trinity and will I doubt not assist you most effectually in any of your academical necessities as he is a senior and popular member of a large and important college.

Tell Mama (with my love) I have almost decided on taking a man and wife for my butler and housekeeper. The latter lived with Mrs. Elliot for some time who gives her an excellent character for activity and authority. She quitted 2 or 3 years ago in order to marry her present husband who has been butler in several respectable families and they set up a greengrocers in London, but it did not answer. So they wish to go to service again. I see no objection to matrimony for if your butler and housekeeper are not, they are sure either to make love or quarrel and in the one case you have at least a chance that they will do neither. I really think them creditable people, tho' he is Irish and she is warm tempered.

Mrs. Heber (Richard's Stepmother) to Richard Heber
Cambridge. 2 *July* 1811

As to the merits of Mr. and Mrs. Downing you only can judge, the character Mrs. Elliot gives of *her* is tempting, The objections

I have heard to a married pair is that they play into each others hands to the frequent vexation of the Family, and if artful and inclined to cheat, may bear each other out and if one is found fault with, both take offence. Not having a family is well, if one could be sure a twelve-month or so might not alter the case. Besides the bedrooms at Hodnet Hall are ill-circumstanced for married people. Would the woman come without the man ?

Mary Heber to Richard Heber
Trinity College, Cambridge. 2 July 1811

The University Breakfast yesterday was very well conducted. 3000 persons were said to have been in the gardens and 200 couples stood up to dance under awnings and festoons of flowers. I danced with Leslie Melville,[1] one of Lord Leven's sons, you may have seen him with the Thorntons, I have been acquainted with him about a year. We went afterwards to the Concert where Catalini[2] surpassed herself. Dr. Raine came in late, over-come (as he himself calls it) with wine, in the highest spirits and very entertaining. We made room for him in our party and were quite delighted with him. The Duke is in extacy with the honours that are conferred on him and bows from morning to night. He was actually encored for his performance in this way and seemed much gratified by such a mark of approbation. There is to be another public breakfast at Trinity College tomorrow which is to surpass the first in every way. The cloisters are most admirably adapted to the purpose.

Dr. Martin Routh to Richard Heber
Magd. Coll. Oxford. 8 August 1811

I saw the Principal of Brasenose lately and gave him my thoughts on our local politics. Kett[3] is here and dined with me

---

[1] Presumably John Leslie Melville (1786-1876). He married in 1812 Harriet, daughter of Samuel Thornton, M.P., of Clapham and Albury Park, and succeeded as Earl of Leven and Melville in 1860.
[2] Catalini, Prima Donna (1779-1849).
[3] Henry Kett (1761-1825), fellow of Trinity College, Oxford.

on Tuesday at the same time as the Dean of Westminster[1] from Islip. The latter has been frequently calling on me and gave me one of his books. But I am not very fond of him altho' I have behaved with all civility to him. Still I suspect my general dislike of the Superiors of my own order which originates not from pride or disappointment, but from other causes. He may be a very honest and good man for what I know of him. But I forget myself when I trouble you with this foolery.

James Ferriar[2] to Richard Heber
Wolverhampton. 4 September 1811

Pray, is this political romance ' the Spirit of the book '[3] really written by the Bp. of W.? It is the vilest trash that I have seen for many years.

Walter Scott to Richard Heber
Ashestial. 17 October 1811

My dear Heber,

My brother Tom whom you may remember in Edinburgh is now in town soliciting a matter in which you can probably serve him. After various misfortunes, he has been induced to accept an offer by Genl. Ross, Colonel of the 70th regiment, to be paym'ter to that Corps, the present paymaster being permitted to retire on full pay in consideration of bad health and long service. There is however some rub in this matter which Tom will himself explain to you, which refers not to his appointment but to the retirement of his predecessor. In the meanwhile he is waiting in London at great expense considering his large family and limited finances and conceives that Lord Palmerston's[4]

---

[1] William Vincent (1739-1815), dean of Westminster 1802-15, rector of Islip 1807-15.

[2] James Ferriar (1761-1815), physician and writer, published *The Bibliomania, an Epistle to Richard Heber Esq*, 1809.

[3] *The Spirit of ' The Book ' or, memoirs of Caroline, Princess of Hapsburgh* (i.e. the Queen Consort of George IV) anon. 1811, was written by Thomas Ashe (1770-1835), miscellaneous writer.

[4] Henry John Temple (1784-1865), third Viscount Palmerston, statesman, was secretary at war from 1809 to 1828.

decision might be accelerated by the proper use of a little personal influence. I think you know Lord Palmerston whose general character is that of a kindly man as well as a man of letters. If you can assist poor Tom in this matter, you will do me a most essential kindness and at the same time do a very good and benevolent action. My brother's misfortunes arise entirely from a good humoured indolence and carelessness of disposition which adversity has I trust effectually corrected. If you see him there are few men whose society will entertain you more for an hour or two.

I have bought a little place by Tweedside[1] and am busy planning ornamenting and scheming a little cottage, where I hope one day we may crack a social bottle of claret, in spite of the merciless distance that separates us. As this letter is only intended to introduce my brother to your memory and his business to your attention, I shall only add that I am very truly yours

W. Scott.

Rev. Thomas S. Smyth to Richard Heber
Macclesfield. 2 October 1811

Copleston has turned charioteer and succeeded in his first attempt in breaking three of his father's ribs and tearing and mangling his own face. Of course the spirited mare he was driving must put in some claim for some part of the exploit.

Dr. Edward Copleston to Richard Heber
Oriel. 28 November 1811

In the meantime let me congratulate you upon the appearance of the ablest number of the Q.R. which (by universal consent) has yet been published.

[1] Abbotsford, near Melrose.

VIII   Letters to
RICHARD HEBER
1812-1817

WE DO NOT know how or when Richard Heber first formed the idea of sitting in Parliament as the representative of Oxford University. He went to the poll in 1806 and in 1814 a canvass was carried out on his behalf, in self-defence against the pretensions of ' Mr. Weatherall '. This opponent is presumably Wetherell, who represented Shaftesbury in 1813 and the city of Oxford in 1820, and went on to have a moderately successful career as a politician and lawyer which was eventually capped with a knighthood. The chief characteristic of his political views was a violent hostility to reform (whether legal, municipal or parliamentary) and to Catholic emancipation. That was the man whom Richard was to oppose. It does not follow, however, that Richard's political views were in all respects the opposite of Wetherell's.

We do not, in fact, know very much about Richard's politics. He was accused of having helped to get Lord Grenville elected Chancellor in 1809. He was contemporary at B.N.C. with Grenville's nephew and we have an early hint (no more) of friendship between them. He was associated with James Stanhope, and Stanhope was both associated with and related to Grenville. Grenville had resigned his ministry in 1807 because he was prevented from emancipating Roman Catholics. It was said of Richard himself that he was on the Catholic side. The evidence so far would seem to be conclusive that Richard stood for Catholic emancipation.

Our judgement, however, is complicated by the fact that Richard apparently denied it. Catholic emancipation was the burning question. Churton, thoroughly bigoted against the Roman church, writes explicitly in this chapter to enquire the truth of rumours that Richard favoured Catholic emancipation. The ' candid and friendly letter ' which he acknowledges in return persuades him that Richard is ' the same true and steady Church and Kingman I always hoped and believed you to be '.

Perhaps Richard did not deal ingenuously with him. Or it may be that his opinions were not firm. We note that his correspondents, from the conservative Stonard to the liberal Copleston, all write as if they took for granted Richard's sympathy with their opinions. It is fairly clear from his subsequent tour in Parliament that he was not a political man. He may have seen too clearly both sides of the question to act decidedly on either.

At all events the canvass was premature. There was no vacancy and Richard did not fight an election until 1821.

*   *   *

Mary Heber to Richard Heber
Hodnet. 19 April 1812

There was a Vestry called this evening to consult on the cheapest means of relieving the poor during the present scarcity, when it was agreed by the farmers that a weekly distribution of soup would be the most effectual. For this purpose they have begun subscriptions, Mr. Clarke giving three guineas, Reginald the same and some of the farmers ten shillings each. The subscribers will be allowed a certain proportion of tickets according to the sum they give, which they will dispose among such poor as they chuse. We guess that a subscriber of ten shillings may expect ten quarts of soup for ten weeks and so in proportion. Reginald wished me to write to you, hoping you will have no objection to the scheme and contribute towards it. Mrs. Williams has engaged to make the soup therefore there is every reason to hope it will be well done.

James Boswell to Richard Heber
24 April 1812

We have just received the glorious news of the capture of Badajos,[1] but our loss has been dreadful.

I went on Tuesday night to hear the Oratorio of *Palestine* and was highly gratified indeed. Crotch[2] has done himself much credit by his composition and was received by the most numerous audience I ever saw in that concert room with robustious applause.

> 'Heber! with much delight thy Palestine
> I've read, and heard it set by Dr. Crotch
> A well concocted poem, not a hotch
> Potch, as some bards have sung, not by the Nine
> Inspired, but smoaky whisky who in brine
> Should have a rod well steep'd and pickled, Scotch
> Irish and Welsh who write full many a botch
> Though Lords and Ladies call their strain divine.'

Richard Heber to his sister Mary
Gisburne. 25 *April* 1812

Your letter reached me at this place yesterday and I have no hesitation in authorising you to set down my name as a subscriber of £5. 5. 0. to your Severn Soup Shop.

James Ferriar to Richard Heber
Manchester. 11 *May* 1812

The lower classes of people are in a most alarming state here. God knows where the mischief will end. The matter has quite a revolutionary appearance.

---

[1] Badajos defied Wellington's attacks in 1811 but was successfully stormed in April 1812.

[2] William Crotch (1775-1847), professor of music in the University of Oxford, in 1812 composed the oratorio *Palestine*.

Archdeacon Ralph Churton to Richard Heber
Middleton, 12 May 1812

Most shocking indeed! poor Mr. Perceval[1] shot at the door of the H. of Commons! God Almighty preserve us!

Robert Southey to Richard Heber
Keswick. 7 September 1812

You will soon see the *Quarterly* sketch of Nelson's *Life* expanded to a little volume, designed as a midshipman's manual.[2]

You gave me some hopes of seeing you in the North this year. I wish you were now on your way, for our Keswick wonder the floating island made its appearance eight and forty hours ago.

James H. Stanhope to Richard Heber
Mongualde. 10 December 1812

When we parted in London I certainly did not expect to be cantoned in the middle of Portugal this winter. I had hopes of sharing in future victories and that expectation certainly occasioned my short stay at home; although I have been disappointed and only arrived in time to witness a bright display of unprofitable gallantry and a repetition of the melancholy scenes unavoidable in every retreat but more prominent in a British one. I by no means regret the determination I have taken as the lesson of the last month is worth an age of pursuit. When one looks back on the campaign, one seeks anxiously for the reason why the tables were so rapidly turned and how it happened that we could hardly keep face before a French army which three weeks before was considered *hors de combat* for the year.[3]

[1] Rt. Hon. Spencer Perceval (1762-1812) Prime Minister since 1809, was assassinated by a lunatic in the lobby of the House on May 11th.

[2] Southey's *Life of Nelson* appeared in 1813, in which year the Laureateship was bestowed on him, Walter Scott having stood aside in his favour.

[3] Wellington's campaign of 1812 secured some important places without which it was impossible to advance from Portugal into Spain. The advance was pushed on to Madrid and Burgos was besieged. It was at this stage that Stanhope joined the army, just in time for the repulse at Burgos and the retreat back to the Portuguese frontier.

I think the prime cause and keystone of our reverses was Lord Wellington's entry of Madrid abandoning thereby the pursuit of an army which he could have been (?right) to bring to action, and secondly, when he remained at Madrid some time returning to the chase of an enemy he had released from his fangs — of all this I know nothing but from reports, but Burgos I saw but a rational prospect of success I never could see. With the perfect want of means under which we laboured, we had no right to expect to take the town work: but British soldiers who could storm the Picorine could storm any single line of defense and we carried in a night what should have cost a month's seige. But the fort itself was a triple range of strong and well constructed entrenchments and infinitely stronger than Badajos. We had but 3 guns and thanks to our Engineers they were speedily dismounted and we were beseiging one of the strongest places of Spain without guns and with no musquet ammunition. When the latter arrived, we again stormed and lost our most valuable officers in attempting what appears to me impossibilities.

At length the long expected army of relief advances and as usual the Spanish intelligence reduces the force to two thirds of the reality. Lord W. occupies a strong position in front of Burgos. The French army appears and we see a most numerous body of men reorganised and formidable in their cavalry. They were not collected. Lord W. heard of Soult's advance and determined on retreat. He had chased them off the night before by moving to attack them. This advantage he possessed and this alone. It is impossible to conceive a situation of more appalling difficulty to an ordinary mind than this retreat presented. The enemy had 4000 cavalry and we had about 1200 and these harassed by unceasing duty. The enemy had 40,000 infantry and we had about 10,000 British something like 7000 Portuguese and the remainder of our force was composed of men whom we suspected and afterwards found could not be relied on.

The Castle of Burgos commanded the high road, the lateral roads were nearly impassable and many (of) the sick and stores were in the front of Burgos.

In one night the whole army was beyond the fort, the 1st Division moved over the bridges within half a musket shot of the fort in a moonlight night without being perceived. The second day the cavalry behaved so ill that nothing but the firmness of two German Batallions saved them from a dangerous pursuit. I will not go through the long detail of the retreat but Lord W. effectually checked and imposed upon the enemy: we halted when and as long as he chose. He effected a retreat over narrow single bridges with a train of baggage unexceeded by all the armies of the East and West without losing a mule and I might have said without the loss of a man, had not the same scenes of intemperance and indiscipline which occasioned the loss of Sir John Moore's army, returned with unabated force.

When we collected at Salamanca our numbers were as you see in the Despatch, but he offered them battle and had they attacked him, the result would not have (been) doubtful, but any movement by their left rendered it necessary to retire and when once in retreat no army can stop short of the agreed on. Here the weather which last winter so wonderfully assisted Lord Wn. coquetted with the Marshals — whilst we wanted rain to swell the Tormes which would have enabled us to hold Salamanca, the sun shone with nearly summer's heat; when we began our retreat over roads of marsh and mud, such torrents of rain fell as hardly ever were experienced before. Here again the indiscipline of the troops made us lose some men and many also sank under the inclemancy of the weather.

Yet the heaviest loss and which you know must most deeply have been felt by me was the loss of Genl. Paget[1] — I was taken ill with a fever at Salamanca and the morning he was taken he insisted on my getting on to Cuidad Rodrigo. To this I owe my liberty.

Nothing could be more interesting to a military man than the whole of these operations, the mode Lord W. took up his positions, the presence of mind, the unshaken firmness, the wonderful nerve he displayed were lessons never to be forgotten.

[1] Sir Edward Paget (1775-1849); second-in-command to Wellesley and taken prisoner 1811; conducted the Burmese War of 1824-5.

But allow me to look back to former events and to touch on a string you know vibrates more strongly than any other in my heart — I mean the much censured retreat of Sir John Moore. Though I regret the events and much more the innate cause of them I cannot but feel a satisfaction in perceiving that such things may occur under the command of the greatest general of his day, the favourite of fortune and the unlibelled commander of a large army who besides has the advantage that no perfidious Government opposes and no visionary minister clogs him with his aid.

One melancholy fact has been established by this campaign, that the French relying either on a military possession of forts and garrisons or on the terror of future punishment or on the weariness the people feel at this protracted war or conjointly on the whole of these causes, can equally despise the regular army, the guerrillas and the hatred of a nation and can assemble for a considerable time at the extremity of Spain nearly their whole effective force; whilst the only army that could have assisted us remains useless and the only General who united the confidence of the army and the country breaks out in an overt act of unheard of rebellion.

We have also seen that regular Spanish soldiers who for two years have been organising in the Galicias cannot stand against French conscripts who had been 20 days from Bayonne though they have British soldiers by their side as an example.

With regard to our future hopes therefore we can only look to ourselves and I think this retreat will give us great advantage next spring. We shall be able to rest the army as long as Lord W. likes, whereas in advance we should have been ' a la dispocision ' of the Marshals. We shall be able to reclothe and rediscipline the army, we shall be able to form magazines for our future operations. Had we remained forward the whole of our transport would have been employed in feeding us as from hand to mouth and this important operation without which no army can advance in the spring would have been impossible. Against this we have our great disadvantage that for the third time we have abandoned the Spaniards and we shall never be considered otherwise than as birds of passage and we cannot expect Vivas from the heart whatever the tongue may utter. It really makes one's heart bleed to think of the poor people of Madrid and Salamanca whom we have left to be tenfold worse plundered and more oppressed in proportion to their attachment to us. I cannot blame the Spaniard for being weary of the war, when sacrifices are so recompensed, and when zeal and kindness so repaid, it must be more than human constancy that does not pray for a cessation of such friendship. I well know that the retreat was necessary and though it justifies our conduct, it cannot remove one's feelings for the poor wretches who are paying for their attachment to us.

If this letter does not put you to sleep, there is no faith in any soporifics.

(Enclosure to above).

The Army is composed of 8 Divisions of Infantry and 2 Brigades of Cavalry.
1st Div. commanded by 2nd-in-Command   9000

1st Brigade	2nd Brigade	3rd Brigade
Mjr. Genl. { Coldstreams Campbell { 3rd Guards	Mjr. Genl. { 42d Foot Wheatley { 79 ,, { 24th ,,	Mjr. Genl. { 1 K.G.L. Low { 2 ,, { 5 ,,

2nd Div. SIR R. HILL

1st Brigade	2nd Brigade
Mjr. Genl. { 91st Foot Howard { 92nd ,, { 50th ,,	{ 28th Foot { 48th ,, { 3rd or Buffs

3rd Div. lately commanded by GENL. PICTON.

1st Brigade	2nd Brigade
{ 5th Foot { 77th ,,	{ 88th Foot { 94th ,,

4th Div. MAJOR GENL. COLE.

1st Brigade	2nd Brigade Fusileer
{	{ 7th Foot { 23rd ,,

5th Div. MAJOR GENL. LEITH.

1st Brigade	2nd Brigade
{ 4th Foot { 30th ,, { 44th ,,	Major { 9th Foot Genl. { 6th Royals Hay { 38th Foot

6th Div. MAJOR GENL. CLINTON.

	1st Brigade		*2nd Brigade*
Major Genl. Hulme	{ 11th Foot 53rd „ 61st „		{ Queens or 2nd Foot 32nd Foot 36th „

7th Div. MAJOR GENL. HOPE.

	1st Brigade			*2nd Brigade*
Major Genl. de Bernes- witz	{ 57th Foot 66th „ Chasseurs	Colnl. Hackett	{ 1st K.G.L. Light 2nd „ „ Brunswickers

Lt. Division. MAJOR GENL. ALTEN.

{ 43rd Foot 4 companies 95th Foot Portuguese		{ 52nd Foot 4 companies 95th Foot Portuguese

1st Division of Cavalry. SIR STAPLETON COTTON.

Genl. le Marchant	{ 3rd Drag. Guards 4th Dragoons 5th Drag. Guards	Genl. Anson	{ 12th 16th
Genl. Books	{ 1 K.G.L. 2 „	Genl. Altens	{ 1st Hussars 14th „

2nd Division. SIR WILLIAM ERSKINE.

Major Genl. Slades	{ Royals	Major Genl. Long	{ 9th Lancers 11th „ 13th „

Walter Scott to Richard Heber
Edinburgh. 4 January 1813
(docketed ' with copy of Rokeby ')

My dear Heber,

I wrote to you some time ago under cover to James Boswell and that again as I was sending some papers under cover to Croker addressing James Boswell, Temple, which I hope reached him and you. The chief purpose of my letter to you was to know the amount of my debt for the Roxburgh books[1] and to express my great delight therein. The romances especially are beautiful copies of I think the best extant. Pray let me have a settlement for the filthy lucre.

I send you a thumping 4to, some part of which I think you will like though it has a much less pleasing interest upon the whole than the *Lady of the Lake*. It cost me nearly about the same labour namely three months pretty light work. It is to be sure very foolish to be so hasty but I have so little patience with my own rhymes that I remind myself of poor Singing Jemmie Balfour who could run a run when he could neither walk nor stand. Let me hear from you my dear Heber and

believe me always yours while

Walter Scott.

Archdeacon Ralph Churton to Richard Heber
Middleton. 12 January 1813

Supposing you may still be in the country (as Talleyrand's books the spoils of the Continent are not yet ready for the hammer) I will direct Turner to wait on you on Monday next.

Have you seen a paper from Ireland in the *Anti-Jacobin* for November, enough to make any man tremble who has either religion, life, liberty or property to lose.[2]

James H. Stanhope to Richard Heber
Headquarters. 13 May 1813

The last letter I wrote to you was at the end of last campaign. During the winter like Munchausen's horse I have been frozen up in a Beotian land and amid Siberian cold with the exception of the last weeks which I passed in an agreeable manner with my

---

[1] John Ker (1740-1804), third Duke of Roxburghe, was a great collector of books and well known to Scott. The fourth Duke died in 1805. The succession was then disputed. James Innes-Ker was recognized in 1812, and the library was dispersed. After the sale the twenty-four chief bibliophiles of the day formed the Roxburghe Club.

[2] A hostile, bigoted account of the Irish Roman Catholic movement for emancipation, in which the writer expresses the familiar view that a man cannot profess the Roman Catholic faith peacefully under a Protestant monarchy, is here referred to.

old friends at Oporto. I arrived here on the 9th. My old General had reached it three days before me, looking infinitely better than he did last year. You will be gratified in hearing that I am again to join him and I am to be personally attached to him in my present department as I was to Sir Edward Paget. At all times this would be most desirable but most particularly interesting is it at the present moment when he is entrusted with a post of great importance in command of the army to the north of the Duera.

You are always so sanguine in England that I supposed you will not be contented without seeing the French armies pushed over the Rhine and the Pyrennees. We have certainly good prospects but how far our hopes will be realised (at least in this part of the world) must depend in a great measure on the improvement of our allies and the confidence which in a military point of view can be placed in them, subjects in no small degree precarious. The great game appears however to be pendent in Germany etc. and I cannot but think that Spain will be won or lost upon the Elbe in preference to the Ebro.

The French army is strong in this country and although our force is in the highest order, we have lost no inconsiderable number of men during the winter by sickness and have received (at least as infantry) no considerable reinforcements. Our cavalry is however good and respectable in numbers and in proportion as we suffered for want of that arm last year, we may hope correspondent advantages from its present state. I suppose we have not less than 6000.

The French army is 'a portée' of the Duera, but whether they will try to defend the line of it remains to be proved. They derive great advantage from the nature of the country, all the towns which command the bridges are on their side and in consequence of that the Duera was no obstacle to the advance of the enemy when we held its line last year in our retreat. I do not believe we could have forced the line of it last year had not Marmont saved Lord Wellington the trouble of trying, by gallantly adventuring first. It is not probable that such an event will reoccur. It appears therefore that the army is to be divided, I think in about equal proportions, that on the North to get the Esla and that on the South the Tormes. This is always a critical movement especially when the enemy have a bridge so near as Zamora which will enable them to throw their whole force against half of ours which must in that case ' rebrousser chemin ', which in the army on the South of the river would be attended with the disadvantage of having the Tormes in its rear, if it communicates with us on crossing the Esla which of course it must do. Still it is not the object of the French to risk much and perhaps we shall bully them out of the line of the Duera. We may then give a view hollow to the Ebro. There is a considerable Spanish force on foot. I suppose the Galician army would join us. The armies of Murcia and Andalusia (the latter under the Conde de Bilbal is in very high order) will of course move and will always act as a diversion. Suchet appears to have enough on his hands, if Sir John Murray is like Caesar and is a man of many blows as well as of many letters. At any rate we shall have an interesting campaign[1] and that is some comfort!

We gain much by Lord Wellington being supreme and not a little by Soult being off.[2] Jourdan has been bilked so often that he will not wish to change at this period of his military life his earlier habits. We shall be in movement in a few days. If I have time I will write you a line. If I do not, you must forgive it. I need not ask for an answer as I am convinced you will never send one.

I was very near sending you home a most valuable book both as to decency of stile and abstruseness of matter, but I conceived you have certainly got it. Don Tome Sanchez de Matrimonia, the learned dissertation *de Debitu Conjugali* is not to be paralleled and tended much to enliven my winter quarters, as I took the liberty of adding notes critical and historical.

I met at Oporto the other day a very extraordinary young man — Mr. Banks[3] who is a great friend of Lord Byron and an

[1] The decisive battle of Vittoria was fought five weeks after this letter was written.
[2] Early in 1813 Bonaparte recalled Marshall Soult (1769-1851) to the German front, sending to Spain in his place Marshall Jean Baptiste Jourdan (1762-1833).
[3] William Bankes (d. 1855), traveller, friend of Byron and Hobhouse.

associate to his Lordship's friend the late Mr. Matthews. I never saw so singular a compound of eccentricity and judgements, of trifling and study, of sound opinions about others and wild speculations about himself, good talents applied to no future object and a most wonderful memory prostituted to old songs and tales of Mother Goose. Do you know him ? but why do I ask as till we meet again I have no hopes of being answered. I like the man much for he appears to have an excellent temper, a good heart and a certain degree of freshness and independence in opinions which I do not think the travellers who come to this country generally possess.

Dr. Martin Routh to Richard Heber
Magd. Coll. Oxford. 14 May 1813.

I also wish to make a present of a pen to a young lady of considerable family. To whom can I better apply myself than to Mr. Heber to select one either of gold or silver or some other metal or composition which will do credit to the taste of the selector ? I should be glad of it as soon as it suits your convenience.

I am approaching the end of my second vol. but of late the work has gone on with less speed principally on account of my occasional absence at my Living.

James H. Stanhope to Richard Heber
Ryde. 25 August 1813

Although you may regret that the papers are not black letter and printed by Aldus, yet I know you still condescend to read them; you therefore may have seen that I was wounded and that I arrived in the *Parthian* at Portsmouth. I meant to have proceeded to town where I should have met you probably before now but Lord Buckingham[1] dissuaded me from jumbling myself and brought me over here with him where I have his

---

[1] Richard Grenville (1776-1839), a graduate of Brasenose College, second Marquis of Buckingham in 1813 and Duke of Buckingham in 1822.

own surgeon to attend me, and every comfort. I am going on exceedingly well but the ball remains in my back under the shoulder blade where it probably will reside all my life without molestation. I shall not be any further service this campaign. Have very little pain and sound slumber of 10 hours.

James H. Stanhope to Richard Heber
St. James's Place. 28 September 1813

I cannot tell you *how I am* as who shall decide when doctors disagree. How *I feel I am*, which is as if I had a decayed tooth in my back; but I must have patience. All the surgeons previous to my coming to town thought that the ball would remain quiet and that the wound would heal. Here they foretell bone coming out, some say the ball, some say by one aperture formed by the ball and others by one which is to be formed by them.

Dr. Martin Routh to Richard Heber
Magd. Coll. Oxford. 18 October 1813

You will be glad to hear that I have finished with the exception of a somewhat long Preface, two volumes of my work. As soon as the first was printed I sent it to Dr. Parr for his inspection and though I must not tell you his judgement of it lest I appear too arrogant, yet I mention the circumstance as it encourages me to persevere in my purpose of dedicating it to the Episcopal Church of Scotland.

You are much better acquainted than I am with most things and can tell me whether it would be presumptuous or informal to address them without having previously obtained their permission. If not, I should be spared some trouble, Nay Mr. Heber, you yourself would be spared the pains of writing to your acquaintance the Bishop of Edinburgh on the subject. If it should be desired, I would communicate to his Lordship my intended address to the Bishops and Presbyters of the Scottish Church previously to the publication of the work, on being assured that no person in this Southern part of the Kingdom would be consulted respecting this address or even on my intention of addressing them.

The Title of the book[1] is:—

Reliquiae Sacrae
Sive
Fragmenta et Opusculae
S.S. Patrum Anti — Nicaenorum
Quorum Scripta
Separatim Edi Non Solent
Accedunt
Epistolae Synodicae et Canonicae
Synodo Nicaena Antiquiores
Cum Libris Scriptis Contulit, Notis Que Illustravit.
etc. etc.

John Richardson to Richard Heber
Wanlip. 21 October 1813

I wish you joy of the brilliant manner in which old Graham[2] has terminated his Spanish career. Lord Wellington's performances are in themselves excellent; I hope they may produce the effects expected.[3]

James H. Stanhope to Richard Heber
15 St. James's Place. 22 November 1813

I was just going to write to you to beg that you would manage to meet me at Althorp[4] soon, but if we now meet it will be across

---

[1] Dr. Routh's great work *Reliquiae Sacrae*. He had issued the Prospectus in 1788, the first two volumes actually appeared in 1814, two more in 1815 and 1818 and the final volume in 1848. He died aged ninety-nine having been resident in Oxford for eighty-four years, for sixty-three of which he was President of Magdalen.

[2] General Thomas Graham (1748-1843), a graduate of Christ Church, A.D.C. to Sir John Moore at Corunna, commanded a brigade in the Walcheren expedition, served under Wellington in the Peninsula, commanded the left wing at Vittoria, was wounded, and in 1814 commanded the British contingent in Holland.

[3] *I.e.* the complete freeing of Spain from French troops and a successful advance into France.

[4] Lord Spencer's seat, near Northampton.

the sea, for the Govt. have urged General Graham to take the command in Holland and I cannot stay behind when the Graeme leads the way. My shoulder is healed, more bone will come out but whenever it does I must lay up for a few days and get a fat fair frow to nurse me. I am so busy buying horses that I cannot write a long letter. Only bear in mind — we must make up for this some day, but I cannot persuade myself to be the only idle person when all hands are employed. I go as Graham's first A.D.C.

James H. Stanhope to Richard Heber
Klundert, near Williamstadt. 1 January 1814

I have not had time to write to you before but I have commenced this huge folio sheet in order to make amends.[1] You will have heard of our having landed at Tholen in consequence of the evacuation of Williamstadt and Breda. We made a reconnaissance on Bergen-op-Zoom the next day but a reinforcement had entered that morning (the 17th). Had the winds not detained us so long in England, I think we should have taken the place by a *coup de main*, as it (is) of immense size and had at one time but a thousand men in it of all sorts. That day is however gone by. On the 18th the French pushed a strong body supposed to be from 6 to 7000 men to and invested Breda where Gen. Benkendorff was with 1200 Russian Infantry and 3000 cavalry.

After amusing themselves with throwing some shot and shells into the town, they retired on the 21st in consequence we suppose of one of their Regiments of Hussars being nearly cut to pieces by a Regiment of Black Prussian Hussars towards Tilburg. This occasioned us to draw ourselves more to the left to be *a portée* to move in support of Breda. A garrison has been left in Tholen. Steinbergen is evacuated and our right is at Williamstadt.

---

[1] Stanhope's cogent description of the campaign in Holland needs little supplementing The force landed at Tholen in December; it was never strong in numbers and always weak in quality. It acted in support of the right wing of the allied advance, Graham putting himself at the disposal of Bulow. With increasing success the allies became less united, and the operations in which Graham was engaged were made more difficult by the vacillation of the Prussians.

In consequence of orders from Gen. Winzengerode, Gen. Benkendorff evacuates Breda tomorrow moving on Dusseldorff to which point the march of the former is directed. We, although not half equipped, weak in numbers and having a most extensive line to defend, nevertheless send a Brigade ' pour le moment ' to keep the French out *if possible* though to one who has never seen these much boasted fortresses, it would be difficult to describe the weakness of these with a small garrison in time of frost. The magnitude of Breda is so great that 12,000 men at least should garrison it for a seige, and frost here is a kind of Death to all sorts which levels alike all ranks of systems. From the scarcity of materials hardly any of these works are revetted, thus the slope of the ramparts is so great that one might ride up them and when the wet ditch is frozen over, the works are not so defensible as field entrenchments. Bergen-op-Zoom is an exception to this. If we can keep Breda for a few days, it will be safe, as Winzengerode's movement protects Bulow's flank from MacDonald and renders his army disposable. A Corps of from 8 to 10,000 men which was blockading Wesel has already been rel'd by the Russians and has joined his main body which is occupying the extensive line from Arnheim and Geertruydenberg. I hope therefore we shall be able to do something.

The allied armies moved towards Switzerland on the 20th, which has shewn the best spirit. Berne has replaced the old Govt. of 1802 under Monsr. de Stiegor — but all this I suppose is old news.

You will expect something about the country. I wish I could send you a better account of it. I used to complain of the want of enthusiasm in Spain (I mean the self devotion which comes forward and becomes organised, not good will of which there is plenty both there and here) but the people here are dull and motionless as their Canals. Till the Hereditary Prince came here a few days ago, the order for the Levy en Masse, circulated some days before at the Hague, never had arrived, and since he published it, nobody has been raised. The country is full of young men more than I ever saw in any country but with the exception of some cries of ' *Orange boven* ', some orange ribbons which begin to fade and some triumphal arches which savour too strongly of French Prefecture and old drilling to Napoleon's victories, no travellers would know there was such a thing as war, much less that their independance was at stake. They fear the Cossacs and *pretty justly* more than the French; of the latter I have seen a good many, but must leave the description of them to another time. The weather is very cold but the air is not so searching as in Spain. The hoar frost hangs like snow up on the trees and rarely can you see your neighbour for fog, but I smoke my segar and am not the worse for it.

My shoulder aches still but I ride 30 miles a day without fatigue and sleep certainly much better — still it remains to be tried how I stand winter operations. I have sent to the Hague for a warm fur pelisse. We have plenty of everything, Burgundy, Champagne, Claret and Curacoa for our friends and a place *always for you* (I can venture to say) at the General's table if you will come and look at us.

P.S. The fever at Cadiz has killed half my Cortes friends, but the best are still alive.

Jan. 3rd. The frost is broke which puts Breda, etc. in safety. ' On dit ' that the Cossacs have taken a French convoy from Antwerp to Bergen.

James H. Stanhope to Richard Heber
Mirxham. 6 February 1814

Since I wrote last I went to the Hague from whence I was suddenly recalled by the preparations for the attempt against the enemy's fleet at Antwerp. On the first we arrived at this village and the Prussians near Dewne pushing one Divn. on Lier and Malines. The Prussians (contrary to the General's disposition) attacked Dewne the same evening and experienced a considerable loss, not taking the whole of it till next day. On the morning of the 2nd we attacked the village which in spite of all the abbatis they had made and the opposition of above a 1000 men strongly posted, was soon carried by the impetuosity of our troops who behaved to admiration. So great were the exertions that were used in the formation of our batteries (animated by knowing that Bulow had rec'd orders to move towards Winzengerode and would leave us today) that we opened 24 pieces of heavy ordnance principally *Vertical fire* among which were 3 huge Napoleon mortars at 3 o'clock on the 3rd. During that evening, the 4th and 5th we threw at and mostly into the basin above 2000 shells and 400 of the large ones. We frequently occasioned flames to burst out in different parts, but the enemy always succeeded in extinguishing them, still the mischief we have done there must have been very great. Our loss was not considerable not exceeding I think 200 men. Our heavy guns were removed last night and we retire today to take up positions communicating with the Prussians and protecting Williamstadt and Breda. I think our campaigns[1] are nearly over. Probably by this time the fate of Bonaparte is decided. I think I shall return to England (in case of peace) before I go to Italy, as Hester does not seem certain what she means to do. I have rec'd highly interesting letters from her of 15 July from Latikia. She is quite well and delighted with the people their character, kindness and even her own dangers.

Dr. Edward Copleston to Richard Heber
Oriel. 20 March 1814

We have all been entranced in ecstasy by Mrs. Siddon's[2] Readings, as they are called or in reality actings. She has answered much better than I expected. I went strongly prepossessed against it, as thinking it would be a spurious mixture of two arts essentially different, but the effect was so powerful as to make you unconscious of the want of stage scenery and accompanying performers. When she exclaimed in Lady Constance's character ' War! War! No peace! peace is to me a War ' (vide the whole passage)[3] the application of the feelings of the day were close. Of course *we* were too well-bred to betray any such vulgar emotion as this would have excited in a London Theatre.

[1] The assault on Bergen-op-Zoom failed on 8 March, but the war terminated on Napoleon's abdication on 30 March.
[2] Sarah Siddons (1755-1831) retired from the stage in 1812 but continued to give private performances and readings.
[3] King John, III, i.

Archdeacon Ralph Churton to Richard Heber
Middleton. 25 March 1814

I abominate premature canvasses; and I fear it is true as you have heard, that Mr. Weatherall[1] has ' declared himself a candidate' or that his friends have done so. If he has done so himself, that single circumstance ought to defeat his views if he had ten times the merit which he may possess.

I think the wisest and best thing any real friend of yours now in the University could do, would be to remonstrate with Mr. Weatherall's friends and put an end at once to what is in Oxford so unprecedented and in itself so improper. What certainty is there that Sir Wm. Scott[2] will be elected to the peerage ? It has been rumoured again and again these half dozen years and more that he and the Speaker were to be made Peers; for ought that is yet known, I suppose both of them may live and die ornaments of the Lower not of the Upper House.

My own opinion is unaltered that an independent country gentleman, especially if he be a man of talent and literature is much the fittest man to represent the University. Such was dear Sir R. Newdigate,[3] Sir W. Dolben,[4] Mr. Page[5] and Lord Cornbury[6] etc., though I do not mean to say that there were all men of shining abilities or of great learning. The first requisite is a gentleman of good family and independant fortune who will give an unbiased constitutional vote, not a professional man, who will barter the honour and interests of his seat for promotion in his profession.

I must advert on this occasion not without anxiety to another point. A friend who wished to retain his vote for you asked me a year or two ago whether you were firm on the Roman Catholic

---

[1] Charles Wetherell (1770-1846), politician and lawyer; demy of Magdalen College, Oxford, 1786-91; a tory of the most conservative school; M.P. for Shaftesbury 1813-8, Oxford 1820-6, Hastings 1826, Plympton Earl 1826-30, Boroughbridge 1830-2. Knighted 1824.
[2] Sir William Scott, see note on page 198.
[3] Sir Roger Newdigate (1719-1806), antiquary, M.P. for Oxford University 1750-80.
[4] William Dolben (1726-1814); fought for the abolition of the slave trade; M.P. for Oxford University 1768-1806.
[5] Francis Page (born 1743), M.P. for Oxford University 1768-1801.
[6] Henry Hyde, Viscount Cornbury (1710-53), M.P. for Oxford University 1732-50; was a friend of Bolingbroke and had the reputation of a Jacobite.

question. If I gave him any answer (which I do not now recollect) it was of course that I trusted you were. I mentioned in a letter on some other business that such a question had been asked me; and you were silent on that point in your answer, as it was then, like the present canvass, premature. It is now however necessary to be explicit. That most woful election of Lord Grenville created an almost universal hostility to our dear Brazenose and cast a suspicion on almost all his partizans and supporters. I greatly fear that any candidate from Brazenose, known to have been friendly with Lord Grenville, will not be very favourably received by the University, but unless it is clearly understood that he does not coincide with his Lordship as to Roman Catholic Emancipation, if he has ten times the talents and recommendations of both our present worthy representatives, he will have no chance whatsoever. As far as I can learn (and I was at Oxford a few weeks ago) the Chancellor contrives to disgust and in truth to insult them more and more in almost all intercourse with them. Whether he did at last go with the late address to the P. Regent I have not heard but it was repeatedly said that he refused to go.

But the matter of the Roman Catholics is truly momentous. Independently of the incurable hostility of that idolatrous Church to Protestants and the innumerable massacres which they have committed in cold blood and the probably still more bitter persecution which from the same quarter awaits the witnesses of truth; — view the matter merely in a political light. To rob the King, as they do, of *half his Prerogative* and as we shall do if we concede what they demand, is a far greater evil than to rob him of *half his Dominions*. If our invaluable Constitution, the source under Providence of all our strength and prosperity, remains entire, we may be free and powerful, though the territory of the sovereign were (as God forbid it should be) less than at present; but if we surrender it, as we should do if we transferred half of the Imperial Prerogative of the Crown to the Pope or to any foreign power, tyranny, slavery, anarchy and confusion would soon ensue. If your principles — though you may have sometimes been in *bad company* — are as I trust firmly and constitutionally settled on this fundamental point in our Protestant Government, I could go through fire and water to serve you. If it is otherwise, though it may not be necessary at present to say whether I *could* give you a silent vote, I most certainly *could not solicit one friend in your favour.*

I was much concerned to hear that the Rector of Hodnet had been drawn into being an advocate of the Bible Society, which I believe to be big with mischief only less than popery. In this County almost all the Clergy keep aloof from that motley association. But the few pseudo-evangelicals that are to be found in some distant parts are to a man I believe friends of the Bible Society and to the claims of the Roman Catholics.

Archdeacon R. Churton to Richard Heber
Middleton. 5 April 1814

I thank you for your candid and friendly letter and am truly glad that *antiquum obtinus.* You are the same true and steady Church and Kingman I always hoped and believed you to be. In consequence of your letter I have written or applied through other friends to most of the gentlemen on your list of names and to many others. I canvassed a friend yesterday for you and he said at once ' Milton politics, I know nothing of Milton politics, Fitzwilliam's thing or something of that sort '.[1] I assured him it was not so but true Church and King or words to that effect. This was at a meeting of Magistrates and Commissioners of Taxes where I could not say much without being heard by all or by several. Today it occurred to me that he had been informed that you had voted for Lord Milton at the Yorkshire Election. I therefore wrote a note to undeceive him, informing him that you were a warm supporter of the opposite party and the Fitzwilliams having by a maneuvre (of which merit was claimed by an East India gentleman who once travelled on the

[1] Charles William Wentworth Fitzwilliam (1786-1857), Viscount Milton, third Earl Fitzwilliam; supported parliamentary reform and was one of the earliest advocates of free trade.

same coach with me from Oxford to London) engaged all the horses for two stages round York, you walked 20 miles to give your vote for Mr. Lascelles,[1] I believe the name was.[2]

Dr. Philip Bliss[3] to Richard Heber
St. John's College. 6 April 1814

Do not think me impertient, but think me what I really am, your firm friend in saying that five or six men in this Common Room are against you because they fancy you are a friend of the Catholic cause. I as an individual feel strongly interested for that cause but I think I once somewhere heard that your sentiments differed: if so, and I had the liberty to make the assertion I think I could secure a few bigots.

In my wish for Heber, I flatter myself I am supporting the man of letters, the independent country gentleman and one who goes to represent the University as she should be represented with ability, integrity and independence.

Dr. Martin Routh to Richard Heber
Magd. Coll. Oxford 13 April 1814

Surely those persons were at a loss for objections who urged that you ought to have been previously in Parliament in order for them to form a judgement whether you would be a proper representative of the University. But this nonsense I am told went down in a neighbouring college to our own — not Queens College but one farther off. Let me hear from you, altho' I am again so circumstanced owing to an intrigue in this place, that I can do you little service or much less than I wish.

---

[1] Henry Lascelles (1767-1841), Viscount Lascelles and second Earl of Harewood.

[2] The Yorkshire Election of 1807 was one of the most expensive, even for those days, and one of the closest. The result was:—

Wilberforce	11,806
Milton	11,177
Lascelles	10,989

[3] Dr. Philip Bliss (1787-1857), Fellow of St. John's College, Oxford : antiquary.

Rev. John Stonard to Richard Heber
East Malling. 15 April 1814

What overpowering events! Surely there never will be any more news as long as we live. The Papers will be as dull as a ledger and Politics insipid as the white of an egg. Only it is to be expected that the amiable spirit of Party will stir up some internal troubles as it did after the Peace in 1763. There will be ground. Provisions are falling in price, therefore Labour must fall and Rents must fall. The taxes cannot be paid, true; but then the establishments will be less expence. True again, but who can suppose that all these matters will be kept in a just equilibrium. Besides, people will soon be tired of peace. Their spirits will flag at the cessation of the violent excitements they have lately received, as gamblers do a quiet life and they will take advantage of anything tending to rouse them from their torpor.

Dr. Martin Routh to Richard Heber
Magd. Coll. Oxford. 16 June 1814

A friend of mine made Collingwood finish my two volumes last night and prevailed on me to send them this morning to our Chancellor with an intimation that I would if he thought proper present another copy or copies elsewhere, at the same time saying that I should be perfectly, nay better, satisfied with his determination to the contrary. To this communication I received a very polite and kind letter from his Lordship in which after congratulating me on having thus far advanced toward the completion of my work, he adds that he has not the smallest hesitation in expressing to me the earnest wish that he may be allowed to submit copies of it not only to His R.H. The Prince Regent but also to one or two other august Visitors ' that it may be known not only here but also in other countries, how those studies which are most peculiarly suited to this place continue to be presented among us '. Such are the terms his Lordship has been pleased to use. I will therefore trespass once more on your goodness for assistance and will if you give me leave and are not afraid of writing to me as you have reason to be in addressing some other persons, send you five copies to be bound as speedily as may be and in the way you shall direct for Their Imperial and Royal Majesties, his Royal H., our Chancellor and Mr. Heber. Could their arms be on the covers ? but I know nothing of this matter.

Mary Heber to her brother Richard Heber
Hodnet. 21 June 1814

I cannot let a day pass at home without thanking you for all your kindness to me in town to which I am indebted for the most interesting part of my excursion and without which I must have lived and died without seeing the Emperor of Russia.[1]

The subscription for Lord Hill's pillar near Shrewsbury is almost universal.[2] You do not intend I hope to omit paying him the same compliment.

The people all seem to have been asleep ever since I left them. I am sure George Walkely has and the weeds have taken advantage of his slumbers and almost out top the larches in your shrubbery.

Walter Scott to Richard Heber
Piccadilly, Thursday (25 May 1815)

Dear Heber,

In consequence of the enclosed I will be at Sir George Beaumont's not however for breakfast but about ten o'clock in the morning. Do come if you can and have a rally with us after old Paradise.

W. Scott.

[1] Visit of Emperor Alexander of Russia to England was from 7 to 27 June.
[2] Rowland Hill (1772-1842) was one of Wellington's outstanding generals who were honoured in 1814. Hill became a baron. The inhabitants of Shropshire, at a cost of £6,000, raised a column in his honour.

(Enclosure)

William Wordsworth[1] to Walter Scott
(postmark) 24 *May* 1815

I begin to fear that we are destined not to meet. I mentioned to Mr. Heber an original picture of Milton recently rescued from a Broker's shop. The sight of this Portrait *I am sure* would delight you. Mr. Heber expressed a wish to see it. Sir George[2] and Lady Beaumont feel the same desire and I now write to beg that if you be at leisure on Friday morning next or any morning next week after Tuesday, you would arrange with Mr. Heber that we might all meet at Sir George Beaumont's at half past nine for breakfast and proceed to the Picture.

Nat. Domett Junr. to Richard Heber
Rotterdam. 23 *June* 1815

Your books are very safe here and Van Cleaf whom I have seen has promised to send the others with the account in the course of next week; as soon as they arrive I will ship the whole for London letting you know at the same time.

Tho' I have been here so long I am not indeed a Dutchman neither should I be one were I to stay here ten times as long: their language tho' not very pleasant could not of course be passed; and what I find to be good in them will if possible copy, but old England is so predominant that I have some difficulty in persuading myself anything can be good that is not English; their want of freedom is one terrible thing, political opinions if prejudicial to the State must not be spoken in public, a gentleman was arrested a few days ago for having mentioned a report that some of the Brabant troops had deserted to the enemy.

When the news first arrived concerning Bonaparte's landing in France, the people were completely terrified imagining that he would immediately march against Holland; had it not been for

---

[1] William Wordsworth (1770-1850).
[2] Sir George Beaumont (1753-1827), art patron and landscape painter.

those seasonable supplies of troops ammunition and money sent
by our Government, many I am sure would have fled to England
without thinking of defending their own country. Till within a
day or two, they were still alarmed; the great news which the
last week has given us and which is, no doubt well known in
London by this time, has driven all their fears and now they
would fain take the honour of those great victories to themselves
which is almost ridiculous.

I may congratulate you, Sir, upon this news so glorious to
Englishmen and which has shewn the world that Wellington is
second to none. No one has denied that the Dutch troops have
fought well, yet they are afraid it will be and so affirm to please
one another that their conduct surpassed that of all other troops.
When it is repeated to me, I do not allow it which makes them
rather angry.

You are so kind as to enquire whether my heart is my own,
it will I assure you never be left as a Vrouw's property in Holland.

James H. Stanhope. Copy of letter to Lady Spencer
Bourget, in front of Montmartre. 3 July 1815

Two things have prevented my writing to you dear Lady
Spencer, want of time and ignorance about the state of poor
Fred Ponsonby.[1] But now the war is over as a suspension of
hostilities has taken place and as I hear that 'hang it' is quite
out of danger, I cannot refrain from giving you an outline of our
campaign[2] which I fear you nevertheless consider as an outrageous attack against the just liberties of a people.

Bonaparte's plan appears to have been as able as anything he
ever did and was not far from succeeding. The collection of his

[1] Sir Frederick Cavendish Ponsonby (1783-1837), son of the Earl of Bessborough, was
wounded when commanding the 12th Light Dragoons at Waterloo.
[2] Stanhope's description of Waterloo is again clear and accurate. He refers first to the
action at Quatre Bras on 16 June, when Picton's division arrived just in time to support
the Prince of Orange's troops. That night the Prussians retreated on Wavre; next morning
Wellington moved back from Quatre Bras. The night of the 17th was spent in bivouac
on the field of Waterloo, and the battle fought on the 18th, in the afternoon and evening.

troops was made in such a manner that either the Duke was lulled into security or, what is more probable, was apprehensive of a false movement and suspected tho' they assembled near Maubeuge they might attack him on the Ath road.

At any rate the Duke left a ball at Brussels at 2 the army began to collect, marching from their different points at daylight and the 5th Division having marched 25 miles had a severe action in the evening and we having moved something more just arrived to save the wood which was the key of the position which the Belgians had all but lost. We were under every disadvantage, the cavalry having all to move 30 and some 45 miles and therefore they were useless on that day. Had the wood been lost the French army was between our corps and we must have retreated that night.

Blucher's retreat the same night left us in no pleasant position, but the Duke eased us off little by little and expressed his joy when he saw all the Infantry gone. We took up the position the Duke will describe in his despatch and endured the most tremendous night troops ever were exposed to, without fires and immersed in all the richness of Belgian mud.

The house was the key of the position as it was at the angle on which the potence rested and was defended by the 2nd Brigade of Guards. The whole hill was covered with a formidable artillery and the infantry were in columns ready to form squares: for this was the most singular feature of the battle, at least on the right and centre that it was fought almost entirely in squares, being exposed to the fire of above 250 pieces of artillery and the united efforts of cavalry and infantry. What past on the left I only know by hearsay, that the heavy cavalry made a most brilliant charge and suffered severely in being led on too far. On our side we were in echellons of squares as I have sketched with my pen most incorrectly but to give a rough idea of it and in two lines supported by cavalry.

Having been pounded by shot and shell till your morning service was about over, we were assailed by a most immense body of cavalry against which our light cavalry made no head and showed a lamentable inferiority of which no one can give a better act. than Lord Uxbridge[1] who by the way showed himself one of the calmest and bravest of men.

The reception of the cavalry by our squares was magnificent, tho' suffering severely from the artillery, every man felt his own security and poured in a fire as destructive as it was well sustained. But the Curassier Lancers were not to be discouraged and for above an hour they continued never retreating above 200 yards and then charging again, Barnes the Adjt. Gen. waving them on and our men at length learning to despise their power over steady infantry. Frequently the enemy sent in Tirailleurs of their cavalry to fire their pistols in our squares hoping that it should fire a volley and that they might charge us with their mass before we could load, but their hopes were disappointed. In the meantime the house and garden had been attacked by a heavy column of infantry, the French cavalry had passed it and were lined on the brow of the hill but nothing shook its defenders and the attacks were successfully and successively repulsed. A heavy column had moved along the high road to the left where supported by an immense cavalry (force), a furious action ensued and two columns of infantry were seen moving over the plain in a concentrating direction, on that front of the line occupied by the 1st Brigade of Guards the 52nd, 71st etc. and some Brunswickers. Here the English infantry did what never was practised before, deploying into line and beating the infantry and then forming four deep to beat the attacks of the cavalry who had been waiting for the moment of our confusion to complete our rout. So stood the battle, when the last desperate effort was made by three columns of Imperial Guards. The Grenadiers of it, accompanied by Bonaparte to the bottom of the hill, came to our share, the right column to that of the 52nd etc. and it is hard to say which was cleaned away the soonest. Our men poured in a fire standing four deep, the men who had fired then went to the fourth rank to load and thus without interruption a destructive

[1] Henry William Paget (1768-1854) succeeded his father as Earl of Uxbridge in 1812. He served in the army with distinction in Flanders, Holland and Spain. For his splendid services as commander of the British cavalry at Waterloo, where he lost a leg, he was created Marquis of Anglesey.

hail was kept up against which nothing could stand and the hill was heaped with their dead. Thus long had the army stood, just keeping their ground and where any link breaking, the whole wd. have been annihilated, for with the superiority of the French cavalry, retreat was out of the question. The first impetus of the French checked, it seems the Duke made up his mind to convert a difficult defence into an attack. Everything advanced and everything before us fled. A French General whom I have met since as a negotiator said that a cry ran through the ranks, ' que la vielle garde fuyait ' and that in an instant as if by magic every-one consulted his own safety by flight. Bonaparte told Count Lebon striking his own forehead, ' Il n'y a rien comme l'infanterie anglaise.'

At this time the roar of the Prussian artillery was heard on our left and soon appeared through the smoke which hung heavily on the field what appeared a fresh army springing from the earth and sweeping on in pursuit of the enemy. Of all sights the plain then presented the most magnificent and of all moments that was the proudest and it is useless to attempt to describe it. To give you an idea how well our artillery behaved, I must tell you the French cavalry frequently charged through the guns but cd. not carry them off, the artillery men ran to the squares for safety and the instant our fire repulsed the enemy, returned to their practice of grape and this was repeated several times.

You will tag me with national vanity if I say that no other army could have kept that hill and stood such attacks but I am well convinced of the fact and that we could not without the Duke who outdid himself and set an example that never was surpassed. How he escaped or indeed how anyone came alive out of that scene of carnage is strange. The field of battle was not large and the killed of both sides could be easily distinguished and I understand above 18,000 French bodies have been buried.

Of our subsequent events I need say nothing as with this exception of our attack on Peronne it has been like a walk through England. These heights on our front were enough to frighten us and I am truly thankful that the business will be settled without the effusion of more blood.

God forbid that I should ever see such a battle again for I hardly dare to ask what friends I have left. Yet it was decisive and we probably should have lost more in several battles to reach this place.

I must now say two words about myself. About two weeks before we moved, another abcess began to form in my back and I suffered so much that I had determined, having got through the 16th, to go to Brussels on the 18th if we had not been attacked. The great exertion of the day commenced my cure and absorption has delivered me for the present of my enemy. I was appointed Asst. Q.M. Genl. to the 1st Divn. a day or two after the battle, which I continue.

I fear you can hardly decypher or comprehend this letter. If you can, pray show it to Heber, for I cannot write any more at present.

James H. Stanhope to Richard Heber
Paris. 30 August 1815

You ask what is the opinion of the most enlightened class of the country. It is impossible to answer it as this is a chaos in which none quite agree or wholly put confidence in one another. The King by his neutral line has disgusted the old royalists and by being compelled to become the instrument of the extortion of the allies has still further irritated the country against him. His wisest act is that of nationalizing the army and making them like our Militia which would destroy the esprit de corps and perhaps wean them back to civil life, but as yet this is only on paper. If the King shoots Ney, it may produce good. He is to be tried by Marshalls.[1] Davout,[2] Moncey,[3] I hear are among the number.

I am convinced the great fault we have committed is having brought Louis in behind, but whose is the blame none can tell,

[1] When Napoleon returned from Elba, Ney was sent by the King to arrest him. Ney, however, deserted to Napoleon and fought at Waterloo. The King on his return had him apprehended and tried for treason.
[2] Louis Nicholas Davout (1770-1823).
[3] Bon Adrien Jeannot Moncey (1754-1842).

but the Dr.[1] says it is not him and I heard Lord C.[2] equally denies it. We should have entered as enemies, have asked for as many millions as we wanted, have occupied as many fortresses as required for guarantees and then, had the nation chose to call to the Throne a pacific King in whom we could trust, we might perhaps relaxed a little in our demands, but we should have left him — instead of which the allies have broken their faith in every way, have brought 500,000 men into France since L was restored, have imprisoned and driven away magistrates of his appointment, have taken from him the revenue of his provinces and instead of being known to the French by his benificence by saving them from the horrors of war, he is considered as the executioner. As for the plundered pictures, it is all very right and they are going fast so you had better come.

I believe Fouché[3] is sincere, nay more, there is every reason to believe he was betraying B. and was at the bottom of the insurrection in La Vendée.[4] Anything is preferable to the Voltigeurs du Roi (the old gouty emigré) who maintain Ferdinand is the best King in Europe and that no King can be firm in France if the people is enlightened. They have returned more blind than they were with every folly and prejudice confirmed. I fear with you our officers will not benefit much by Paris. The houses where play and women are combined attract all, and the former makes large gaps in fortunes: l'autre va sans dire !

As to myself I like to prostitute myself to about a dozen parties. The Jacobins treat me as a natural colleague from being the son of —[5], the others with many shrugs and ah ah! at my relationship with Mr. Pt. Les savants m'acceuillent avec bonté au rapport de Sir J.B.[6] and between the one and the other, I see a good deal of their society, which is all I wish to do that one may be able to form some opinion for oneself.

I have heard from the Doc. He is for the destruction of all palaces and public edifices but for the preservation of every

[1] The Doctor is Addington, created Viscount Sidmouth, 1805.
[2] Lord C. is presumably Castlereagh, the Foreign Secretary.
[3] Joseph Fouché (1759-1820), Police Minister under Napoleon.
[4] A Royalist insurrection in La Vendée during the Hundred Days.
[5] 3rd. Earl Stanhope, ardent supporter of the Revolution.
[6] Presumably Sir Joseph Banks (1743-1820), president of the Royal Society.

peasant's cottage, a charming theory but reversed in practice, for the Generals live in and preserve the one, the soldiers break into and destroy the other. People are apt over their firesides to talk of destruction and pillage with tranquillity, but if they were to see a specimen they would change their opinion. Nothing can equal the admirable conduct of our army, it has gained the respect of all.

Mrs. Reginald Heber (sister-in-law) to Richard Heber
24 September 1815

Mary and I went to our Ball (at Shrewsbury) and returned the same night or I should say the next morning for we were in good time for breakfast. Lord Hill, Sir Noel and Sir Francis[1] added much to the ornament of the ballroom by the brilliancy of their numerous stars and orders. The two former are much thinner and browner than when they left England. They have only a fortnight's leave of absence but Lord Hill thinks we shall soon see him in England again as the armies will be shortly dispersing. He told me that the Regent longing to share with Blucher in the spoils of the Louvre has signified his wishes to the Pope that the *Apollo* and the *Venus* may be presented to him, with which request His Holiness is most ready to comply.

Ney's trial and probable execution[2] would have long since been over but for some informalities in the proceedings of the Court Martial of which the President had laid hold of to delay the business. But the general belief is that he will be shot.

Robert Southey to Richard Heber
Keswick. 9 January 1816

I regretted much that you were not in London during my late visit to the great city on my return from the Netherlands, During a five weeks journey, I saw many interesting places and

---

[1] General Sir Rowland Hill (1772-1842), cr. Baron 1814 and Viscount 1842 and his two brothers, Sir Francis (1779-1842) and Sir Noel (1784-1832).
[2] Ney was shot 7 December 1815.

some beautiful country. My course was Ostend, Brussels, Water-loo and the three fields of battle at La belle Alliance, Les Quatre Bras and Ligny, Namur, Huy, Liege, Spa, Aix-la-Chappelle, Maestricht, Tongres, Tirlemont, Louvain, Brussels, Mechlin, Antwerp, Ghent, Courtray, Ypres, Dunkirk and Calais.

As I could not avoid writing upon the last year's great events, I have endeavoured to avoid all possible competition with Scott. My title is ' A Poet's Pilgrimage to the Field of Belle Alliance '; my metre and six lined stanza consisting of a quatrain and a couplet. This stanza (has) a slight Spencerian tint of language in keeping with the title. About 900 lines are written and I am yet far from the conclusion of my task. You will conclude that it has not proved an irksome one or that it would not have been thus prolonged.

Majr. General Sir John Malcolm[1] to Richard Heber
Hotel de Londres, Place Vendome, Paris. 10 August 1816

This is an extraordinary scene but I doubt whether you do not know more in London than we do who are in the midst of it. It appears to me that there is only one course for the allies which is to take the best security they can against future danger. The reaction will be as great as the means left to France will permit. As little should be left as is consistent with preserving her as one of the great nations of Europe. I pity the poor King. He should quit Paris and fix his residence elsewhere. He should increase his Swiss Guards and raise an army of Vendeans and Bordelais and fatten them with the plunder of every turbulent rascal in his Kingdom. As to Chambers, Constitution and Liberty of the Press[1] about which fools in France and greater fools in England speak, I shall say nothing about them. Materials must be

---

[1] Major-General Sir John Malcolm, G.C.B. (1769-1833).
[2] Louis XVIII on his return from exile in May 1814 granted France a liberal Con-stitutional Charter. After his second restoration however, the Chamber of Deputies (" la Chambre Introuvable ") was controlled by the Ultra-Royalists who were loud in their endeavours to destroy the Charter, abolish the freedom of the Press and to restore the position and estates of the aristocracy and the Church. In November 1816 a new and moderate ministry was formed which, thanks to the Duc de Richlieu was able to secure a reduction in the Allied army of occupation.

prepared before a structure can be reared and these are at present wanting for anything but a military Government. Security of property and a just administration of the Law is essential.

The French desire change as much at the moment as they did the day the revolution commenced, but the people are at present more speakers than actors. They appear to me (but I am yet a stranger) totally incapable of a government at all resembling ours. Force will decide and it is very problematic which will be the strongest the day the allies quit. Louis is considered as having been raised to the throne by the conquest of his country. He cannot remove that impression but he may gain strength by exercising the rights of a conqueror. I fear the gout will stop him.

James H. Stanhope to Richard Heber
Paris. 15 January 1817

The distress in the country among *les paysans* unrelieved by the rich is not to be exaggerated, but from all I can collect, the financial difficulties are more feigned than real. It resembles the squeals of a child for fear he should be hurt. The Govt. will succeed in raising their 12,000,000 (without guarantee) in bits and the payment of the Contributions will be continued. The military payments have been stopped. The King is going to have 12,000 Swiss but as yet has 2. This step has not produced a good effect anywhere and there are already quarrels of which nothing is said. There is an ' on dit ' that 1/5th of the Contingent is to be withdrawn. There is another of a quarrel between Portugal and Spain. The former is fitting out an expedition to occupy one side of the Rio de Plata and say it is with Ferdinand's consent, which the Spanish Embassy here denies. ' On dit ' and from pretty good authority that the Royalists in Mexico have got ahead but at Chile the insurgents are so.

The Emby. gave a ball last night but I do not think we assimilate much yet with the natives, but the tone of Society is better than when I was here last. Madame de Staël[1] is more odious

---

[1] Madame de Staël (1766-1817). She was a daughter of the financier Necker.

than ever and her daughter surpasses the mother. There is an Ultra, la Duchs' d'Ecave who battles her handsomely and who finished the other night, ' Je vous laisse vos 25 années des crimes mais laissez vous nos 25 années des malheurs.' 'Pour le reste', all goes on the same. 'Le Roi mange et les grands ont leurs amours'. Talleyrand cuts jokes and praises the ministry ' surtout pour le " budget " qui est inpayable '. The *beau monde* slide down les Montagnes Russes and real Russian mountains, Kofsolofsky, etc. enchant them by quadrilles. The *piece du theatre* most in the fashion is called Susanne who comes forth from her bath pursued by a dozen bearded elders. Sir S.S. and family attend for philosophical causes as he thinks his anti-terraqueous unsubmergible machine might be of use to her.

IX   Letters to

RICHARD HEBER

1818-1823

AT LONG LAST, in 1821, Sir William Scott received the peerage for which he had been angling for more than sixteen years and there was a by-election at Oxford. Richard, after a very spirited contest was elected. Unfortunately these letters throw no light on the methods used to gain votes for him. Was he represented as a progressive ? Did parliamentary reform or Catholic emancipation figure in the programme? Or was the fight not rather one between rival factions in the university? ' Let forty B.N.C. men go up and vote !' commanded Richard's election manager at the critical moment of the battle. One thing alone seems certain: that the voters were not encouraged to cast their voice according to their private opinions about the principles (if any) involved. Whether Richard found the House of Commons as interesting from the inside as he had expected is another matter.

In Shropshire the peace of Moreton Saye was disturbed by the arrival of a new curate. He and Mary Heber were married in 1822. It appears that Mary had a shrewd head for business. Old Mrs. Heber left Moreton Saye vicarage to the newly married couple and moved to Whitchurch, where she ended her days in 1834, aged 82.

In 1823 Reginald said goodbye to Hodnet and sailed away to India as Bishop of Calcutta.

Rev. Charles P. Burney[1] *to Richard Heber*
Greenwich. 2 February 1818

My friends have urged me forward to offer myself as a candidate for the vacant Professorship of Ancient Literature in the Royal Academy, but as I think with extremely slender chance of success. The Post is highly honourable and for reasons which you must feel, I may be excused for coveting it greatly. I wish if you come across Mr. Phillips[2] or any others of the Academicians you would edge in a word in my recommendation.

Rev. Charles P. Burney to Richard Heber
7 February 1818

The situation in the Academy is one of *pure* honour without salary, without duty. My friends put me on the canvass for it before I knew all which is connected with the history and dignity of the Post.

Dr. Edward Copleston to Richard Heber
Oriel. 20 April 1818

The proposition you have conveyed to me in so handsome and flattering a manner was indeed quite unexpected — and you can imagine the surprise with which I read it. For the office you suggest I have no pretensions whatever, for I presume that a modest acquaintance at least with the materials of such a work is indispensable in him who is regarded as the superintendant of its progress. Now in this respect I am deficient beyond even what you are prepared to believe. The fondness I have expressed for English Antiquities and the occasional attention I have paid to very limited subjects of that kind has perhaps led you to think that I have made it a serious study. Nothing I can assure you is farther from the truth. My serious studies are directed to Theology and what is called Metaphysics in both of which departures I

[1] Rev. Charles Parr Burney, son of Dr. Charles Burney.
[2] ? Thomas Phillips (1770–1845), portrait-painter, R.A. 1808.

fancy I see much that remains to be done. I have a vast field before me and I never expect to beat one third part of the ground. You can form some judgement of the cares which such a post as mine involves, if besides being guardian of the College ' tam in spiritualibus quam in temporalibus ' as our statutes tell me I am, a personal intercourse also is to be maintained with every member of the Society and with the duties of the University and the pulpit in their turn — to say nothing of a memory which compels me to read over every two or three years whatever I have need to bear in mind for use.

Walter Scott to Richard Heber
Abbotsford. 27 April 1818

I wrote generally to Mr. Elliot when I received his announce to thank him for the undeserved honour which the Club has confer'd on my unworthy person and which I prize very highly as much on account of its living as of its departed members. I will certainly be most happy when my residence in town will permit to avail myself of the privilege confer'd on me.

If anything could render it more wellcome, it would have been its procuring the means of my again seeing your *pieds de mouche* as our poor Ellis used to call your characters.

Why will you not come down to Scotland and brighten the charm of friendship? Edinburgh you will hardly know and me you will hardly know so much is the former altered for the better and the latter for the worse. I have escaped from my disease however very nearly and almost entirely from my doctors who proceeded entirely on the *Tirtea-Fuera* system. I have been building a sort of old-fashioned though modern messuage here and intend one day to complete it with a Library — and I have land and trees as well as any Justice Shallow in the land, 1200 good acres of which 200 are woodland. But alas! all my trees are in their infancy and it is a future age that will enjoy them otherwise than in the mind's eye.

Pray do come next season that is this summer and leave all your wonted haunts for a month or two. You will like them

better on your return. I say particularly this summer for next
I have thought of going abroad for a few months. Your old
friends will be delighted to see you and none more so, dear Heber.

Yours in sincere friendship,

Walter Scott

So I see our friend Sir Jo. Malcolm is setting up his banners and
shouting among the Mahrattas. It is enough to endure him in
his love and kindness, but when he roars in wrath, Achilles'
shout which overturned twelve curricles will be a joke to it.

Major General Sir John Malcolm to Richard Heber
Camp Chittore. 15 July 1818

Amid wars, negotiations and all the turmoil of camp occupation
I seize a moment to write to a friend in whose society I hope soon
to enjoy myself all the more for having in this life of incessant
toil learnt to place an increased value in comparative rest.

You will see by the public papers I have had my share in the
Battles of Negopatam.[1] The peace I lately concluded with Holkar
works well and has been the forerunner to quiet in this distracted
quarter, Jeswint Row Khan, a chief of Scindeahs who has long
plundered Mewar was attacked by us for harbouring Pindarries
and fled. He gave himself up to me the day before yesterday and
awaits very patiently the decisions of our Govt. and his Masters.
Kurreem the celebrated Pindarry chief gave himself up to me
yesterday begging mercy and subsistance. Duleep Khan a pre-
datory chief who for years had laid waste the territories in this
vicinity had the option of entering our service or being attacked.
He and 500 well mounted followers chose the former and I mean
to send them in a few days towards Poonah to aid in the reduction
of our treacherous ally the Paishwah whose fate now we have
conquered all our enemies cannot be long protracted.

Amid these scenes I cherish my passion for research which
however I have little time to indulge. I left my Division and took a

[1] The third Maratha war, 1817-8, is here referred to. It was embarked on because
the Maratha rulers, of whom Holkar of Indore was one, had lent their support to the
pindaris, freebooters whose existence could not be tolerated in the orderly British
dominion which India was becoming.

ride of twenty two miles to this place. I wish I could have met you on the road first to have introduced you to my Escort and next to have shewn you the ancient Capital of the noblest (in birth) of Hindu Princes. The Escort would have amused you. It did not amount to more than one hundred and fifty men but it included Coast Sepoys from Madura near Cape Comorin, Nizars from Hyderabad, Native Cavalry from Arcot, Rohillas (Native Hussars) from Delhi, men of a Dromedary Corps from Turshabad(?) irregular horse from Mysore, Holkari horse, some of Duleep Khan's Pindarry's and a few dismounted Rajpoots from Chatra sharing the road. This is a picture of my troops and my condition and I assure you I consider the task of making these elements more kindly and of aiding to convert the late instruments of anarchy into firm defenders of order to be as serious and as glorious a duty as any I have had hitherto to perform. As far as my character is concerned as an L.L.D. I imagine it will be considered as one of the most honourable.

Chittore still is one of the most magnificent objects I ever saw. It is very high, in length between four and five miles, in breadth from half-a-mile to a mile and surrounded with lofty ramparts of stone and frequent bastions. The fortifications winding with the varied shapes of the cliffs on which they are built. Over the top of this mountain (which is about twelve miles round) there is an abundance of water and tracts of cultivation. It once, when Chittore was the seat of Empire, contained one hundred thousand houses (if Rajpoot legends are to be believed) and there are still ruined Palaces, Minarets and Temples and many marks of former grandeur, but it has now a small garrison of five hundred men instead of fifty thousand who once defended it, and the town on the mountain is reduced to five hundred houses and that below having little more than double that number. The Princes of Mewar ever since Ackbar took Chittore have resided at Oudipore where they have nothing left but their rank. Their daughters on account of their terrible *high blood* are courted by Rajpoot Princes at the head of armies. The hand of one of them was contested twelve years ago by the Rajahs of Joudpore and Jypore; after a war of four years during which their country was desolated and their revenue exhaused, Meer Khan gave the Rajpoot Helen a dose of poison and the war terminated accordant to the honour of both parties with its object.

Rev. Sydney Smith to Richard Heber
20 Saville Row. 7 March 1819

Many thanks, dear Heber, for your kind note and present. Poor Leyden was a very highly gifted man and I never hear his name mentioned without remembering the many pleasant days I have spent in his society. Friendships grow in youthful soils; their progress is much slower in ground that has been much stirr'd about and cultivated.

George Crabbe[1] to Richard Heber
18 Brewer Street. 19 June 1819

The note which you were so obliging as to send to me from Bond Street, gives me pain, though I am proud of the attention, for it tells me that I had forgotten your invitation. No indeed I had not: I have not that shame. I have only inadvertency to answer for, a kind of Parson Adams-like confusion of ideas, that sent me to Pimlico instead of to the place where I had dined with you before and where reason would have informed me I should dine again.

Do, dear Sir, inform such of those pleasant gentlemen as you may meet again that the man for whom they waited so long was only inadvertent and was punished for that.

Mary Heber to Richard Heber
Moreton Saye. 1 December 1819

Mama desires her love; is sorry she sent her letter to you folded notewise, but as our household can none of them read (strange to say in this age of improvement) we grow rather careless about such matters.

---

[1] George Crabbe (1754-1832), the poet, was at this time at the height of his fame.

Mary Heber to Richard Heber
Moreton Saye. 28 May 1820

You may have heard that young Charles Cholmondeley[1] has taken the curacy of Moreton and means to live at the Oak Cottage which we are very glad of, after all our changes and ill luck in curates. He likes the place himself very much and I think we are in high luck to get what the poor Dean would have called a ' thorough gentleman '.

Mary Heber to Richard Heber
Alderley Rectory. 3 August 1820

Our new Chaplain at Moreton, young Charles, goes on remarkably well and is very much liked by all his parishioners high and low. He is a rather shy odd fellow, but when well known is highly to be valued for his numerous good qualities and excellent disposition. He staid with us at Moreton till the Oak Cottage was ready for his reception and we were quite happy to have such an opportunity of becoming thoroughly acquainted with his character. Old Charles[2] goes slinging on in the old way and cannot understand why his son prefers a profession to the honourable idleness he has himself persevered in so many years.

On the 22nd I proceeded to Astle for ten days which included the Knutsford Races. The Parkers were remarkably well and had a gay and pleasant party of twenty. Mrs. Shakespeare Phillips was there, as handsome I think and agreeable as ever. Her daughter is come out a nice pretty girl but rather too like Papa. The Balls were very good and I had a full share of the best partners. There was a grandee party at Tatton which we therefore named the House of Lords and our Astle party being enlivened by a large proportion of military called itself the Horse Guards.

The current report of the week is that Vale Royal is to be made a Peer,[3] but none of his family believe in it and are at a loss to guess the origin of the rumour.

[1] Rev. Charles Cholmondeley (1795-1831). He and Mary Heber were married in June 1822.
[2] ' Old Charles,' father of the new curate of Moreton Saye, second son of Thomas Cholmondeley of Vale Royal (1770-1846).
[3] Thomas Cholmondeley became Lord Delamere, 1821.

Lord Milton[1] to Richard Heber
19 December 1820

What is the news from the North Pole for tho' all the world is intent upon other matters I cannot help having a little curiosity about the world itself, its ways and its shape.[2]

What an extraordinary event it will be, if after so much despair on the subject of a North-Western Passage, it should at length be discovered and yet if we cannot dissolve the ice with which it is impeded, one knows not what commercial benefits can be derived from it, but perhaps some commercial Hannibal may start up and remove the impediments, the love of gain is as great an incentive as the love of fame.

Sir Walter Scott[3] to Richard Heber
Edinburgh. 21 June 1821

I trust you are to be true of promise and come to Abbotsford this season. I have just lost my facetious friend and private agent John Ballantyne and I shall miss him much. The gratified creature bequeathed me £2,000 to build a Library. This was part of the profits of our smuggling adventure.

Yours always, my dear Heber,

Walter Scott

Mary Heber to Richard Heber
Moreton Say. 25 June 1821

Charles Cholmondeley has had a grievous disappointment at being prevented by his father from taking his degree this term. There is no managing old Charles, tho' he has persuaded his son to give up the greatest part of his future expectations under the promise of clearing him now, yet he delays performing his part very unhandsomely.

[1] Lord Milton, later third Earl Fitzwilliam (1786-1857).
[2] In 1818 government encouraged polar exploration by an act offering rewards for finding the north-west passage and for reaching latitude 89 degrees north. In October 1820 Edward Parry's third expedition sailed into the arctic.
[3] Baronetcy conferred on him in 1820.

We are happy to hear there is so good a prospect of a vacancy at Oxford. If I can be of any use to you in making or copying alphabetical lists, I shall be happy to be employed in your service, but I cannot help hoping you will have no antagonist and slip in like Mr. Peel.[1]

Sir Watkin has been very busy making Wynnstay fit for his Royal Guest and now it is reported the King is not coming this way into Scotland. All Sir Watkin's friends however are very glad he has a motive at last for furnishing his house which has long been a by-word among them.

Reginald and Emily are well and so is our nice little niece who I think you will admire, she is very like Reginald.

Dr. George William Hall, Vice-Chancellor of Oxford to Richard Heber
Oxford. 24 August 1821

Sir,

It is with much satisfaction that I announce to you the result of the Election of a member to represent the University in Parliament in the room of Sir William Scott, now Lord Stowell. The members of Convocation after three days polling have this day elected you, Richard Heber Esq., by a majority of ninety three, the numbers of the Poll being for

Sir John Nicholl[2]	519 for
Rd. Heber Esq.	612

I have the honour to remain, Sir

Your sincere friend and Servt.

Geo. Wm. Hall, V.C.

Draft of letter to the Vice-Chancellor from Richard Heber, M.P.
in reply.

Mr. Vice-Chancellor,

With feelings of no ordinary kind I have just received the information contained in your obliging letter. To say that the

---

[1] Sir Robert Peel, the statesman (1788-1850), was adopted M.P. for Oxford University on account of his record of opposition to Catholic Emancipation.

[2] Sir John Nicholl (1759-1838), fellow of St. John's College, Oxford; judge; opponent of Catholic Emancipation and parliamentary reform.

present moment is the proudest of my life would be doing the occasion no more than justice. I will not however attempt to bury my sense of the honour conferred on me under an unnecessary accumulation of words. The little that I have to offer in return may be shortly expressed — respect and affection to the University of Oxford where I am grateful to have received my education (believing as I do that the studies there prescribed of Ancient Literature, the Evidences of Christianity and the Volume of Holy Scriptures are of the utmost importance to our National character, our present and future happiness), a fixed resolve to protect to the utmost of my means its academical rights, privileges and interests, an anxious wish to perpetuate our Constitution in Church and State, cemented as it is with the blood of Patriots and Martyrs: such are the principles in which I have been born and bred and in which I hope to die. By acting up to them to the best of my judgement in the station to which the partiality of the University has raised me, I trust to obtain that favourable construction of my endeavours of which the insufficiency of my abilities might otherwise tempt me to despair.

These abilities, such as they are, together with my time my zeal and my energies are at the disposal of the University and I trust that the honest and disinterested exertions of a plain unprofessional gentleman (however they may shrink from comparison with the splendid talents and accomplishments which have adorned and still adorn your Representation) may even yet be deemed no unsatisfactory discharge of the duties imposed upon me or the trusts committed to my care.

To yourself, Mr. Vice-Chancellor, may I be permitted to add, my best thanks are justly due for the polite and obliging terms in which you have done me the honour to convey the decision of the University.

I have the honour to subscribe myself with a full conviction of the importance of the honour conferred.

Sir,

Your obliged and very obedient humble servant,

Richard Heber

Lady Spencer[1] to Richard Heber
Whitfield. 26 August 1821

I cannot allow a moment to pass without heartily shaking your hand, my good friend on your success. It has been a hard foughten field and a very handsome result has been the event. But never let my Cantab ears be assailed with the superior dignity which darkly envelopes the awful mysteries of Oxonian election, when put into comparison with our homely and vulgar proceedings on such occasions. No — Your Big Whigs may run and hide their dishonoured Buzzes — they are shamed and disgraced beyond all our hopes and Cambridge for ever say I. Who ever could have thought of doubting your being a most villainous Tory?

James Boswell to Richard Heber
29 August 1821

My dear M.P.,

You have no doubt had congratulations without number but I question if any one have given you a circumstantial narrative of our proceedings so here goes. Nothing particular occurred on Tuesday when I reached Oxford travelling in the inside while Dr. Dodson[2] was on the out. I told him this was emblematical of the coming contest. We dined in B.N.C. about a hundred in number. I did not see Hodson that day as I thought it best not to disturb him. You have heard of the opening of the proceedings on Wednesday when Thomas[3] delivered a second edition of his pamphlet gratis, Churton to whom in the knowledge of the world Parson Adams was a perfect Brummell, made a very foolish reply and was followed by Reginald whose simplicity and feeling evidently produced a great effect which was not diminished by a filthy attack from Hamer.[4] The Johnians were much elated at

---

[1] Lady Spencer, wife of second Earl Spencer, d. 1831.
[2] Dr. (later Sir) John Dodson (1780-1858) of Oriel College.
[3] Presumably Dr. Vaughan Thomas (1775-1858), sometime a fellow of Corpus Christi College, who in 1816 wrote *A sermon on the impropriety of conceding the name of Catholic to the Church of Rome.*
[4] ? James Hamer (born 1783), fellow of Corpus Christi.

their small majority on the first day's poll[1] and held a sort of Belshazzer's feast upon the occasion. I had engaged myself to dine with the President of Magdalen to meet Parr who came he said to do honour to his son Heber, but Hodson had made a party for Sir Archy[2] in the Common Room where he required me to preside and I found him so tetchy from sickness that I was obliged to give way. Sir Archy was in high glee and very narratively and jocosely disposed but I was obliged to sufflaminate him towards the close of the evening or he would have astonished Churton's weak mind.

On Thursday morning I began to have some misgivings but after seeing Hodson and being let a little into the secret of things, I felt confident, and my live port and awe-commanding face struck terror into our adversaries. As the poll advanced the countenances of Hamer, Knatchbull[3] and Co. became strictly academical ' colore sub fusca '. Jasper, I and some others dined with Rechel but I joined the B.N.C. party where I found Carollus Grant who has gained the appellation of a heaven-born Chairman.

When the result was announced on Friday I called on Routh who would not take one hand, but made me drop my hat and give him two. We had a grand symposium at the King's Hall and College of Brasenose. Hodson, I thought imprudently, attended but seemed a new man. He made one or two speeches which were admirable and Bosanquet[4] whose health we drank was truly eloquent and affecting. Kinsey[5] made a good bluff harrangue and told us that he wished no higher toast than that it should be recorded of him that he was Junior Proctor the year of Mr. Heber's election. Dean[6] who had the activity of a parched pea and the loquacity of a popinjay proposed the health of Churton

---

[1] The voting during the three days' poll was as follows :—

	Nicholl	Heber
1st day	208	205
2nd day	270	383
3rd day	41	24
	519	612

[2] Sir Archibald Macdonald (1747-1827) of Christ Church, judge.
[3] ? Dr. Wyndham Knatchbull (1786-1868), fellow of All Souls.
[4] Sir John B. Bosanquet (1773-1847), formerly of Christ Church; judge.
[5] William Kinsey (1788-1851), fellow of Trinity College.
[6] ? John Dean (1770-1833), sometime fellow of BNC.

just at the moment when Stonard and I had projected a speech in which he was to introduce it articularly, and the old gentleman babbled o' green fields.

I forgot to tell you that on Wednesday it was directed that the household troops should be kept in reserve till next day but at half past ———, the following words on a slip of paper were produced in the handwriting of General Hodson, ' Let forty B.N.C. men go up and vote ' which was obeyed with military precision. The General is not quite satisfied, he thinks our majority should have been 150. I think it quite as well as it is.

Sir John B. Bosanquet to Richard Heber
Montague Place. 17 September 1821

I always thought it desirable that the election should take place during the absence of the undergraduates, lest the junior part of the University should be scandalized by the bickerings of their seniors, but till I witnessed the uproarious proceedings in Brasenose I was not aware of another reason for preferring the vacation for the assembling of the graver members.

Sir Archibald MacDonald to Richard Heber
Connaught Place. 24 September 1821

It was a glorious struggle and a triumphant victory. Waterloo was a joke to it and not more decisive. Poor Jemmy Boswell was only intelligible till the cloth was removed and the ex-chief seemed to exult very much in his mastery of him for in retiring from Brasenose Common Room he said, if he thought Jemmy could speak another word he would instantly return.

Mary Heber to Richard Heber
14 February 1822

You will have received my mother's letter respecting my future prospects. I hope for the happiness of your approbation and that you will find your new brother worthy of your regard.[1]

[1] See footnote on page 286.

Richard Heber to his sister, Mary
Westminster. 15 February 1822

Nothing connected with your present or future happiness can be a matter of indifference to me, on the contrary it touches my heart most closely. To have you married to an honourable and well-principled man must be a sincere gratification and from all that I have heard or seen of Ch. Cholmondeley such I consider him to be. As to settlements, from what I have heard from your mother Charles's fortune and expectations are less than I cd have expected. However if you are both satisfied I have no right or wish to object. I will attend to all the points in your and your mother's letters as speedily as possible and you shall hear from me again in a day or two.

In the meantime, I tell you for your private satisfaction that I shall be glad to assist your income by presenting Charles to the Rectory of Marton which is fortunately still within my own command unfettered by any positive promise. This, it is true, is no great matter (say £100 into pocket curate paid) but every little helps.

As to Waters Upton, we will see what can be done, but I am not very sanguine as to anything in that quarter. However, we will take soundings immediately. Your mother talks of Sir John Leech the V.-Chancellor, what can he have to do with it? Old Lord Eldon[1] is the man and a very impracticable one, too.

Richard Heber to his sister, Mary
Westminster. 20 February 1822

As to Waters Upton, the most likely channel to be successful with the Chancellor to whom I could have access appeared Ld. Sidmouth[2], Ld. Powys[3] and Ld. Lonsdale.[4] The first has already obtained two livings for his own son-in-law[5] and is promised

[1] John Scott (1751-1838), Earl of Eldon; lord chancellor.
[2] Henry Addington (1757-1844), Viscount Sidmouth, a member of the Cabinet.
[3] Edward Clive (1754-1839), son of the famous Robert Clive, became Earl of Powis through his wife's inheritance.
[4] William Lowther (1757-1838), Earl of Lonsdale 1807.
[5] Lord Sidmouth's son-in-law was Rev. George Pellew, later Dean of Norwich.

more; the second has been sometime soliciting Shropshire preferment (not improbably Waters Upton) for young Clive of Styche[1] of the Chancellor: the third has undergone an operation and cannot be molested. Under these circumstances as seemed proper I was advised to apply myself with a better chance of success than by any circuitous course. The Vice-Chancellor, Lord Eldon hates like poison and it is believed would not listen to Lord Cholmondeley whose family have taken rather a saintly turn which is also Lord E's aversion. He has occasionally been induced by a frank open-hearted application to bestow preferment in quarters where it was little expected. Accordingly I have ventured to try my fortune. Do not be sanguine as to the result.

Richard Heber to his sister, Mary
Westminster. 21 February 1822

I enclose the Chancellor's answer which tho' queerly worded is civil and to the purpose. If he does not accede to our request at least we cannot complain at being kept long in suspence. I am sorry you and Charles cannot have Waters Upton which would have been a snug house and place to start in. As it is you must be content with Moreton and Marton.

(Enclosure)

Dear Sir,

I regret that on account of what has passed respecting the Living you mention, since it became vacant and one or two other small Livings in Shropshire since they became vacant, I fear I cannot possibly make any of them the means of consulting the welfare of those whose welfare you have at heart or of testifying the respect with which I am,

Dear Sir,
Yr faithful servant,
Eldon

Lin. Inn Hall, 20 *February* 1822

[1] Lord Powis's candidate was probably Rev. William Clive (1795-1883), later Archdeacon of Montgomery.

Mary Heber to Richard Heber
23 February 1822

Between ourselves old Charles is a slippery fellow and as he has not scrupled to diddle his son, he would not have much conscience in imposing on us unless you are a match for him.

Mary Heber to Richard Heber
Moreton Saye. 27 February 1822

After the example of your kindness, Reginald has offered to give up all the emoluments of Moreton to Charles and if we can get Fordhall to live at, we shall do pretty well. But you must follow up old Charles for the £1,000 down or we shall never furnish it.

Mary Heber to Richard Heber
Moreton Saye. 8 March 1822

Charles has had puzzling letters from his father about settlements. He declines having any correspondence on the subject and begs you will manage all for us with his father in the manner of the first proposal which was made namely (I repeat lest you should have mislaid the letter) that his 10,000 and my 14,000 shall be settled on us both, the Interest jointly and the whole Interest to the survivor for life, each to have the disposal of their own principal in case of no family. I abhor the name of jointure and will not consent to giving up any part of my fortune to old C. C. on any such condition. The odd thousand which old C. C. ought to pay down, he will I daresay object to : if he does, you must make it surely and certainly settled on his son at his death or he will spunge it out of him like the former sums. He is not to be trusted and I will not be dependent on him for anything.

Dr. Edward Copleston to Richard Heber
Oriel. 10 March 1822

Grenfell's[1] speeches please me best of any that I read in the papers on financial questions. He is a thoroughly honest man and ought to be supported more zealously than he is in his measures relating to the Bank. I am heartily glad to see that he succeeded Friday night in throwing out the Clause for remuneration to the Bank in this business of reducing the 5 per cents. That Corporation has fattened on the distresses of the Country and has acted towards the Government just as a Jew moneylender to a foolish spend-thrift. It is high time that the whole of their system should be faithfully exposed.

Sir Walter Scott to Richard Heber
Undated (March 1822)

I cannot tell you how shocked I was at the unexpected evil tidings which your letter conveyed. Our stock of harmless mirth and useful information is at once impoverished by the death of poor Jamie Boswell.[2] I missed seeing him in Scotland as we just crossed each other, I arriving in Edinburgh almost the day he left it. I little then thought I was missing the only chance of seeing that kind-hearted and excellent creature which was ever to be offered to either of us. But these are the deprivations which we must expect when we have passed the meridian of life and verge towards its sunset.

I who must extend my view to a period which I may never see save in prospect, am now looking anxiously to the education of my children. Walter, whose regiment was reduced, is spending a year at Berlin for the languages and in prosecuting his military studies. But I must have some of your advice about my younger son Charles as with much quickness and vivacity of talent, he

[1] Pascoe Grenfell (1761-1838), politician, merchant, expert on finance. Government had introduced a measure for the reduction of the national debt by the commutation of 5 per cent. into 4 per cent. stock. Grenfell was very anxious that the Bank of England should not profit from this transaction which carried no risk.
[2] James Boswell died 29 February

shewed indolence and indifference to his classical studies, I had made up my mind reluctantly enough to let him go to India. Since he has been settled with Mr. Williams[1] at Lampeter, his disposition has taken a different turn and he has become studious and desirous of knowledge. This inclines me with much pleasure on my part to alter my views for him and I am therefore desirous to afford him the opportunity of a good classical education with a view to his going to our bar.

In about a twelve month he will be fit for college and I am desirous he should have the great advantage of some residence in Oxford. I must be indebted to you for your advice as to the College he should be sent to and the steps preliminary, for I understand his name should be put on the books some time before joining. Will you favour me with your opinion on this subject ?

If it is not a secret, I should like to know the author of an epistle to you on a certain interesting subject. The author has managed the matter so like a scholar and a gentleman that I cannot guess who, being possessed of powers so superior to the subject he has chosen, should have taken so much pains about such a matter, unless it be your brother Reginald. The whole is very ably written and I am sure both the unknown author and I have not a little reason to be proud of the manner in which we are treated. I am particular sensible of the great delicacy which he has exercised towards myself and which so few could have preserved in the course of such a discussion.

I hope we are to see you this summer, *sans faute*. You will find me among lime and mortar but with plenty of accommodation still standing. Lady Scott says nothing will give her more pleasure than to renew a friendship which is now somewhat ancient like herself.

Bezonian speak or die![3]
What is the date of the 1st Editn. of *Adventures of a Guinea*.[2]

[1] John Williams (1792–1858), classical scholar and schoolmaster; his school at Lampeter was later called St. David's College. Partly through the influence of Scott, Williams became the first headmaster of the Edinburgh Academy.

[2] *Chrysal or the Adventures of a Guinea*, by an Adept (Charles Johnston ?1719–?1800, barrister). His work went into many editions.

[3] King Henry IV. Part Two, v, iii.

What of the 2nd Edition.

What of the additional two volumes.

Who the devil is Charles Johnson who is said to have written it ?

Sir Walter Scott to Richard Heber
Abbotsford, Melrose. 24 March (1822)

I write immediately as you desire having indeed nothing to direct my partialities to any of the Colleges you mention in particular. *Caeteris paribus* indeed Charles would meet at Balliol with some of his countrymen destined perhaps to pursue the same path with himself, but I am so little certain whether I should regard this as an advantage or otherwise that I leave the matter entirely with you. I have no idea (if) he can be fit for College sooner than in about 18 months. But as my mind is made up for sending him there, the sooner I get him through your goodness put upon the list, the better chance I can have of getting him forward.

I am very much flattered at what you tell me of young Adolphus.[1] I would write to him but the subject is too tickelish. Of course you will leave the main question undecided and just say that as he chose a subject in which it was necessary to mention me so often, I am much flattered to see that he possesses a much more exact acquaintance with my publications than I do myself:— that I am particularly sensible of his great personal delicacy and that I hope he will soon exercize his evident talents on a more important and interesting a subject than either the novels or the poems. I should very much like to know him. I daresay he is a very joyous companion. I wish you would bring him with you when you come.

I want by the way to have your coat of arms without quarterings or impalements. I am constructing a little tower with six small shields on it, and I want yours, the peerless blade's, Merritt's and one or two others to adorn my design.

---

[1] John Leycester Adolphus (1795-1862), barrister and author; published anonymously in 1821 *Letters to Richard Heber Esq. containing critical remarks on the series of novels beginning with Waverley, and an attempt to ascertain their author.* This work, in which he identified Scott, made Adolphus's reputation, and earned Scott's friendship.

P.S. If you have by you *El Diabolo Cijuelo* I should be obliged by the loan of it. I want to compare it with *Diable Boiteux*. Freeling[1] will give you a frank for me.

Sir Walter Scott to Richard Heber
Abbotsford. 28 March 1822

I feel it a duty to transmit to you a letter which I have this morning received from my son-in-law[2] with particulars of the unhappy affair which is likely to deprive us of Sir Alexander Boswell[3] so soon after poor Jamie. The previous circumstances are as follows:— Andrew Stewart[4] of Dunearn a violent Whig had been severely attacked in the *Beacon* newspaper about a year ago and had an affair with the printer in which he came off poorly enough — first asking the name of the author of the obnoxious paragraphs — then refusing to receive the said name, because the discovery was coupled with the condition " If Mr. Stewart's intentions were honourable," then backed by two servants fetched from the country on purpose, attempting to beat the printer while his assistants held him, and getting beat himself instead. All this and a subsequent bravado attempt to fix a quarrel on the Lord Advocate had given rise to much picquering[5] which was enhanced by party animosity. Poor Sir Alexander had it seems been busy on the occasion and had written several songs which appeared in a Glasgow Tory paper called the *Sentinel* in which Stewart was — they say, for I never saw the paper even by chance — repeatedly attacked. I always foresaw that he would do mischief for there is no animal so dangerous as a man thus driven to bay.

Stewart contrived to get possession, I cannot well tell how, of some debt due or said to be due by the Editor of the *Sentinel* and under pretence of legal execution seized on the desks and papers

---

[1] Sir Francis Freeling (1764-1836), Secretary of the Post Office, member of the Roxburghe Club, Fellow of the Society of Antiquaries.
[2] John Gibson Lockhart (1794-1854), wrote a biography of Scott, edited Motteux's *Don Quixote* 1822 and translated *Ancient Spanish Ballads* 1823.
[3] Sir Alexander Boswell (1775-1822), elder brother of James died on 29 March.
[4] James Stuart (1775-1849), whig polititian, was acquitted of the killing of Boswell.
[5] i.e. Skirmishing or wrangling.

in the office of the paper, a sort of distress I should think illegal. He thus came into possession of Sir Alexander's manuscripts and the result you will find in the enclosed letter.

I am deeply concerned. The poor fellow dined with me just about a month ago and was extravagantly joyous, lightly thinking what a blow his own feelings were to receive in Jamie's death and those of his family in this bloody catastrophe.

It is some comfort to me that I had remonstrated with all my young friends about continuing this skirmishing war and had kept by dint of authority my son-in-law out of it. You will see something of this in a hint in his letter.

Mary Heber to Richard Heber
29 April 1822

I fancy old Charles will do little or nothing more. He has given Charles one hundred which he tries to persuade me is outfit enough, if he is induced to double it, it is the very utmost that can be looked for, *I* think.

Archdeacon Ralph Churton to Richard Heber
Middleton. 29 April 1822

I give you joy in the pleasing prospect of a renewal of the connection between the Hebers and the Cholmondeleys. I may possibly have seen but not I believe know young Mr. Ch. Cholmondeley. His Father I have seen sometimes once in particular at Harthill when our ever lamented friend[1] lived there. I see the young clergyman is already by preferment connected with Heber in Yorkshire and Heber in Shropshire. His future residence will I presume be the latter county which will on many accounts I can readily suppose be most acceptable to the young lady who is about to change her name.

---

[1] Hugh Cholmondeley, late Dean of Chester.

Dr. Edward Copleston to Richard Heber
Oriel. 9 May 1822

There was a rumour here (how it began I know not) that you intended to speak on Canning's Motion.[1] The House appears to have been so impatient that no prudent man would knowingly chuse such an opportunity for making his first display. Your vote was as I expected — and I am not sure it was not as I would have voted myself — for Canning does not seem to me to have succeeded in establishing his distinction between a restoration of privilege to the Peers and an admission of Commoners to eligibility. Besides it looks like beginning at the wrong end, to give seats in the Legislature before other immunities are conceded.

The plot is thickening in regard to agriculture and finance. I am perfectly sure that currency is the main source of the embarrassment and that Ricardo[2] has overlooked that part of the operation of the Bank Restriction, which I take to be the hinge of the whole question.

Judging from the report in the *Courier*, Sir Francis Burdett's[3] must have been a powerful speech. His allusion to Lethbridge was particularly happy ' unless he thinks political economy' means low prices. The *Courier* reports appear to be among the best which is a great change. Shall we see you in its pages this session ?

Richard Heber to his sister Mary
Essex Court Temple. 31 May 1822

In fact (between ourselves) Sidebottom has all along from his long experience of Ch. Ch. and his habits anticipated much difficulty and cavilling on his part owing in some degree to the

[1] To introduce a Bill to allow Roman Catholic peers to sit in Parliament, from which they were disabled by an act of Charles II. Canning claimed that the peers' right to sit was a different question from that of Catholic emancipation in general. The motion was carried by 249 votes to 244, but later lost in the Lords.

[2] David Ricardo (1772-1823), classical economist. Elected Radical M.P. for Portarlington, 1819.

[3] The government spokesman Lethbridge, in introducing a motion for import duties on agricultural produce in order to relieve the English agricultural interest from the low prices which then prevailed, had referred to ' the abominable theories of political economists '. Sir Francis Burdett's (1774-1844) forcible opposition speech contained the rejoinder which the House, as well as Copleston, so enjoyed.

great delight he takes in mooting legal points and also to the custom he indulges in of writing so much and so long upon every matter that comes before him as to perplex and bewilder himself.

George Canning, M.P. to Richard Heber
14 September 1822

My dear Heber,

The proposal which I told you was the only one that I should think it a duty to accept, has been made — and I have accepted it.[1] God send me a good deliverance.

Ever sincerely yours,
G.C.

Mrs. Charles Cholmondeley to Richard Heber
20 October 1822

We thought Hoylake a very dull place. The bathing is good but that takes up only half an hour in the day which seems long enough as you may suppose on such a dreary sand-bank.

Were you among the disappointed visitors at Fonthill ?[2] or did you see it before Mr. Farquhar had bought the whole ? Mr. Beckford must have raised a great sum by merely showing his fine furniture independant of the sale. Edward Stanley[3] compares the fine Gothic building with all its ornamented embellishments to a Cathedral fitted up by a Lunatic Bishop.

Rev. John Stonard to Richard Heber
Aldingham, Ulverstone. 31 December 1822

I wish you would turn Baring,[4] Ricardo and Rothschild[5] and the whole gang of Jew speculators and moneylenders and

---

[1] Canning becomes Foreign Secretary.

[2] William Beckford (1759-1844), collector, sold Fonthill in 1822. John Farquhar (1751-1826) the millionaire bought it.

[3] ? Edward Stanley (1779-1849), bishop of Norwich 1837.

[4] Alexander Baring (1774-1848), M.P. and financier; son of the founder of the financial house of Baring.

[5] Nathan Meyer Rothschild (1777-1836) was naturalized in 1804. He was not, however, a member of Parliament.

loanraisers out of Parliament. I hate to see their names in the newspapers, a set of vagrant Countryless Ragamuffins, ' Dead to glory, only burn for gold '.

Sir Walter Scott to Richard Heber
Castle Street. 25 February 1823

I send the enclosed to Dibdin[1] under a slip seal that you may read it and if you think it will answer the purpose, forward it — if not I will modify the answer as you think will be more agreeable.

To be sure to offer my own society instead of that of the author whom it has delighted the Roxburgh to honour is much on a footing with the honest publican who altered the ingenious distich which a predecessor named Little John had placed beneath the sign of Robin Hood. The distich originally ran:—

> Ye gentlemen and yeomen good
> Come in and drink with Robin Hood
> If Robin Hood be not at home
> Come in and drink with Little John.

Instead of the last line his successor inserted his own so that it runs thus:—

> Come in and drink with Simon Webster.

Pray bestow some of your *pieds des mouches* to tell us why your brother goes to Calcutta when he could have a Bishopric in this nook-shotten isle of Albion when his time comes. Also whether you have been able to get any hope for Charles as you were kind enough to promise your interest on that score. He will soon be fit to join.

We have been all well here. My son-in-law is going up to London this spring. I will give him a letter to you. I think you will like him when you get over his shyness. Have you seen his *Spanish Ballads* ? It is a beautiful book.

---

[1] Thomas F. Dibdin (1776-1847), bibliographer; original member of the Roxburghe Club. The Club had invited the anonymous author of *Waverley* to become a member. Scott consented to join as proxy for this great man.

I am weary of saying 'Why come ye not to Skotland?'

I shall be anxious to do something smart for the Club as well as to settle all dues and presentations etc.

Bye the bye Petrie[1] has sent me his plan. I cannot approve those loppings and toppings he proposes. It is scarce possible for one man to guess the purpose for which another made such chronicles. I pray you will let this be well considered.

Thomson[2] is now in London and might surely help your deliberations very much.

Lord Grenville to Richard Heber
Dropmore. 2 May 1823

The advice of one so ignorant as I am of all our political objects and relations can be of little value in the case you mention.

Not knowing what objections there may be against it, I should say, *prima facie* that as long as the King thinks fit to acknowledge the gentlemen in question as the public Ministers of independent and friendly sovereigns, the University has no occasion to enquire whether in fact that independence is exercised on a throne or in a prison, but ought to shew to those ministers the same marks of attention and respect, precisely in the same mode and to the same degree as to any other public ministers of like rank attending the commemmoration on the present as on former occasions.

But Mr. Peel is on every account the proper person to be consulted in this case. If any doubt were officially mentioned to me, my answer would be to recommend an official reference to him as the Home Secretary of State and in his relation to the University as well as to the Government, no other person can be so fit to give confidential advice upon it.

---

[1] Henry Petrie (1768-1842), antiquary, keeper of the records in the Tower of London, had set on foot a scheme, never completed, for a *corpus historicum* of early English history.

[2] One George Thomson (1782?-1833) was tutor in Scott's household between 1811 and 1820.

ICHARD'S Parliamentary career was not a success. He never
once spoke in the House. Doubtless, with his extreme short
sight, catching the Speaker's eye was a difficult matter and
his inability to read anything beyond the range of a few inches
must have made the use of notes almost an impossibility. Had he
entered Parliament when he was younger he might have overcome these disabilities, but to start thus in a new milieu at the
age of forty-seven was too difficult. He resigned in 1826.

Amelia Heber, writing mostly to her mother-in-law, described life in India from the woman's point of view during Bishop
Reginald's short ministry. He died suddenly in 1826. She, on
her return to England, published his *Life* and *Journal*.

The Rev. Charles and Mary Cholmondeley moved in 1826
to Hodnet Rectory where he died in 1831 at the age of thirty-six.

*   *   *

Sir Walter Scott to Richard Heber
Abbotsford, Melrose. 17 July (1823)

My son Charles's instructor and friend Mr. Williams pro-
nounces that he will be fit to enter College next Easter for
Residence and that he should for that purpose be put on the
books if possible this season. I have made no motion in the
matter relying on your kind assistance but am now under the
necessity of jogging your memory a wee bit. I wish I could set
you jogging so completely that you would not stop till you had
crossed the Border. Sure it would be more sensible than Reginald

jogging away to be a Bishop *in partibus infidelium* for I fear
Calcutta is little better. I wish he had let the Nullifidian Europeans
and the pagan Gentoos[1] go to the devil in their own way and
stayed with us in old England.

Mrs. Charles Cholmondeley to Richard Heber
Moreton Saye. 27 July 1823

Mr. Alcock says he wrote to you some time since to know your
decision about some repairs in Marton Church which have been
ordered by the Archdeacon on his visitation. Charles made
particular enquiries about this when we were at Marton and
found that the Archdeacon had ordered all the open seats to be
new floored. They belong I understand to you, Mr. Roundell
and Mr. Baldwin and these two latter worthies are trying to
encroach on your property and to obtain a new division by which
you will be the loser. Some of the people want to have their
open seats pewed, but Charles and Mrs. Hall and all the rational
part of the congregation think they are much better as they are.
It appears that these seats are at present all appropriated, but as
there are no sittings for the poor, Charles wishes you would
order *one* seat to be given to them and perhaps Messrs. Baldwin
and Roundell may follow your example and so afford accommodation to those cottagers who are at present shut out. Mr. Wilson
advises your writing immediately to decide about the repairs of
your seats or Mr. Roundell that *arch-fiend* will take advantage.

Mrs. Reginald Heber to her mother-in-law
Fort William, Calcutta. 15 October 1823.

Altho' we hope you will have received a large packet from us
announcing our safe arrival in India[2] but a very short time

---

[1] i.e. Hindus.

[2] The main dates of Bishop Heber's ministry in India:—Consecrated Bishop of
Calcutta 1 June 1823. Sailed for India 10 June: arrived in Calcutta in October. His first
visitation of N. India commenced on 15 June 1824. His Chaplain Mr. Stowe died at
Dacca on 17 July. He arrived in Bombay 20 April 1825. Mrs. Heber left Calcutta on
2 March and joined him in Bombay on 26 April. Together they left Bombay on 15
August, reached Ceylon on 27 August and arrived back in Calcutta on 21 October 1825.
He left on his second visitation of S. India on 2 February 1826, reached Madras on
25 February and died in Trichinopoli 3 April 1826.

before this reaches England, yet as I am sure you will like to hear as often as possible of our proceedings, I shall employ the very short time allowed me (the ship being on the point of sailing) in giving you some account of ourselves and all about us. We had just entered the river up which we proceeded to Diamond Harbour, about 60 miles from Calcutta, when Lord Amherst[1] sent down the Government yacht to meet us, a beautiful ship with royal accommodations. Our fellow passengers went up in a steam-boat and were only a few hours on the voyage, but we paid dearly for the honour done us for in consequence of very heavy rains that had fallen all over Bengal, the Hoogly was become a torrent against which even a spring tide had no effect and we crawled on at the rate of six miles in the 24 hours for five days, till Government had pity on us and sent down small boats which took us the remainder of the way speedily and we landed on Friday evening a few miles from Calcutta, where we found carriages ready for us which brought us to a most excellent large house in the Fort assigned to us by Lord Amherst till we removed into our own. Here we found sundry Chaplains ready to receive us and a troop of servants amounting to 40, a good dinner and every possible comfort, but the whole scene was so new to me, everything appeared on such a magnificent scale after being so long accustomed to ship accommodations that I was quite bewildered and scarcely knew which way to move.

After dinner I was introduced to the Head Servants (most of the 40 had lived with the late Bishop) and was acquainted with their offices, names etc. etc. but even yet I am scarcely acquainted with their faces and am perpetually ordering them to do things which would be followed by loss of caste were they to obey me. Fortunately with such a tribe of household domestics, there is one confidential agent, a kind of native gentleman who manages them all for us, settles their wages and pays them and to whom I make all complaints and who is answerable for everything that may be lost in the house; this man bears a very high character, and at least if he cheats himself he will not suffer others to do so

[1] William Pitt Amherst (1773-1857), governor-general of India, 1823-8; Earl Amherst of Aracan, 1826.

which must inevitably be the case with such a crowd and with our imperfect knowledge of the language. We must yet increase the number not having the Stable department yet supplied.

The house consists of ground floor of which I know nothing, it being in this country always if possible given up to the servants; of two magnificent rooms loftier than you have any notion of, with large Venetian windows and doors all round, and seven other rooms all good, high and airy. We have a beautiful bed-room, dressing room and baths for our suite of appartments, Emily has an excellent nursery and two of the other rooms are occupied by some friends, ship-mates to whom we are giving temporary houseroom — for here there are no Inns and it is customary to take your (friends) into your own house till they can provide for themselves.

We are all at present perfectly well and as the cool season has begun, we do not expect to be more annoyed by the heat than we have been. Reginald was installed on Saturday and preached on Sunday — the Cathedral is a light airy Church kept quite cool by 21 Punkahs constantly going. These are indispensable in every house and are pulled by the Palanquin bearers who take it in rotation.

We dined at Government House the day after our arrival *en famille* and find the Amhersts disposed to be extremely friendly and good natured; on Friday we dine there to meet all Calcutta which we expect to be a formal dull business; however the Palace is an immense building and proportionately cool. I have already between thirty and forty morning visits to pay which I dread and really the confusion so many new names and faces makes in my poor head is sad.

We rise early every morning, take a drive and then come in to bathe and breakfast, have tiffin at one, if we drive late (but when we are alone, four is our dinner hour) drive and walk again in the evening and are in bed by ten. The forms and the utter want of privacy are as yet the most disagreeable things we have to endure. You must not stir without two or three attendants and every room in the House is open and an entire view into the appartment only prevented by a large screen being placed at the entrance. Men walk in and out of the room with more freedom than women in England. When I am in bed and tucked under the Mosquito curtains by my ayah, two men arrive, one to perform the same office by Reginald and the other to put out the candles or rather high lamps, and everyone submits to this with the most perfect indifference; in time I expect to become equally callous but as yet it does seem strange. Emily has a black nurse to play with and attend upon her and with some difficulty I got rid of another who had the same office. She is delighted with all she sees and calls the natives ' pretty black men '.

Sir Walter Scott to Richard Heber
Abbotsford. 29 October (1823)

I have been hoping for some time to hear from you the probabilities of my son Charles getting to Oxford about Easter next when he leaves his present residence in Wales. In your kind wishes on his behalf are like to prove ineffectual which may surely be the case even with your powerful interest, I must either think of applying to ' England's other eye ' or of sending him on the Continent for which I have a good opportunity. Either course will be much better than his coming home to me till the giddy time is a little passed by. I am more anxious about him than his brother. Walter is just the sort of fellow who is in his element in the military — remarkable athletic and excellent at all his exercises, good drawer, good mathematician, a fine person and just the stuff out of which would have been made in former times a verie parfite gentil knight.

Although entering a rollicking regimt. of Irish dragoons at eighteen he has been always attentive not to go out of limits in expense and in his little warfare with the Irish Kerne behaved with great temper and spirit. So he is in his place studying at the Royal College at Sandhurst in the senior department with a good chance of getting on the Staff.

But Charles costs me more anxiety being very lively and imaginative and having much of what papers might call genius, with its concomitant of indolence and love of the pleasure of the moment. I know too well the dangers of this sort of character by experience being precisely that which my Scotch friends said of me namely that ' I would either make a spoon or spoil a horn '. So I must think about disposing of him and think early that I may act to purpose and so I am obliged to be pressingly troublesome on your leisure so far as to beg you will let me know whether there is any chance of Oxford for him, that if otherwise I may look about elsewhere.

We have had a vile broken season. I never saw so much bad weather.

My last amusement has been Dr. Meyrick's treatise[1] on old armour which is got up with much information though with some few inaccuracies.

Lady Scott sends kind compliments.

Sir Walter Scott to Richard Heber
Abbotsford, Melrose. 12 *November* (1823)

I received both your kind letters and the enclosure from the President of Brasenose and I paused on the contents for a couple of days that I might reply with mature deliberation. Upon the whole I think I cannot do better for Charles than to embrace the advice which Dr. Gilbert[2] has so kindly given and adopt such arrangements as shall enable Charles to commence his residence in October. I trust he will then be ready to go to his studies with the advantage of a good foundation and as he has quick and lively spirits, I am fully sensible of the advantage of his becoming resident at a long term when the minds of the young men are turned more decidedly to their studies than in summer. The arrangement will require him to make his act of Entrance after Christmas. My son-in-law Lockhart will write to an intimate of his who is high in the University to see him through the forms of his act which will save you any trouble on that account,

---

[1] Dr. Samuel Meyrick (1783-1848), antiquary; wrote a history of arms and armour, 1824; knighted 1832.
[2] Ashurst Gilbert (1786-1870), became vice-chancellor of the university and later bishop of Chichester.

unless you will have the kindness to send him a note of introduction to Principal Gilbert that he may thank him in my name and his own for his uncommon kindness and receive a hints which he may be favoured with concerning his line of study till October. If you think Charles's doing so would be proper his address is Falcondale, Lampeter, Cardiganshire.

If we are alive and well I entertain serious hopes of seeing him settled at Alma Mater in October which I thought I might surely manage if you were in the neighbourhood at the time ' there will be a play filled '. Or why should you not take your promised tour and visit us here and we could see you back to your own Southern land. I assure you Don Quixote might be pardoned if he took Abbotsford for an absolute Castle, though perhaps except in bringing to the landlord no profit, it is a good deal more of our own.

I beg you to express my very grateful thanks to Dr. Gilbert. I should rejoice to think that the mode he has suggested of availing myself of his great kindness should be convenient to him as I know well how great a favour he has conferred on me, and how many solicitations he is subjected to, deservedly high as the reputation of the College stands.

Dr. Thomas F. Dibdin to Richard Heber
27 November 1823

There was a report that you were thrown from your horse had fractured your skull — got your spectacles jammed into your eyes. You write on Sunday and say nothing of this. It cannot therefore be true.

All London is ringing with certain congratulations and my house is beleagured with Candidates for the Curacy, Clerkship, Lectureship and Pew-Opener-ship.[1] A whole regiment of females, middle aged and frightful, have passed in rank and file before me for the latter. 'Tis a noble Church, nearly double the size of Kensington. Of rents and profits, when we meet: only

---

[1] Dibdin was first rector of St. Mary's, Bryanston Square.

the Dibdin caravan moves on — not for Mecca but for Marylebone in the early spring. The Church will be consecrated on
the 30th of next month: then I shall in right earnest begin my
Metropolitan career! I believe there is no doubt of my retaining
Exning, too — there to make a philological retreat for three
months every year.

Sir Walter Scott to Richard Heber
Edinburgh. 13 December 1823

A thousand thanks to you my dear Heber for one of the
greatest favours you could possibly have done, in paving
Charles's path to Alma Mater. If I may trust the report of
Mr. Williams, himself an excellent scholar as well as very candid
in his communications, (it) gives me the comfortable assurance
that he is possessed of the learning and at present of the disposition
to make a good use of your patronage. He will of course attend
religiously on the first day of the Lent term and I trust he will feel
the ' strong contagion of the gown '. From April to October he
will worship the Domestic *Lares* and in October he will offer
up his time to the *Dei Majores* of Isis.

Mrs. Reginald Heber to her mother-in-law
Calcutta. 1 January 1824

My last letter was to dear Mary, acquainting her with the
illness of my darling Child and that she was recovering from it —
since that I sent you a message through by Aunt to say how much
better she was and that I had taken her out to sea for a fortnight
for her more complete recovery. I am just returned bringing
the dear girl quite well and with her usual excellent temper and
spirits. Indeed so rapid a change I never before witnessed and
it is the surprize of everyone to see what a fortnight's airing has
done for her.

As soon as my confinement is over, which I may now daily
expect, we shall leave Calcutta to go for a few miles out of
reach of its dust and heat for the hot months of March, April,

May and part of June, when we shall begin our travels up the country which will occupy us till the end of the year.

We have not yet had a single line from a creature in England and are just now very much mortified at the arrival of a ship of so late a date as the middle of August without receiving a letter; it has however brought Reginald the Act of Parliament to which we have been so long looking, decisive of Government's finding him a house and paying his Visitation expenses, so that we shall soon now I hope move into a comfortable residence of our own which will be a great advantage to us in many respects: — for it seems a decided thing that the air of the Fort does not agree with Emily and tho' the house is a good one, it is oppressively hot when the weather is warm and now I am really almost suffering from cold; — it is one of the few remaining in Calcutta with more than half the windows unglazed and only venetians to supply the place of glass. Luckily our bedroom and Reginald's study have windows and the sleeping nursery is an inner room with no outward communication, a very common and desirable thing during the hot months; — there is not a grate in the house.

I have been endeavouring to get a white woman for a wet nurse, but could not succeed, so I am forced to put up with a blacky, which however disagreeable in some respects, is reckoned better and wholesomer than soldiers wives generally are, which is the only description of person to be met with here.

January 5th. Since I wrote on Jan. 1st we have settled on leaving Calcutta immediately, a good natured acquaintance having lent us an excellent house on the banks of the Ganges, about 14 miles from here, where we go on the 7th. We are very anxious to get Emily out of the Fort as soon as possible, and the river affords a most comfortable mode of communication for Reginald whenever he wishes to return to Calcutta, as Visitor of the College, he is allowed a very nice covered boat or as it is called here a Bhaliah, a ten-oared boat with a comfortable room quite new and nicely fitted up, in this we can go up in four hours and down in half the time. The house is lent us to the end of February when we shall either rent one in the same neighbourhood or return to our own here.

I believe I told you all about our servants: — when our Stable establishment is complete we shall have 53 and their wages form no small part of our expenses: with the exception of turbands and cummerbunds or sashes we have however no clothing to find and no taxes. The privilege Reginald has of franking is some saving for all letters are paid for on being put in the post; he is also allowed stationery of every kind, medicines and a weekly newspaper; these are his perquisites.

We are obliged to keep four carriage horses and a groom runs by each horse's head — not that we shall often drive four at once, but in this climate they can only go out once a day, and our work is much more than that, walking being so quite out of the question. A good horse will cost £200!!

Mrs. Charles Cholmondeley to Richard Heber
7 January 1824

I write in little Tom's[1] name to thank you for your kind remembrance in sending him a New Year's gift of a nice warm pair of boots to comfort his little cold feet. You will be glad to hear he grows a fine stout boy and but for an unlucky cold he has caught which annoys him with a rash, he would be quite well.

I have been to Hodnet to arrange your Fonthill purchases; and have found room in the Drawing Room for both the ebony table and the cabinet. They are very beautiful and so is the china; I found very great difficulty in selecting some of the latter for myself which you were so kind as to say I might do, and the remainder I have arranged very ornamentally on the Cardinal's Table[2] and placed it under Bishop Cleaver, between the windows.

Mrs. Reginald Heber to her mother-in-law
Calcutta. 31 March 1824

Reginald has not been quite so well lately as he had been previous to our last letter to you, but he is now quite recovered

[1] Thomas Cholmondeley, eldest son of Rev. Charles and Mary Cholmondeley, born 21 November 1823.
[2] An ebony table that belonged to Cardinal Wolsey.

and only a little thinner than he was. I am happy to think that this indisposition was brought on entirely by what may be so easily guarded against that I do not feel the least uneasiness for his future health. No persuasion of mine, of any of our medical acquaintance or of the old established Indians here could induce him to live as he ought to live in this relaxing climate. He had taken a fancy into his head that low living would ensure his preserving his health and the consequences have been that tho' never seriously ill, he had brought himself into so low a way as to require medical advice for some time. The evident change that a few days generous living having made in him was quite surprising; he is now perfectly aware of his mistake and will never fall into it again.

This is our manner of life, we are on our horses long before daybreak, come home before the sun is much above the horizon, bathe and breakfast, dine at three or $\frac{1}{2}$ after, take a drive in the carriage when it becomes cooler and are in bed very soon after nine and sometimes earlier. We have each of us a comfortable sofa in our rooms on which we frequently take a nap between breakfast and dinner. The children are out in the carriage by five, the baby always and Emily sometimes fast asleep. They are both quite well, the latter running about as she would do in England, apparently not sensible of the heat, except that she is paler than in England and little Harriet as healthy and fine a child as you can see and as good tempered as her sister was at her age. I continue nursing her and it agrees with us both perfectly well.

The heat is now become very very great: from $\frac{1}{2}$ after eight till six every window in the house is shut to exclude the hot air which blows as from an oven: — with this and keeping oneself quite quiet under the Punkahs one may be reasonably cool, but the least exertion is distressing. I am wet through all day; probably my being a nurse increases this as Reginald is not so much annoyed by it. I pity those whose necessary avocations take them out during the heat; fortunately Reginald never need go from the house except on Sundays and it is quite surprising to feel how cool the Churches are; service too is early in the morning and late in the evening whereby the great heat is avoided.

On Thursday we move into one of the coolest houses in Calcutta which Reginald has taken for two years; it has five large rooms, two of them 68 feet long and the other three 54 square, the three latter are Study, Drawing Room, and nursery and the two former Dining and another Drawing Room: does not this sound magnificent ? Large rooms are of the utmost consequence in this climate where no exercise can be taken especially for children and the furnishing them is hardly a 4th of what it need be in England. We have been returned to Calcutta about a month and have resided in a small but comfortable house while our own has been repairing; very sorry we were to leave the country, but the distance was too great for Reginald's duties. All committees and episcopal meetings are held in his house which saves him much trouble and fatigue.

We shall go up the country in a most patriarchal way with our flocks and our herds. I mean that we take goats for milk, poultry for food and indeed a little of everything that can be wanted in a domestic establishment. We are told that when we are off, the trouble to ourselves will be nothing, but the preparation will be no little fatigue.

Mrs. Reginald Heber to her mother-in-law
Calcutta. 21 May 1824

We are very busy making preparations for travelling but it is a subject that makes me unhappy. The medical men as well as those who know what travelling is in the Country strongly dissuade us from taking the children and what to do I know not. My own feelings are that however painful it will be to leave the children I shall suffer more at being so long separated from my husband. He, on the contrary, will not hear of my being so long away from them, especially from Emily who would almost break her heart at losing me; and he is very pressing with me to consent to remain behind and let him go with Archdeacon and Mrs. Corrie[1] and Mr. Stow. That he should have such companions would indeed set my mind quite at rest as to his welfare for the Corries are delightful people and would take every possible care of him, as much as I could do; but to be left behind in a strange land for seven or eight months is what I cannot bear to think of! — but yet I fear must be. However, it is not quite settled and could I find a loophole to creep through I would most certainly lay hold of it. You will be sorry to hear I have lost Nurse, who is married to a Sergeant Vernon and married just at the moment when her loss would be most felt and also left me when I had barely filled her place (supply it I never can) and when my baby was ill with her teeth; so that I cannot say she has used me well. I have a married woman now who I hope may suit me but I am not half reconciled to her; a native nurse I will never have if I can help it.

I can hardly describe the atmosphere in which we are existing. This is said to be the hottest summer that has been known for some years. We are forced to exclude the outside air still all day and sitting quite quiet all day under the Punkah I am bathed in perspiration. The nights however are generally cool.

Mrs. Reginald Heber to her mother-in-law
Barrackpore. 2 July 1824

You will be sorry to hear that I am really left in this strange land by myself ! It is a sad sad disappointment to me and to my beloved husband too for we had promised ourselves so much gratification from travelling together ! On the 15th he embarked in a very comfortable pinnace with Mr. Stow and accompanied in another by Archdeacon and Mrs. Corrie, both of them experienced travellers in India and both of them anxious to increase his comfort and smooth his path in every possible way.

In January I hope to embark and join him with the children at Bombay, to finish the rest of his visitation together. Immediately on his departure I left Calcutta, not being able to endure our large melancholy house without him and came down with the

[1] Daniel Corrie (1777-1837), bishop of Madras 1835.

children and Miss Stow to Barrackpore where I have taken a
small bungalow close to the river and also very close to Government House, one of my principal objects in chusing this place,
for the Amhersts are much more here than in Calcutta and they
are nearly the only people with whom I am at all intimate.

The children are perfectly well, the climate certainly agrees
better with Emily than England, especially when she is out of
Calcutta; there she must be confined to the house the greatest
part of the day, whilst here she is in the open air, under the
shade of the verandah during the whole of it.

Sir Charles Grey[1] to Richard Heber
Madras. 1 August 1824

I have had an intention for more than a year of asking you for
some advice and you can hardly have a better illustration of the
influence of the tropic of cancer than this indolence which has
made me put off for so long what was so easy to be done at any
time. The case is that I believe myself to have discovered in
Horace Walpole the real *Junius* and not only to have made the
discovery but to have established it almost beyond dispute. I
may have found a mare's nest, and am about to point out what
many others have perceived as well as myself but have not chosen
to notice. Indeed I sometimes half suspect that Francis[2] was
requested to father *Junius* in order that the aristocracy might be
saved the disgrace. The office which I ask of your friendship is
that you cast your eye over the papers which I am about to send
to Murray,[3] and without taking upon yourself the responsibility
of advising the publication, that you will if you see fit, put a veto
on the publication. This I fully authorise you to do or to shew the
papers beforehand if you will to any whom they may concern.

Reginald's appointment, though you may be sure I am glad
to see him in the same hemisphere with me, did not give me so
much satisfaction. To say the truth if I could have whispered in

---

[1] Sir Charles Grey (1785-1865), Justice of the Supreme Court.
[2] Sir Philip Francis (1740-1818).
[3] John Murray (1778-1843), publisher, editor of the *Quarterly Review*. Sir John
Murray cannot trace any references to these papers in his archives.

his ear, it would have been ' don't come ' and I sometimes blame myself for not having written to him on Bishop Middleton's death, but it never entered my head that he would come to India. He and Mrs. Heber have borne the climate hitherto very well and of course you know that they are now on a visitation of the northern provinces where they will find a temperature almost European. We have hopes of seeing him here in 1825. He is well away from Calcutta at this time of the year. The hot season has been unusually severe throughout India, but we have had the very worst of it at Madras in consequence of the rains having entirely failed in November and December.

We are *en pleine guerre* with the King of Ava[1]: Lord Amherst I fear has been rather hasty in declaring it; perhaps I should say too generous. He has given the vermin too much ' law ' and we shall have a deal of trouble to run them down. In the absence of the Commander-in-Chief and of the only efficient member of his Council and without any preparation, he suddenly put forth a formal declaration which was of course to be immediately acted upon and the consequence has been that excepting the taking of Rangoon, their principal seaport, we have hitherto done the enemy no harm; but on the contrary have had rather the worst of it in our skirmishes on the frontiers. They have a method of field fortification which must make an advance into their country very tedious and the retreat of an unsuccessful army almost impossible. I believe the best way would have been never to have thought of doing more than giving them sharp raps on the knuckles if they put their paws over the border. Now, however the die is cast and we must beat them thoroughly.

It is rumoured with some probability that a large force will be assembled about Dacca under the command of Sir Edward Paget[2] in person and will advance through Munnipoor upon the Birman Capital in October, November and December. The expense will be enormous and we shall probably be obliged to encumber

[1] First Burmese War, 1824-6. The Burmese, like the British, were a proud and expanding people. For some time there had been incidents and provocation in Assam and the Arakan. The British declared war in March 1824. The main operation was a slow advance from Rangoon to Pagan. Peace was made on British terms, which included the cession of the Arakan.

[2] Sir Edward Paget (1775-1849), commander-in-chief in the East Indies, 1822-5.

ourselves with the management of a large additional territory, having already more than enough for all the waste energies of the British Empire

Rev. Sydney Smith to Richard Heber
Firton, Yorks. 20 August 1824

When my merits are properly understood and rewarded in the Church, I will subscribe to the Athenaeum[1] or any other Club you please but I have not risen at present (nor shall I ever rise) beyond mutton chops and the Gray's Inn coffee house. Many thanks for the intended honour.

I have had no opportunity of telling you that the last time we met you helped me very badly to asparagus, no toast and only 3 heads of the vegetable. I don't suppose you meant anything by it, but it had an unfriendly appearance.

Sir Charles Grey to Richard Heber
Madras. 15 September 1824

The war with Ava is at a standstill. I hope we shall be contented with clearing the valley of the Bramahpootra — taking possession of Aracan and so making the mountains that divide the vallies of the Bramahpootra and the Irawaddy our Eastern boundary. I heartily wish we had never thought of doing more than driving these poor obstinate creatures beyond it. It is a time of moral as well as physical reparation. The expedition to Rangoon is accused of having acted with great severity and it is certain that the whole population have the greatest horror of us and shew no inclination to submit or be reconciled.

Mrs. Reginald Heber to her mother-in-law
Barrackpore. 20 September 1824

You will be sorry to hear that since I wrote last I have been for days hanging over what I conceived to be the deathbed of my

---

[1] Richard was one of the founders of the Athenaeum Club and many notabilities were asked at his instance to become members.

baby. She was seized with a severe attack of water on the head, what is technically called Acute Hydrocephalus, precisely the same as carried off my first child. For nine nights I never was in bed and Dr. Abel[1] who attended her expected every hour to be her last; he was astonished at the extraordinary degree of strength and vital powers she possessed which enabled her to bear the remedies used and to resist the disease which after a long struggle gave way; and thanks to a Merciful God no trace of it remains, but from being a fat child, she is reduced to a mere skeleton; teething which in this climate is far more serious than in our happy one was the cause of this attack and she is still obliged to have her gums repeatedly lanced to prevent any fresh irritation.

. . . The writing of home brings all its comforts and all its happiness so strongly to my mind, contrasted with my present lonely situation, sitting in my Bungalow, children gone to bed, utterly alone, and a storm of thunder, lightning and rain without that it makes me feel more than usually forlorn.

Mary asked me if the gooseberries arrived safe; they were in perfect preservation and been very useful to us, so that we shall be most thankful to have a few sent out to us each year; but above everything cheese is the most valuable present that can be made us; what we can get here is ruinously dear and very bad, yet it is in high requisition.

W. Wilberforce[2] to Richard Heber
Nr. Uxbridge. 24 September 1824

I return your many thanks for your very friendly letter and I yield to the attractive force which you have brought into action on me. Tho' commonly peeping at the Great Babel thro' the loophole of retreat, your society will constitute a channel of communication with the elite of the British World. I should immediately have written to you but for my conceiving that I

---

[1] Clarke Abel (1780-1826), botanist; physician to Lord Amherst.
[2] Wilberforce was in 1824 on the verge of retirement from public life. It may be noted that he was chiefly responsible for the foundation of the bishopric which Reginald held in India.

might be passing, spare you possibly the trouble of another letter and I was encouraged in my dilatoriness by considering that silence was to be understood assent.

Mrs. Reginald Heber to her mother-in-law
Calcutta. 14 November 1824

Reginald was at Lucknow when I last heard from him the 1st inst., where he had been most honourably received by the King of Oudh, who requested him to sit for his picture to an English artist living there; how Lawn sleeves will look in a Musselman palace I do not know. It is an Eastern custom for any person of distinction to be attached by a man who notes down all the particulars of his day, such as when he rises, bathes, when he breakfasts and what he eats, down to the most minute possible details; this honour has been conferred on Reginald and the notes taken are first sent to the King and then published in the Court Circular. I have been most anxious to procure these papers, it would amuse Reginald so much when we meet to find me informed of all his movements. As it also is a custom for the King to send his visitors a couple of his wives, I am accused here of jealousy in wishing to get these papers ! ! !

Dr. Philip Bliss to Richard Heber
New College Lane. 12 December 1824

By the way, though I want nothing for myself, I would gladly interest you again for my poor brother. He is now in the Mediterranean station in the *Sybille*, a midshipman of twelve years and more standing and with no earthly chance of promotion, although he has seen more service than half the lieutenants and bears the best character as an officer and a gentleman from every captain with whom he has served. I remind you of him because he writes me word that unless he is made shortly, he shall have no other chance for three years and by that time he will be almost too old to wish it and retire.

Mrs. Reginald Heber to her mother-in-law
Calcutta. 20 January 1825

Emily has had better health for the last three months than she has ever enjoyed; I know that it has been more uninterrupted, never requiring medicine or any care but that of diet in which I am as particular as ever. Nothing sweet, no fruit and very little vegetable, a plain mutton chop and a pudding compose her dinner; children here are generally fed with hot currie, onions, fruit and all kinds of unwholesome trash. Harriet has eight teeth now and in perfect health, her severe illness has prevented her being a forward child but she is very intelligent with a sweet temper.

I have heard two or three times from poor Miss Stow since she left me; her last letter was from Macao where she and all her female fellow passengers were to remain whilst the ship went on to Canton; no Christian woman being allowed to land in China.

Mrs. Reginald Heber to her mother-in-law
Calcutta. 2 March 1825

You will be surprized and I hope glad to hear that I am actually on the eve of embarking on board the *Lowjee Family* to join Reginald at Bombay; this was a very short time ago a thing perfectly unexpected to me as I was assured by Government that no vessel was likely to sail this season from this Port to Bombay. However about a week ago I was informed that this ship was actually taken up for that purpose by Govt. and that if I could get ready in time I might have a passage in her. My poor baby was my only hindrance, she has had since I wrote last another attack in her head and tho' from being taken at its very earliest stage, the danger was not so great as in the former instance, yet it has served very much to increase my reluctance to taking her from Dr. Abel's care, till the period of dentition is quite over which if it please God she survives, I have no doubt but that she will be a very healthy child. This was a most serious distress to

me for I felt I was running a very great risk in removing her from
Dr. Abel's care and yet I could not bear to lose so good an
opportunity of joining Reginald.

At last my difficulties were ended by a most kind and friendly
offer of the Pearsons[1] to take charge of my baby till we returned.
They live in a very good part of Calcutta and within five minutes'
drive of Dr. Abel's and as they are people I like extremely as I
have seen a great deal of them and have received much kindness
at their hands, I accepted their offer without reluctance — and
have just been fixing my darling child in her new habitation.
It has been a very heavy trial to part with her especially anticipating as I do one more severe illness before I see her again, but
I feel I am acting for the best as far as human foresight goes and
by the best advice; and as Mrs. Pearson has brought up a large
family herself and has remarkably sensible and pleasing manners,
I am quite at ease as to the hands in which I leave her. Mr. Pearson
himself made the proposal and though his manners are not good,
yet I am sure he has a kind heart and will do whatever was in his
power to promote her welfare. The whole family are a great
acquisition here; he has a very well stored mind on almost every
subject and talks well and unaffectedly. They are general
favourites.

I have now left Calcutta and am writing on my way down the
river to get on board at Diamond Harbour, which I hope to
do before night.

Dr. Martin Routh to Richard Heber
Magd. Coll. Oxford. 18 March 1825

There is nothing about the chance which Church and State
have of getting rid of the claims of the Roman Catholics to
political power. I believe that after a time England will be ruined
by her sects and that the true Church will have to seek for protection and safety elsewhere.

---

[1] John Pearson, Judge-Advocate of Calcutta.

Dr. Edward Copleston to Richard Heber
Honiton. 2 April 1825

When I returned to Oxford after seeing you in London, I was so full of business that it was impossible for me to look at *Junius*. As soon as that was over I was obliged to set out for Devonshire and I brought the MS. with me. I have just finished the perusal of it and I hesitate not to say that it will rekindle the interest about *Junius* and that it will probably convince the world that Horace Walpole was the author.

At any rate the argument is ingenious and the coincidences pointed out are very curious. I am sure that anything from Sir Charles Grey's pen would be worth reading and I did not expect to find so much matter in support of his hypothesis as he has brought together.

Mrs. Reginald Heber to her mother-in-law
Bombay. 2 May 1825

I landed here on the evening of the 20th and had the inexpressible delight of once more joining my beloved husband, after a separation of nearly eleven calendar months and of seeing him tho' thinner, which I could not but expect after so long and fatiguing a journey, in perfect health, in excellent spirits, and looking back to the tour (with exception of the melancholy scene at Dacca) with every feeling of pleasure and gratification.

A few days before I left Calcutta I wrote to you to say that an opportunity had occurred very unexpectedly for coming here. I embarked on the 4th of March and had a most tedious and wretched voyage of nearly seven weeks. The heat was intense and we never had a favourable wind from the moment we rounded the island of Ceylon; think of the thermr. standing for weeks at 89 and often much higher without a possibility of using the common means of alleviating the heat. The consequences as one might naturally anticipate was a great deal of illness on board; a remittant fever made its appearance, which Emily first had, but very slightly hardly worth the naming but enough to make me very uneasy and I should think to contribute in no small degree to the severity of my subsequent attack, which confined me to my bed nearly a fortnight and of course left me in a very weak and reduced state. Such an illness on board ship where I was the only woman, without a creature belonging to me but my child, was most distressing but thank God my good constitution prevailed and I am now perfectly well in health, having recovered since I landed in a surprizing way. I am however a severe sufferer from one of the plagues of the climate which often appears without a cause and which invariably follows fever. I have no fewer than eleven boils, some of them extremely painful and from which I suffer a good deal, as in a new place I am forced as long as I can to receive and return visits and to bear the pain of having my stays on.

Emily is uncommonly well, quite stout and rosy; at this time of year, the climate of Bombay, and from its being on an island, is very superior to that of Calcutta, there are no hot winds and she is able to run about all day out of doors with impunity, merely using the precaution of keeping in the shade.

We have three bungalows handsomely furnished and provided with everything including servants that we can want, found by the Government here. Mr. Elphinstone,[1] the Governor of Bombay, has behaved in the handsomest manner possible to Reginald (far more so than the Governor-General will ever do). When he heard that he was coming by water from Surat, which you will find to the north of Bombay, he sent a vessel to bring him down, had the bungalows ready for him and has promised a cruiser to take us to Ceylon, wait our movements there and then take us on to Calcutta, where we purpose arriving about the middle of October when the unhealthy season is over.

To add to our pleasure at meeting here, I found letters with the most excellent accounts of our dear baby who has not had a moment's illness since I left her; the Pearsons are truly kind friends to us. I am told she has one of the best rooms in the house given up to her and is treated in every respect just as if she were their own child. She runs about and begins to speak and Mrs. Pearson says she is just the same sweet tempered child I left and

[1] Mountstuart Elphinstone (1779-1859), governor of Bombay 1819-27.

the pet of the whole family. Miss Pearson is going to marry Capt. Greville,[1] a cousin of Lady Combermare's; this may be news at Buntingsdale; it is a pretty good match and promises still better when Lord C. comes out who will doubtless push him on in his profession.

I must now answer some of your questions; the Directors do find us a house at a rent not exceeding 600 rupees or £60 a month, which is quite sufficient to procure us an extremely good one; they do allow Reginald a certain sum, 1,000 rupees per mensen to pay his travelling expenses; this is not so handsome as the former allowance, for tho' it was enough when he was travelling alone, it will not near cover our joint expenses, still we could always save on these occasions about 2,000 rupees a month out of our annual income, his visitations will therefore be the time when we can save anything worth talking about.

I have mentioned that we have three bungalows, we have also Reginald's tents pitched in the Compound for various purposes and they are all on the sea beach. Indeed our sleeping room is very little above high water mark; this ensures us a fresh sea breeze during the greater part of the day, and therefore instead of being shut up from sunrise to sunset as we should be in Calcutta, we admit as much outward air as possible and Emily runs about all day in the shade with visible advantage, she is rosy and rather fat. But tho' this sounds very superior to Calcutta, yet as a residence I like nothing that I have yet seen so well as the latter; in no part of the South of India (where alone we are likely to live) have we the three or sometimes four months of delightful cold weather save in Calcutta; and consequently people get relaxed and have no means of bracing but of going to the Upper Provinces. The whole climate of India is to be sure miserable enough at times, but take it with all its advantages of Society, etc. etc., Calcutta is preferable.

You can have no idea of the publicity in which we live here. Our sleeping bungalow opens with a verandah which is merely closed by a very open rush fence which has merely the name of shelter without the reality, and even if we were willing to sacrifice

[1] Major George Greville (1793-1834).

the comfort of breathing to decency which we cannot do, it would be impossible to effect it for we have no means of shelter, so I suppose in time I shall perform my toilette in public with perfect composure.

Dr. Edward Copleston to Richard Heber
Oriel. 12 May 1825

One or two phrases in your letter, which I have just received and for which I beg you to receive my thanks, make me apprehensive that I did not express myself exactly as I intended or as I ought to have done. It is sometimes unknown to the individual most concerned what the feeling and expectation in whose zealous support is of great consequence. I felt that you probably were in this predicament and that a trifling sacrifice on your part would set all right, if one of your friends of whose sincerity and attachment you could not doubt would undertake to communicate with you.

Let me add that nothing was further from my thoughts than to advise a set speech upon this or upon any subject. It is not the way by which the dissatisfaction to which I alluded is to be overcome. It is merely some *public* evidence of attention to the political feelings of the University, which those who know you as I do stand in no need of, but which will always be demanded of them by others who disapprove our choice.

The Cause has certainly lost ground in the Country and I conclude the majority in the Upper House will be greater than last year. Surely the conduct of the French Government since the re-establishment of the Church is enough to tell us that the spirit of the Romish Church is the same as ever and will always shew itself intolerant in proportion to the power it acquires.

Lord Holland[1] to Richard Heber
Richmond. 19 July 1825

Truth must be told, I have not yet read Sir Ch. Grey's paper which lies in my room with many others which gout first,

---

[1] Henry Fox (1773-1840), third Baron Holland.

lazyness second, absence and heat have indisposed me from examining. The internal evidence against Walpole is very strong indeed and the private papers correspondence and journal of the year in which *Junius* appears, all tend to confirm me that he could not be the author. Everyone named, Gibbon excepted, is more likely than H. Walpole.

Mrs. Reginald Heber to her sister-in-law Mary Cholmondeley
Colombo. 4 September 1825

We left Bombay on the 16th August and made an eleven days voyage of it here, a time as usual of suffering for me but of enjoyment to Reginald and our little Emily. I should like you very much to see her just now, though (in) England she might be called a little pale, yet here she looks one of the healthiest children in the Island and she has none of the tyrannical ways that most children have here owing to their having two or three servants whose business it is to humour them and follow them about. But to return to our proceedings.

We landed at Point de Galle, the southern extremity of Ceylon where we were received with military honours and all the noisy tokens of respect by the natives. We remained there four days and then set off on our journey to Colombo, partly in palanquin and partly in carriages. We were a large party, being escorted by the principal inhabitants of the place, our own party consisting of six palanquins and preceded by a band of spearmen, flags and music. I headed the procession and I am quite sure from this circumstance that I was taken for the Bishop travelling in his robes; another Pope Joan!

The road lay close to a beautiful sea, tumbling and foaming over rocks and thro' a grove of palms with the ground covered with beautiful flowers and underwood. We slept one night on the road in what is called a Rest House, this only consists of walls and roof with perhaps cane bedsteads on which you put the mattresses of your own palanquin and sleep as we did comfortably as in a good bed; where there are none of these the palanquins supply their place.

The last sixteen miles we went in the Governor's carriage, which with four beautiful horses and four more as relays and a body guard he kindly sent to meet us. We are settled in a good house, provided and furnished by Government and have never met with more kindness and attention than we have here. Sir Edward and Lady Barnes[1] (Governor) do all they can to make us comfortable, there are no horses to be hired in the Island and we have the entire command of his stables and as Lady Barnes is near her confinement, she sends me every day her saddle horse.

The Cingalese differ in many respects from the Bengalese, the latter think it a mark of the greatest disrespect to appear with bare heads before their superiors, while the former dress their long hair like women's, with a large tortoiseshell comb and wear no turbans. They speak a quite different language but almost all the servants speak a little English.

You know this is the place whence all the elephants come and formerly there was an annual hunt to catch them, but since almost all the petty rajahs have been put down, there has been no demand for them and consequently they have increased in such numbers as to do much mischief in the corn-fields — to make it dangerous to travel in the interior without a large escort and lights at night to frighten them away. You are also aware that this is called ' the spice Island ' from the immense quantity of cinnamon which is exported. The shrubs (for they are not allowed to grow higher than a common sized lilac bush) are planted in gardens which cover a space of 17,000 acres and their smell is most fragrant; in the Dutch laws, the loss of a hand was the penalty for cutting one of these, now a fine is substituted.

Richard Heber to his sister, Mary
15 September 1825

Will it surprise you or will it not to learn that I have written to the V.-Chancellor declining all future views towards the repr. of the Univ. of Oxford in Parlt. Towards this I have been turning onward for some time and the impending Dissolution

[1] Sir Edward Barnes (1776-1838), governor of Ceylon, 1824-31.

seemed the proper moment to decide. Not taking an *active* part in its proceedings, I found the House somewhat of a fag and a bore and the time it took up unprofitably spent. All things considered I do not think I shall repent my resolution.

Mrs. Reginald Heber to her sister-in-law Mary Cholmondeley
Calcutta. 25 October 1825

We landed on the 21st after a very tedious and latterly stormy voyage and had the comfort of finding our dear baby in perfect health, much grown and improved in our absence. She evidently knew my voice and kissed me as if she was glad to see me again tho' nearly eight months have elapsed since I left her. Emily is delighted to see ' sister ' again. We are all thank God perfectly well, very happy in being once more an united family. Calcutta, too, is grown healthy and people look cheerful and happy.

The cheese even after its long imprisonment proves excellent, the bottles of fruit were, alas! all smashed from being ill-packed, there being nothing to prevent the cheese from falling upon them when the box was turned, their contents falling on the hams of course destroyed them, but still the magnificent cheese pays for all.

We keep two pairs of carriage horses, two saddle horses and a pony for Emily, but certainly riding does not agree with me as it did in England. I have two very nice English maids who are a real acquisition to me.

Mrs. Reginald Heber to her mother-in-law
Calcutta. 12 December 1825

We are in a good deal of a hurry just now, having in a short space of time to make preparations for a long journey which we intend commencing early in February, to remove into a new house, to give large dinner parties and our ' squeeze ' besides having these latter to return.

The time we are able to spend in Calcutta is so short that we are anxious to get all the civilities over which we feel to be due before we leave it again for eight months. The lease of our house is nearly out and as its owner Mr. Leycester is anxious to return to it and as on many accounts we wish to leave it, we have fixed on another in a more airy and I should hope a more healthy situation. The house is a very good one tho' the rooms are not so large as those we now occupy and we have a third storey which in the hot season is of incalculable benefit. We sail for Madras early in February. Sir Charles Grey, who knows that Presidency better than most people, says there are parts in which it may be difficult for children and all their numerous attendants to find conveyances. We therefore propose that Reginald should leave me and them in the Nilgirey Hills, a fine healthy situation while he makes this part of the tour and this advice we shall probably follow. I hope not to be separated from him for more than three weeks or a month and this will be not a little better than remaining here alone for four or five months.

We have very uncomfortable news from the Aracan of the dreadful sickness which still prevails, as well as from Prome of our troops having sustained a partial defeat. This war is indeed the most unfortunate that we ever undertook in India and as all our pacific terms have been rejected by the Burmese, I see no end to it. They are wise to avoid coming to an open general engagement with us, but keep drawing us on into their deadly country, certain that climate will produce effects which their arms could never do. All this increases, however undeservedly, Lord Amherst's unpopularity. Indeed I should (say) that nothing save some brilliant and decisive victory would prevent his speedy recall. Lady Amherst has been for some time very unwell and I cannot help thinking that neither of them would be sorry to have a pretext of that sort for leaving India.

Mrs. Reginald Heber to her mother-in-law
Calcutta. 11 *January* 1826

We are all perfectly well and that we may all continue so, we have again come to the painful resolution of being separated for a five months from each other! I will state how we are situated

and will then leave you to judge whether for all our sakes we
have not chosen the wisest part. Our long and unexpected
detention in Bombay, our subsequent tedious voyages to and
from Ceylon, made our arrival here so late, as to render it
impossible for Reginald to get his business done so as to allow
of our setting out in time to travel in the Madras Presidency
during the cool season; those who have travelled at the hot time
of the year say that to children it is very prejudicial tho' not so
much so as travelling in the rains, the natural consequence of
being so late in setting out. The heat when dry never disagrees
with Reginald and it was only in going from Bombay to Poonah
during the rains that he ever suffered inconvenience. By our not
accompanying him, he will of course move much more expedi-
tiously, so much more as to enable him to escape all rain whatever
and to be safely housed in Madras before the wet season sets in.
This therefore is what reconciles me, more perhaps than anything
else even the welfare of my children, to another separation,
I trust of a much shorter duration than the last. He expects and
I most ardently hope that he will be here early in July, in time
to take me and our children to a more healthy situation during
the rains.

My dear Reginald has for his companions a medical man from
Madras and his Chaplain Mr. Robinson, a person who from his
long residence in India, his having frequently travelled on that
side of the Continent, his not being at all an adventurous person
and above all, from the attachment I am certain he feels after an
intercourse of many months with his Bishop, is an admirable
compagnon de voyage, whilst his learning, his good disposition and
temper make him the best Chaplain, whether travelling or in
repose, I have yet seen here.

Reginald has grown almost fat, and I am complimented by
everyone on his renewed good looks; but he grows grey fast
and I am sorry to say which is of more consequence that he
grows a little deaf, this annoys me from knowing how much it
is in his family. I trust however that with care, it will not become
serious.

Lord Combermere[1] has been now some time before Bhurtpore with a large army and a train of artillery; it is a strong
well-fortified place and bravely defended by the usurper, Darjunt
Sing, but we have already made rapid approaches and it is generally supposed that three weeks will see the demolition of the
fortress. Lord C. is popular beyond everything with the army
and with all who know him generally. His extreme activity
excites the surprize and admiration of the soldiers who work
under his orders with an enthusiasm that has perhaps rarely
been surpassed. He is remarkably judicious in the manner with
which he treats the native officers, holds levees for them, enquires
into their histories and seems to consider them as his equals,
instead of despising them as has been and still is the case amongst
old Indians.

W. Gregson to Richard Heber
London. 30 January 1826

I have only just returned from the North where the commercial
distress is at its highest; in the cotton, silk and woollen trades the
depression is dreadful: cotton in particular, such is the glut is
actually selling below the price at which it can be grown; in this
branch at least there must soon be a favourable reaction. The
Liverpool Bank, whose failure you will see in the papers, is a
small affair and likely only to affect shopkeepers and the lower
orders.

Mrs. Reginald Heber to her mother-in-law
Calcutta. 9 February 1826

The seige of Bhurtpore has been one of great glory to Lord
Combermere and I hope will be also productive of considerable
emolument; he expects that his share of prize money will amount
to £200,000, if the whole of the treasure taken is adjudged to the
captors, but of this there seems to be some doubt.

---

[1] Sir Stapleton Cotton (1773-1865), Viscount Combermere; commander-in-chief in
India 1825-30; captured Bhurtpore and installed a puppet ruler in 1826.

Sir Charles Grey to Richard Heber
Calcutta. 16 April 1826

The Burmese war is well ended for the present. I still think it would have been infinitely better if we had never passed our old frontier; but having got into the heart of the enemy's country, roused them into activity and rage, and drawn the attention of the world to the contest, it was right to take something from them; and if we could have communicated the change of conditions to England immediately as they arose, my own opinion at last would have been to put them *hors de combat* for ever whilst we were about it. To this it must come at last, for I am satisfied you will find them a more formidable people henceforth than they have been hitherto.

Mrs. Heber (stepmother) to Richard Heber
Whitchurch. 21 April 1826

I cannot delay in informing you that our dear Mary on Thursday morning the 20th April presented us with a fine Boy.[1] She and the baby have every prospect of doing well. Miss Congreave is to be a godmother and requested that if a boy, she might name him. Cholmondeley trusted to her discretion and she calls him Reginald, a name most dear to us all.[2] May the Almighty give his Grace to our new born still further to adorn it.

Mrs. Charles Cholmondeley to Richard Heber
10 June 1829

We are all well. Cholmondeley has no symptoms of any indisposition whatever and the 4 boys all grow fast. Richard Hugh[3] is a noble lad indeed and promises to be the giant of the family.

---

[1] Birth of Reginald Cholmondeley, born 20 April 1826, third son of Rev. Charles and Mary Cholmondeley.

[2] Bishop Reginald Heber died suddenly on 3 April 1826 at Trinchinopoly.

[3] Richard Hugh, fourth son of Rev. Charles and Mary Cholmondeley, born on 24 August 1828.

Mrs. Charles Cholmondeley to Richard Heber
17 July 1830

I hardly know how to tell you the strange and unlooked for event which has taken place. Perhaps you may not think so ill of it as I do for I confess it has shocked me quite beyond anything I can express. I have recd. a letter from Emily from which I conclude (for it does not actually state it) that she is married to Count Valsamachi, the Secretary of the Ionian Islands. Her acquaintance with him has been very short and she knows nothing of him but what he tells her himself and he by all accounts has been tempted by the idea of her having a fortune which he easily might suppose seeing her style of living in town. He appeared so intimate with her in June that I warned her of her danger and received a positive assurance from her that she would be cautious and think nothing of him. Since that time she has never mentioned his name in her letters till today when she says, ' before you receive this I shall be his wife '. She has kept the whole a secret from her own friends and all ours and seemed determined no expostulation shd. divert her purpose. All Reginald's property is in her power, for most inadvisedly poor fellow, thinking her as good as himself, he left her sole guardian of his children and executor of his affairs, so these poor children will now be dependent upon a foreigner whom nobody knows. Some say he is a Greek, some a Venetian, nobody knows what his fortunes or expectations are. For her, I hope I may never see her again; to have lived sixteen years with such an angel as Reginald and in four little years after his death to forget him and so far disregard his children as to give up her independant power of protecting them is what no woman of principle to say nothing of feeling and delicacy could have done. But with all her fine writing and publishing,[1] she has never shewn any real feeling and devotion to his memory since his loss. The world has long cried shame on her manners and flirting, but I was unwilling to believe anything against her until now.

[1] *The life of Bishop Heber*, by his widow, was published in 1830.

I hear that Count Valsamachi and his wife are gone to Paris to find and see you; no doubt to obtain your sanction and approval. She is very artful but I trust and hope that whatever you might be prevailed on to do in bounty and affection to the children for Reginald's sake may be amply secured by guardians and trustees. Nothing can be trusted to her discretion and prudence, still less to her Greek helpmate. They are to reside the next two years in Cefalonia.

RICHARD LIVED ABROAD after leaving Parliament. His political activities were ineffectual and it is as a Book Collector that he is remembered now. He used to say that it was his ideal to secure three copies of each book: one to read, one to place on his shelves and one to give to his friends. Moreover, he was far from being an indiscriminate buyer, who needs must buy for the buying's sake. He was the greatest expert of his time on rare books; he knew all about his purchases and was a source to which his book loving friends could and did turn for information. He was very well read himself, and his knowledge of edition dates was undefeatable.

But book collecting is one of the most expensive of all arts. Richard Heber was a wealthy man when his father died, but as year followed year Marton was mortgaged and so was an estate at Wicklewood, in Norfolk, which he had inherited from his mother. He contracted loans at interest from friends and relations. No one knows for certain how many books he had, but there were more than 200,000. Hodnet contained 12,000; there were two houses in London and another at Oxford, stacked from garret to cellar. Other of his libraries were at Ghent, Antwerp and Brussels, and a particularly large one in Paris. There were also collections in many other places in the Low Countries and in Germany. While he had agents in England attending sales, the foreign book market occupied his personal attention in the years after his resignation from Parliament, and as a consequence he lived abroad.

Mary Cholmondeley made many and urgent appeals to him to return. 'Let me not feel as if I had *no* brothers' she cried. Two of the three were dead; her sister-in-law had, in Mary's opinion, made a most injudicious remarriage, and Mary's husband was dead also.

At last Richard returned: an ill and ageing man. We may picture him in his old house in Pimlico, wrapped up in rugs with his thick-lensed spectacles on his nose, poring over an agent's enquiry of how best to forward a cargo of books lately bought at Nuremburg; or writing to pacify an agitated Parisian landlady who was threatening to evict him and to throw his precious volumes out of her house into the street; or studying the political news that tells of the passing of the Reform Bill, that first step that led to a new and different England.

Francis Moore to Richard Heber
Hotel de Hollande, Rue Neuve des bons Enfants, Paris, 2 April 1832

We have the cholera at present in all the arrondissements of Paris, it will of course terminate the very inconvenient quarantine at Calais. One wonder is, by what route it came here, for it seems to have perched in the Metropolis, without having had a 'stepping stone' in any part of France.

The 'Mauvais Sujets de Paris, — et il y en a tant!' are endeavouring to get up little insurrections on the strength of it; and as the French Ministry is detested by all parties, the Mob finds partizans wherever and whenever it stirs. It is really curious to see how the hated Ministry is supported by its enemies — merely from their greater antipathy to each other; and another political curiosity is the existence of more liberal sentiments in the Government than even in the Chamber of Representatives, whom you might have imagined to have had the most high bred tory Nurses 'et d'avoir sucé l'aristocratie avec le lait' from their dignified tenacity in repulsing any popular alleviations attempted to be introduced by the Ministers into the Corn Laws!

Great emigrations from Paris through fear of the cholera. The Malles-postes and Diligences are full. For my part, I fear it not, tho' it will certainly decimate all the dirty parts and people of Paris.

Francis Moore to Richard Heber
Hotel de Hollande, Paris, 1 May 1832

The Cholera still clings to Paris, as if loth to leave it; but the great absorbing question now is the Ministerial revolutions now operating in England. I hope sincerely that all may end well; it is evident that all which concerns England now, affects the whole civilized world.[1]

Mrs. Charles Cholmondeley to Richard Heber
Hodnet. 10 June 1832

I had on Friday what Miss Powell calls a ' Feat Shampeter' under the lime trees, the wives and daughters of some of your farmers, about 18 — together with Mrs. Taylor and the Clergy and we all drank tea under that magnificent canopy being (children included) a party of 26.

One day last week I had a morning call from the Queen of Hamburg, old Mrs. Smyth-Owen,[2] the relict of the late owner of Condover. She always makes it a rule when in the neighbourhood of calling upon me and is a civil good natured old Dowager on the whole, tho' she is a living representation of the 'Pomps and Vanities of this wicked world' in the gossip of which her sole joy seems to be.

Francis Moore to Richard Heber
Paris. 15 June 1832

You will have had such copious and various accounts of the late Rebellion in Paris, I need not intrude my gossip on you. The fact is I kept close quarters while the gentry were fighting

[1] The first Reform Bill was reintroduced by Lord Grey's ministry in March 1832. It was fought hard in the Commons and at length defeated. Immediately, in April, parliament was dissolved. The general election returned a majority for the Bill. It remained only to overcome the opposition of the Lords, accomplished by the threat to create new peers. The Reform Bill (by now somewhat altered and modified) received the royal assent in June.

[2] The Smyth-Owen's of Condover were cousins of the Cholmondeleys, Thomas Cholmondeley and later his brother Reginald inheriting the property in the sixties.

and saw nothing of the ephemeral warfare, excepting the disarming of the lower guard of the Bank, whilst I was looking out of Silvestre's windows. There being a suspension of his *Sale* for that evening (the 5th inst), I returned home by the Rue de Valois and having written till 11 o'clock went to bed and slept most soundly until past 7 the next morning, tho' as I learned, there was tremendous fighting and firing in the Place des Victories and Rue des fossés Montmartres. The Rebels fought fanatically — but I am told the conduct of the King was above all praise. Marshal Soult is now shewing to the Jesuits and their tools, the Jacobins, that he has been brought up in an energetic school. [1]

Francis Moore to Richard Heber
Paris. 24 September 1832

The book trade is not very lively in Paris at present tho', as I learn, there are so many English arrived here lately, as to have filled most of the great hotels. I imagine these visitors are but 'birds of passage,' such as some of the higher classes on their autumnal migration to Italy; and persons of the legal profession who avail themselves of the long Vacation in the English courts to seek a momentary amusement in this capital — now a truly dismal scene, compared to what it was in more tranquil times. I hear on the contrary the town of Boulogne-sur-Mer is a focus of bustle and business, full of active idleness and dissipation, crowded with foreigners and the mart to which the remains of French gaiety is transferred.

In politics we continue in the same feverish state of uncertainty which has existed for the last two years. The Government as anxious to preserve peace as if its existence depended on it — the people equally solicitous to be at war. A new incident in public affairs has just occurred — the death of the King of Spain — which perhaps may gratify the war party without endangering

[1] The bourgeois monarchy of Louis-Philippe having shewn itself as conservatively attached as the legitimist monarchy of Charles X to the forms of royal power, it was not surprizing that the republican elements of the population should begin to show their dissatisfaction. The cholera had killed the only minister who might have contented all parties. Nicolas Jean de Dieu Soult (1769-1851), Napoleonic marshal, republican and now royalist, took command of the government.

its opponents in France, as it is possible that the Heiress of Ferdinand may be placed in a position analogous to that of Dona Maria. These young Queens seem to be 'providential dispensations in favour of the sons of the ' Citizen-King ' '.

Richard Heber to his sister Mary
Westminster. 13 December 1832

For myself I have passed 18 hours out of every 24 snug at roost; the only place where I find myself warm and comfortable. My gout has not been attended with severe pain and inflammation but shewed itself chiefly in weakness in the ankles and extreme soreness and tenderness in the soles of the feet; so I have found it the best plan to remain quietly recumbent till two hours before dinner, after which I usually remain in my great chair in my dressing room till towards 10 at night.

What say you to our elections in London and its adjacent districts ? On the whole I am well satisfied and think we have set a good example to the radically disposed towns and boroughs. It seems to me that the Government or Moderate Liberal Party is likely to take the decided lead in the new Parlt.[1] which in the present state of men's minds throughout the Empire is better for any lover of peace and stability than a larger admixture of ultra Tories and ultra Radicals who might excite to mischief, but are not likely to be listened to by the mass of respectable inhabitants, and would either create desperate quarrels or form together still more ill fated alliances. Shropshire however seems likely to distinguish itself as the first of Conservative Counties.

Richard Heber died on 11 October 1833

---

[1] The reformed parliament was opened in February 1833. It contained, as Richard Heber expected, a great majority of ministerialists — the moderate men who regarded the Reform Act not as the first stage of democracy but as the last stage of parliamentary reform.

INDEX

Thin
6 Oct. 1955.